The Collected Works
of
J. Krishnamurti

Volume IV

1945–1948

The Observer Is The Observed

KENDALL/HUNT PUBLISHING COMPANY
2460 Kerper Boulevard P.O. Box 539 Dubuque, Iowa 52004-0539

Photo: J. Krishnamurti, ca 1945

Copyright © 1991 by The Krishnamurti Foundation of America
P.O. Box 1560, Ojai, California 93024

Library of Congress Catalog Card Number: 90–62735

ISBN 0–8403–6237–4

Printed in the United States of America
10 9 8 7 6 5 4 3 2 1

Contents

Preface

Jiddu Krishnamurti was born in 1895 of Brahmin parents in south India. At the age of fourteen he was proclaimed the coming World Teacher by Annie Besant, then president of the Theosophical Society, an international organization that emphasized the unity of world religions. Mrs. Besant adopted the boy and took him to England, where he was educated and prepared for his coming role. In 1911 a new worldwide organization was formed with Krishnamurti as its head, solely to prepare its members for his advent as World Teacher. In 1929, after many years of questioning himself and the destiny imposed upon him, Krishnamurti disbanded this organization, saying:

Truth is a pathless land, and you cannot approach it by any path whatsoever, by any religion, by any sect. Truth, being limitless, unconditioned, unapproachable by any path whatsoever, cannot be organized; nor should any organization be formed to lead or to coerce people along any particular path. My only concern is to set men absolutely, unconditionally free.

Until the end of his life at the age of ninety, Krishnamurti traveled the world speaking as a private person. The rejection of all spiritual and psychological authority, including his own, is a fundamental theme. A major concern is the social structure and how it conditions the individual. The emphasis in his talks and writings is on the psychological barriers that prevent clarity of perception. In the mirror of relationship, each of us can come to understand the content of his own consciousness, which is common to all humanity. We can do this, not analytically, but directly in a manner Krishnamurti describes at length. In observing this content we discover within ourselves the division of the observer and what is observed. He points out that this division, which prevents direct perception, is the root of human conflict.

His central vision did not waver after 1929, but Krishnamurti strove for the rest of his life to make his language even more simple and clear. There is a development in his exposition. From year to year he used new terms and new approaches to his subject, with different nuances.

Because his subject is all-embracing, the *Collected Works* are of compelling interest. Within his talks in any one year, Krishnamurti was not able to cover the whole range of his vision, but broad amplifications of particular themes are found throughout these volumes. In them he lays the foundations of many of the concepts he used in later years.

The *Collected Works* contain Krishnamurti's previously published talks, discussions, answers to specific questions, and writings for the years 1933 through 1967. They are an authentic record of his teachings, taken from transcripts of verbatim shorthand reports and tape recordings.

The Krishnamurti Foundation of America, a California charitable trust, has among its purposes the publication and distribution of Krishnamurti books, videocassettes, films and tape recordings. The production of the *Collected Works* is one of these activities.

Ojai, California, 1945

———————————————— ✳ ————————————————

First Talk in The Oak Grove

To understand the confusion and misery that exist in ourselves, and so in the world, we must first find clarity within ourselves, and this clarity comes about through right thinking. This clarity is not to be organized, for it cannot be exchanged with another. Organized group thought becomes dangerous however good it may appear; organized group thought can be used, exploited; group thought ceases to be right thinking, it is merely repetitive. Clarity is essential for without it change and reform merely lead to further confusion. Clarity is not the result of verbal assertion but of intense self-awareness and right thinking. Right thinking is not the outcome of mere cultivation of the intellect, nor is it conformity to pattern, however worthy and noble. Right thinking comes with self-knowledge. Without understanding yourself, you have no basis for thought; without self-knowledge, what you think is not true.

You and the world are not two different entities with separate problems; you and the world are one. Your problem is the world's problem. You may be the result of certain tendencies, of environmental influences, but you are not different fundamentally from another. Inwardly we are very much alike; we are all driven by greed, ill will, fear, ambition, and so on. Our beliefs, hopes, aspirations, have a common basis. We are one; we

are one humanity, though the artificial frontiers of economics and politics and prejudice divide us. If you kill another, you are destroying yourself. You are the center of the whole, and without understanding yourself you cannot understand reality.

We have an intellectual knowledge of this unity, but we keep knowledge and feeling in different compartments, and hence we never experience the extraordinary unity of man. When knowledge and feeling meet there is experience. These talks will be utterly useless if you do not experience as you are listening. Do not say, "I will understand later," but experience now. Do not keep your knowledge and your feeling separate, for out of this separation grow confusion and misery. You must experience this living unity of man. You are not separate from the Japanese, the Hindu, the Negro, or the German. To experience this immense unity be open, become conscious of this division between knowledge and feeling; do not be a slave to compartmental philosophy.

Without self-knowledge understanding is not possible. Self-knowledge is extremely arduous and difficult, for you are a complex entity. You must approach the understanding of the self simply, without any pretensions, without any theories. If I would understand you I must have no preconceived formulations about you, there must be no prejudice; I must be open, without judgment, without comparison. This is very difficult for, with most of us, thought is the result of comparison, of judgment. Through approximation we think we are understanding, but is understanding born of comparison, judgment? Or is it the outcome of noncomparative thought? If you would understand something, do you compare it with something else or do you study it for itself?

Thought born of comparison is not right thinking. Yet in studying ourselves we are comparing, approximating. It is this that prevents the understanding of ourselves. Why do we judge ourselves? Is not our judgment the outcome of our desire to become something, to gain, to conform, to protect ourselves? This very urge prevents understanding.

As I said, you are a complex entity, and to understand it you must examine it. You cannot understand it if you are comparing it with the yesterday or with the tomorrow. You are an intricate mechanism, but comparison, judgment, identification prevent comprehension. Do not be afraid that you will become sluggish, smug, self-contented if you do not compete in comparison. Once you have perceived the futility of comparison, there is a great freedom. Then you are no longer striving to become, but there is freedom to understand. Be aware of this comparative process of your thinking—experience all this as I am explaining—and feel its futility, its fundamental thoughtlessness; you will then experience a great freedom, as though you had laid down a wearisome burden. In this freedom from approximation and so from identification, you will be able to discover and understand the realities of yourself. If you do not compare, judge, then you will be confronted with yourself, and this will give clarity and strength to uncover great depths. This is essential for the understanding of reality. When there is no self-approximation, then thought is liberated from duality; the

problem and the conflict with the opposites fall away. In this freedom there is a revolutionary, creative understanding.

There is not one of us who is not confronted with the problem of killing and non-killing, violence and nonviolence. Some of you may feel that as your sons, brothers or husbands are not involved in this mass murder, called war, you are not immediately concerned with this problem, but if you will look a little more closely, you will see how deeply you are involved. You cannot escape it. You must, as an individual, have a definite attitude towards killing and non-killing. If you have not been aware of it, you are being confronted with it now; you must face the issue, the dualistic problem of capitalism and communism, love and hate, killing and nonkilling, and so on. How are you to find the truth of the matter? Is there any release from conflict in the endless corridor of duality? Many believe that in the very struggle of the opposites, there is creativeness, that this conflict is life, and to escape from it is to be in illusion. Is this so? Does not an opposite contain an element of its own opposite and so produce endless conflict and pain? Is conflict necessary for creation? Are the moments of creativeness the outcome of strife and pain? Does not the state of creative being come into existence when all pain and struggle have utterly ceased? You can experience this for yourself. This freedom from opposites is not an illusion; in it alone is the answer to all of our confusion and conflicting problems.

You are faced with the problem of killing your brother in the name of religion, of peace, of country, and so on. How shall you find the answer in which further conflicting, further opposing problems are not inherent? To find a true, lasting answer, must you not go outside of the dualistic pattern of thought? You kill because your property, your safety, your prestige are threatened; as with the individual, so with the group, with the nation.

To be free from violence and nonviolence, there must be freedom from acquisitiveness, ill will, lust, and so on. But most of us do not go into the problem deeply and are satisfied with reform, with alternation within the pattern of duality. We accept as inevitable this conflict of duality and within that pattern try to bring about modification, change; within it we maneuver to a better position, to a more advantageous point for ourselves. Change or reform merely within the pattern of duality produces only further confusion and pain and hence is retrogression.

You must go beyond the pattern of duality to solve permanently the problem of opposites. Within the pattern there is no truth, however much we may be caught in it; if we seek truth in it, we will be led to many delusions. We must go beyond the dualistic pattern of the 'I' and the not 'I', the possessor and the possessed. Beyond and above the endless corridor of duality lies truth. Beyond and above the conflicting and painful problem of opposites lies creative understanding. This is to be experienced, not to be speculated upon, not to be formulated, but to be realized through deep awareness of the dualistic hindrances.

Question: I am sure most of us have seen authentic pictures in movies and in magazines of the horrors and the barbarities of the concentration camps. What should be done, in your opinion, with those who have perpetrated these monstrous atrocities? Should they not be punished?

KRISHNAMURTI: Who is to punish them? Is not the judge often as guilty as the accused? Each one of us has built up this civilization, each one has contributed towards its misery, each one is responsible for its actions. We are the outcome of each other's actions and reactions; this civilization is a collective result. No country or people is separate from another; we are all interrelated; we are one. Whether we acknowledge it or not, when a misfortune happens to a people, we share in it as in its good fortune. You may not separate yourself to condemn or to praise.

The power to oppress is evil and every group that is large and well organized becomes a potential source of evil. By shouting loudly the cruelties of another country, you think you can overlook those of your own. It is not only the vanquished but every country that is responsible for the horrors of war. War is one of the greatest catastrophes; the greatest evil is to kill another. Once you admit such an evil into your heart, then you let loose countless minor disasters. You do not condemn war itself but him who is cruel in war.

You are responsible for war; you have brought it about by your everyday action of greed, ill will, passion. Each one of us has built up this competitive, ruthless civilization in which man is against man. You want to root out the causes of war, of barbarity in others, while you yourself indulge in them. This leads to hypocrisy and to further wars. You have to root out the causes of war, of violence, in yourself, which demands patience and gentleness, not bloody condemnation of others.

Humanity does not need more suffering to make it understand, but what is needed is that you should be aware of your own actions, that you should awaken to your own ignorance and sorrow and so bring about in yourself compassion and tolerance. You should not be concerned with punishments and rewards, but with the eradication in yourself of those causes that manifest themselves in violence and in hate, in antagonism and ill will. In murdering the murderer you become like him; you become the criminal. A wrong is not righted through wrong means; only through right means can a right end be accomplished. If you would have peace you must employ peaceful means, and mass murder, war, can only lead to further murder, further suffering. There can be no love through bloodshed; an army is not an instrument of peace. Only goodwill and compassion can bring peace to the world, not might and cunning nor mere legislation.

You are responsible for the misery and disaster that exist, you who in your daily life are cruel, oppressive, greedy, ambitious. Suffering will continue until you eradicate in yourself those causes that breed passion, greed, and ruthlessness. Have peace and compassion in your heart and you will find the right answer to your questions.

Question: At this time and in our present way of life, our feelings become blunted and hard. Can you suggest a way of life that will make us more sensitive? Can we become so in spite of noise, haste, all the competitive professions and pursuits? Can we become so without dedication to a higher source of life?

KRISHNAMURTI: Is it not necessary for clear and right thinking to be sensitive? To feel deeply must not the heart be open? Must not the body be healthy to respond eagerly? We blunt our minds, our feelings, our bodies, with beliefs and ill will, with strong and hardening stimulants. It is essential to be sensitive, to respond keenly and rightly, but we become blunted, hard, through our appetites. There is no separate entity such as the mind apart from the organism as a whole, and when the organism as a whole is ill-treated, wasted, distracted, then insensitivity sets in. Our environment, our present way of life blunts us, wastes us. How can you be sensitive when every day you indulge in reading or seeing pictures of the slaughter of thousands—this mass murder reported as though it were a successful game. The first

time you read the reports you may feel sick at heart, but the constant repetition of brutal ruthlessness dulls your mind-heart, immunizing you to the utter barbarism of modern society. The radios, magazines, cinemas are ever wasting your sensitive pliabilities; you are forced, threatened, regimented, and how can you, in the midst of this noise, haste and false pursuits, remain sensitive for the cultivation of right thinking?

If you would not have your feelings blunted and hard, you must pay the price for it; you must abandon haste, distraction, wrong professions, and pursuits. You must become aware of your appetites, your limiting environment, and by rightly understanding them you begin to reawaken your sensitivity. Through constant awareness of your thoughts-feelings, the causes of self-enclosure and narrowness fall away. If you would be highly sensitive and clear, you must deliberately work for it; you cannot be worldly and yet be pure in the pursuit of reality. Our difficulty is we want both—the burning appetites and the serenity of reality. You must abandon the one or the other; you cannot have both. You cannot indulge and yet be alert; to be keenly aware there must be freedom from those influences that are crystallizing, blunting.

We have overdeveloped the intellect at the cost of our deeper and clearer feelings, and a civilization that is based on the cultivation of the intellect must bring about ruthlessness and the worship of success. The emphasis on intellect or on emotion leads to unbalance, and intellect is ever seeking to safeguard itself. Mere determination only strengthens the intellect and blunts and hardens it; it is ever self-aggressive in becoming or not-becoming. The ways of the intellect must be understood through constant awareness, and its reeducation must transcend its own reasoning.

Question: I find there is conflict between my occupation and my relationship. They go in different directions. How can I make them meet?

KRISHNAMURTI: Most of our occupations are dictated by tradition, or by greed, or by ambition. In our occupation we are ruthless, competitive, deceitful, cunning, and highly self-protective. If we weaken at any time we may go under, so we must keep up with the high efficiency of the greedy machine of business. It is a constant struggle to maintain a hold, to become sharper and cleverer. Ambition can never find lasting satisfaction; it is ever seeking wider fields for self-assertiveness.

But in relationship quite a different process is involved. In it there must be affection, consideration, adjustment, self-denial, yielding—not to conquer but to live happily. In it there must be self-effacing tenderness, freedom from domination, from possessiveness; but emptiness and fear breed jealousy and pain in relationship. Relationship is a process of self-discovery in which there is wider and deeper understanding; relationship is a constant adjustment in self-discovery. It demands patience, infinite pliability, and a simple heart.

But how can the two meet together—self-assertiveness and love, occupation and relationship? The one is ruthless, competitive, ambitious, the other is self-denying, considerate, gentle; they cannot come together. With one hand people deal in blood and money, and with the other they try to be kind, affectionate, thoughtful. As a relief from their thoughtless and dull occupations, they seek comfort and ease in relationship. But relationship does not yield comfort for it is a distinctive process of self-discovery and understanding. The man of occupation tries to seek, through his life of relationship, comfort and pleasure as a compensation for his wearisome business. His daily occupation of ambition, greed, and ruthlessness lead step by step to war and to the barbarities of modern civilization.

Right occupation is not dictated by tradition, greed, or ambition. If each one is seriously concerned in establishing right relationship, not only with one but with all, then he will find right occupation. Right occupation comes with regeneration, with the change of heart, not with the mere intellectual determination to find it.

Integration is only possible if there is clarity of understanding on all the different levels of our consciousness. There can be no integration of love and ambition, deception and clarity, compassion and war. So long as occupation and relationship are kept apart, so long will there be endless conflict and misery. All reformation within the pattern of duality is retrogression; only beyond it is there creative peace.

May 27, 1945

Second Talk in The Oak Grove

We are confronted every day, are we not, with dualistic problems, problems which are not theoretical or philosophical but actual. Verbally, emotionally, intellectually we face them every day; good and bad, mine and yours, collectivism and individualism, becoming and nonbecoming, worldliness and nonworldliness, and so on—an endless corridor of opposites in which thought-feeling shuffles back and forth. Are these problems of greed and nongreed, war and peace, to be solved within the dualistic pattern, or must thought-feeling go above and beyond to find a permanent answer? Within the pattern of duality there is no lasting answer. Each opposite has an element of its own opposite, and so there can never be a permanent answer within the conflict of the opposites. There is a permanent, unique answer only outside of the pattern.

It is important to understand this problem of duality as deeply as possible. I am not dealing with it as an abstract, theoretical subject, but as an actual problem of our everyday life and conduct. We are aware, are we not, that our thought is a constant struggle within the pattern of duality, of good and bad, of being and not-being, of yours and mine. In it there is conflict and pain; in it all relationship is a process of sorrow; in it there is no hope but travail. Now, is the problem of love and hate to be solved within the field of its own conflict, or must thought-feeling go above and beyond its known pattern?

To find the lasting solution to the conflict of duality and to the pain involved in choice, we must be intensely aware, in silent observation of the full implication of conflict. Only then will we discover that there is a state in which the conflict of duality has ceased. There can be no integration of the opposites—greed and nongreed. He who is greedy, when he attempts to become nongreedy, is still greedy. Must he not abandon both greed and nongreed to be above and beyond the influence of both? Any becoming involves nonbecoming, and as long as there is becoming, there must be duality with its endless conflict.

The cause of duality is desire, craving; through perception and sensation and contact, there arise desire, pleasure, pain, want, nonwant which in turn cause identification as mine and yours, and thus the dualistic process is set going. Is not this conflict worldliness? As long as the thinker separates himself from his thought, so long the vain conflict of the opposites will continue. As long as the thinker is concerned only with the modification of his thoughts and not with the fundamental transformation of himself, so long conflict and sorrow will continue.

Is the thinker separate from his thought? Are not the thinker and his thought an inseparable phenomenon? Why do we separate the thought from the thinker? Is it not one of the cunning tricks of the mind so that the thinker can change his garb according to circumstances, yet remain the same? Outwardly there is the appearance of change, but inwardly the thinker continues to be as he is. The craving for continuity, for permanency, creates this division between the thinker and his thoughts. When the thinker and his thought become inseparable, then only is duality transcended. Only then is there the true religious experience. Only when the thinker ceases is there reality. This inseparable unity of the thinker and his thought is to be experienced but not to be speculated upon. This experience is liberation; in it there is inexpressible joy.

Right thinking alone can bring about the understanding and the transcending of cause-effect and the dualistic process; when the thinker and his thought are integrated through right meditation, then there is the ecstasy of the real.

Question: These monstrous wars cry for a durable peace. Everyone is speaking already of a Third World War. Do you see a possibility of averting the new catastrophe?

KRISHNAMURTI: How can we expect to avert it when the elements and values that cause war continue? Has the war that is just over produced a deep fundamental change in man? Imperialism and oppression are still rampant, perhaps cleverly veiled; separate sovereign states continue; nations are maneuvering themselves into new positions of power; the powerful still oppress the weak; the ruling elite still exploit the ruled; social and class conflicts have not ceased; prejudice and hatred are burning everywhere. As long as professional priests with their organized prejudices justify intolerance and the liquidation of another being for the good of your country and the protection of your interests and ideologies, there will be war. As long as sensory values predominate over eternal value, there will be war.

What you are the world is. If you are nationalistic, patriotic, aggressive, ambitious, greedy, then you are the cause of conflict and war. If you belong to any particular ideology, to a specialized prejudice, even if you call it religion, then you will be the cause of strife and misery. If you are enmeshed in sensory values, then there will be ignorance and confusion. For what you are the world is; your problem is the world's problem.

Have you fundamentally changed because of this present catastrophe? Do you not still call yourself an American, an Englishman, an Indian, a German, and so on? Are you not still greedy for position and power, for possessions and riches? Worship becomes hypocrisy when you are cultivating the causes of war; your prayers lead you to illusion if you allow yourself to indulge in hate and in worldliness. If you do not eradicate in yourself the causes of enmity, of ambition, of greed, then your gods are false gods who will lead you to misery. Only goodwill and compassion can bring order and peace to the world, and not political blueprints and conferences. You must pay the price for peace. You must pay it voluntarily and happily, and the price is the freedom from lust and ill will, worldliness and ignorance, prejudice and hate. If there were such a fundamental change in you, you could help to bring about a peaceful and sane world. To have peace you must be compassionate and thoughtful.

You may not be able to avert the Third World War, but you can free your heart and mind from violence and from those causes that bring about enmity and prevent love.

Then in this dark world there will be some who are pure of heart and mind, and from them perhaps the seed of a true culture might come into being. Make pure your heart and mind, for by your life and action only can there be peace and order. Do not be lost and confused in organizations but remain wholly alone and simple. Do not seek merely to prevent catastrophe but rather let each one deeply eradicate those causes that breed antagonism and strife.

Question: I have written down, as you suggested last year, my thoughts and feelings for several months, but I don't seem to get much further with it. Why? What more am I to do?

KRISHNAMURTI: I suggested last year, as a means to self-knowledge and right thinking, that one should write down every thought-feeling, the pleasant as well as the unpleasant. Thus one becomes aware of the whole content of consciousness, the private thoughts and secret motives, intentions, and bondages. Thus through constant self-awareness there comes self-knowledge which brings about right thinking. For without self-knowledge there can be no understanding. The source of understanding is within oneself, and there is no comprehension of the world and your relationship to it without deep self-knowledge.

The questioner wants to know why he is not able to penetrate within himself deeply, and discover the hidden treasure that lies beyond the superficial attempts at self-knowledge. To dig deeply you must have the right instrument, not merely the desire to dig. To cultivate self-knowledge there must be capacity and not a vague wish for it. Being and wishing are two different things.

To cultivate the right instrument of perception, thought must cease to condemn, to deny, to compare and judge, or to seek comfort and security. If you condemn or are gratified with what you have written down, then you will put an end to the flow of thought-feeling and to understanding. If you wish to understand what another is saying, surely you must listen without any bias, without being distracted by irrelevancies. Similarly, if you wish to understand your own thoughts-feelings, you must observe them with kindly dispassion and not with an attitude of condemnation or approval. Identification prevents and perverts the flow of thought-feeling; tolerant disinterestedness is essential for self-knowledge; self-knowledge opens the door to deep and wide understanding. But it is difficult to be calm with regard to oneself, to one's reactions, and so on, for we have set up a habit of self-condemnation, of self-justification, and it is of this habit that one must be aware. Through constant and alert awareness, not through denial, does thought free itself from habit. This freedom is not of time but of understanding. Understanding is ever in the immediate present.

To cultivate the right instrument of perception, there must be no comparison, for when you compare you cease to understand. If you compare, approximate, you are being merely competitive, ambitious, and your end then is success in which inherently is failure. Comparison implies a pattern of authority according to which you are measuring and guiding yourself. The oppression of authority cripples understanding. Comparison may produce a desired result but it is an impediment to self-knowledge. Comparison implies time and time does not yield understanding.

You are a complex living organism; understand yourself not through comparison but through perception of *what is,* for the present is the doorway to the past and to the future. When thought is free of comparison and identification and their uncreative burden, it is then able to be calm and clear. This habit of comparison, as also the habit of condemnation and approval, leads to conformity and in conformity there is no understanding.

The self is not a static entity but very active, alertly capable in its demands and pursuits; to follow and to understand the endless movement of the self, a keen, pliable mind-heart is necessary, a mind capable of intense self-awareness. To understand, mind must delve deeply and yet it must know when to be alertly passive. It would be foolish and unbalanced to keep on digging without the recuperative and healing power of passivity. We search, analyze, look into ourselves, but it is a process of conflict and pain; there is no joy in it for we are judging or justifying or comparing. There are no moments of silent awareness, of choiceless passivity. It is this choiceless awareness, this creative passivity, that is even more essential than self-observation and investigation. As the fields are cultivated, sown, harvested, and allowed to lie fallow, so must we live the four seasons in a day. If you cultivate, sow, and harvest without giving rest to the soil, it would soon become unproductive. The period of fallowness is as essential as tilling; when the earth lies fallow, the winds, the rains, the sunshine bring to it creative productivity and it renews itself. So must the mind-heart be silent, alertly passive after travail, to renew itself.

Thus through self-awareness of every thought-feeling, the ways of the self are known and understood. This self-awareness with its self-observation and alert passivity brings deep and wide self-knowledge. From self-knowledge there comes right thinking; without right thinking there is no meditation.

Question: The problem of earning a decent living is predominant with most of us. Since economic currents of the world are hopelessly interdependent, I find that almost anything I do either exploits others or contributes to the cause of war. How is one who honestly wishes to achieve right means of livelihood to withdraw from the wheels of exploitation and war?

KRISHNAMURTI: For him who truly wishes to find a right means of livelihood, economic life, as at present organized, is certainly difficult. As the questioner says, economic currents are interrelated and so it is a complex problem, and as with all complex human problems, it must be approached with simplicity. As society is becoming more and more complex and organized, regimentation of thought and action is being enforced for the sake of efficiency. Efficiency becomes ruthlessness when sensory values predominate, when eternal value is set aside.

Obviously there are wrong means of livelihood. He who helps in manufacturing arms and other methods to kill his fellow man is surely occupied with furthering violence, which never brings about peace in the world; the politician who—either for the benefit of his nation or of himself or of an ideology—is occupied in ruling and exploiting others is surely employing wrong means of livelihood which lead to war, to the misery and sorrow of man; the priest who holds to a specialized prejudice, dogma or belief, to a particular form of worship and prayer is also using wrong means of livelihood, for he is only spreading ignorance and intolerance which set man against man. Any profession that leads to and maintains the divisions and conflict between man and man is obviously a wrong means of livelihood. Such occupations lead to exploitation and strife.

Our means of livelihood are dictated, are they not, through tradition or through greed and ambition. Generally we do not deliberately set about choosing the right means of livelihood. We are only too thankful to get what we can and blindly follow the economic system that is about us. But the questioner wants to know how to withdraw from ex-

ploitation and war. To withdraw from them he must not allow himself to be influenced, nor follow traditional occupations, nor must he be envious and ambitious. Many of us choose some profession because of tradition or because we are of a family of lawyers or soldiers or politicians or traders; or our greed for power and position dictates our occupation; ambition drives us to compete and be ruthless in our desire to succeed. So he who would not exploit or contribute to the cause of war must cease to follow tradition, cease to be greedy, ambitious, self-seeking. If he abstains from these he will naturally find right occupation.

But though it is important and beneficial, right occupation is not an end in itself. You may have a right means of livelihood, but if you are inwardly insufficient and poor, you will be a source of misery to yourself and so to others; you will be thoughtless, violent, self-assertive. Without that inward freedom of reality, you will have no joy, no peace. In the search and discovery of that inward reality alone can we be not only content with little, but aware of something that is beyond all measure. It is this which must be first sought out; then other things will come into being in its wake.

This inward freedom of creative reality is not a gift; it is to be discovered and experienced. It is not an acquisition to be gathered to yourself to glorify yourself. It is a state of being, as silence, in which there is no becoming, in which there is completeness. This creativeness may not necessarily seek expression; it is not a talent that demands an outward manifestation. You need not be a great artist nor have an audience; if you seek these you will miss that inward reality. It is neither a gift, nor is it the outcome of talent; it is to be found, this imperishable treasure, when thought frees itself from lust, ill will and ignorance, when thought frees itself from worldliness and personal craving to be; it is to be experienced through right thinking and meditation. Without this inward freedom of reality, existence is pain. As a thirsty man seeks water, so must we seek. Reality alone can quench the thirst of impermanency.

Question: I am an inveterate smoker. I have tried several times to give it up but failed each time. How am I to give it up once and for all?

KRISHNAMURTI: Do not strive to give it up; as with so many habits mere struggle against them only strengthens them. Understand the whole problem of habit, the mental, emotional, and physical. Habit is thoughtlessness and to struggle against thoughtlessness by determined ignorance is vain, stupid. You must understand the process of habit through constant awareness of the grooves of the mind and of the habitual emotional responses. In understanding the deeper issues of habit, the superficial ones fall away. Without understanding the deeper causes of habit, suppose you are able to master the habit of smoking or any other habit, you still will be as you are—thoughtless, empty, a plaything of environment.

How to give up a particular habit is surely not the primary question, for much deeper things are involved. No problem can be solved on its own level. Is any problem solved within the pattern of opposites? Obviously there is conflict within the pattern, but does this conflict resolve the problem? Must you not go outside the pattern of conflict to find a lasting answer? The struggle against a habit does not necessarily result in its abandonment; other habits may be developed or substituted. The struggle merely to overcome habits, without uncovering their deeper significance, makes the mind-heart thoughtless, superficial, insensitive. As with anger, as with armies, conflict exhausts, and no major issue is solved. Similarly conflict

between opposites only blunts the mind-heart, and it is this dullness that prevents the understanding of the problem. Please see the importance of this. Conflict between two opposing desires must end in weariness, in thoughtlessness.

It is this thoughtlessness that must be considered, not the mere giving up of a habit or conflict. The abandonment of a habit will naturally follow if there is thoughtfulness, if there is sensitivity. This sensitivity is blunted, hardened, by the constant struggle of opposing desires. So if you want to smoke, smoke; but be intensely aware of all the implications of habit: thoughtlessness, dependency, loneliness, fear, and so on. Do not merely struggle against habit, but be aware of its full significance.

It is considered intelligent to be in the conflict of the opposites; the struggle between good and evil, between collectivism and individualism, is thought to be necessary for the growth of man; the conflict between God and Devil is accepted as an inevitable process. Does this conflict between the opposites lead to reality? Does it not lead to ignorance and illusion? Is evil to be transcended by its opposite? Must not thought go above and beyond the conflict of both? This conflict of the opposites does not lead to righteousness, to understanding; it leads to weariness, thoughtlessness, insensitivity. Perhaps the criminal, the sinner may be nearer comprehension than the man who is self-righteous in his smug struggle of opposing desires. The criminal could be aware of his crime so there is hope for him, whereas the man in self-righteous conflict of the opposites is merely lost in his own petty ambition to become. The one is vulnerable while the other is enclosed, hardened by his conflict; the one is still susceptible while the other is made insensitive through the conflict and pain of constant struggle to become.

Do not lose yourself in the conflict and pain of the opposites. Do not compare and strive to become the opposite of that which you are. Be wholly, choicelessly aware of *what is,* of your habit, of your fear, of your tendency, and in this single flame of awareness, that which is, is transformed. This transformation is not within the pattern of duality; it is fundamental, creative, with the breath of reality. In this flame of awareness all problems are finally resolved. Without this transformation life is a struggle and pain, and there is no joy, no peace.

June 3, 1945

Third Talk in The Oak Grove

Is it not important to understand and so transcend conflict? Most of us live in a state of inner conflict which produces outer turmoil and confusion; many escape from conflict into illusion, into various activities, into knowledge and ideation, or become cynical and depressed. There are some who, understanding conflict, go beyond its limitations. Without understanding the inward nature of conflict, the warring field which we are, there can be no peace, no joy.

Most of us are caught up in an endless series of inward conflicts, and without resolving them life is utterly wasteful and empty. We are aware of two opposing poles of desire, the wanting and the not-wanting. The conflict between comprehension and ignorance we accept as part of our nature; we do not see that it is impossible to resolve this conflict within the pattern of duality and so we accept it, making a virtue of conflict. We have come to regard it as essential for growth, for the perfecting of man. Do we not say that through conflict we shall learn, we shall understand? We give a religious significance to this conflict of opposites, but does it lead to virtue, to clarification, or does

it lead to ignorance, to insensitivity, to death? Have you never noticed that in the midst of conflict there is no understanding at all, only a blind struggle? Conflict is not productive of understanding. Conflict leads, as we have said, to apathy, to delusion. We must go outside the pattern of duality for creative, revolutionary understanding.

Does not conflict, the struggle to become and not to become, make for a self-enclosing process? Does it not create self-consciousness? Is not the very nature of the self one of conflict and pain? When are you conscious of yourself? When there is opposition, when there is friction, when there is antagonism. In the moment of joy, self-consciousness is non-existent; when there is happiness you do not say, "I am happy"; only when it is absent, when there is conflict, do you become self-conscious. Conflict is a recall to oneself, an awareness of one's own limitation; it is this which causes self-consciousness. This constant struggle leads to many forms of escape, to illusion; without understanding the nature of conflict, the acceptance of authority, belief, or ideology only leads to ignorance and further sorrow. With the understanding of conflict, these become impotent and worthless.

Choice between opposing desires merely continues conflict; choice implies duality; through choice there is no freedom, for will is still productive of conflict. Then how is it possible for thought to go beyond and above the pattern of duality? Only when we understand the ways of craving and of self-gratification, is it possible to transcend the endless conflict of opposites. We are ever seeking pleasure and avoiding sorrow; the constant desire to become hardens the mind-heart, causing strife and pain. Have you not noticed how ruthless a man is in his desire to become? To become something in this world is relatively the same as becoming something in what is considered the spiritual world; in each, man is driven by the desire to become and this craving leads to incessant conflict, to peculiar ruthlessness and antagonism. Then to renounce is to acquire, and acquisition is the seed of conflict. This process of renouncing and acquiring, of becoming and not becoming, is an endless chain of sorrow.

How to go beyond and above this conflict is our problem. This is not a theoretical question, but one that confronts us almost all of the time. We can escape into some fancy which can be rationalized and made to seem real, but nevertheless it is delusion; it is not made real by cunning explanations nor by the number of its adherents. To transcend conflict the craving to become must be experienced and understood. The desire to become is complex and subtle, but as with all complex things it must be approached simply. Be intensely aware of the desire to become. Be aware of the feeling of becoming; with feeling there comes sensitivity which begins to reveal the many implications of becoming. Feeling is hardened by the intellect and by its many cunning rationalizations, and however much the intellect may unravel the complexity of becoming, it is incapable of experiencing. You may verbally grasp all this but it will be of little consequence; only experience and feeling can bring the creative flame of understanding.

Do not condemn becoming but be aware of its cause and effect in yourself. Condemnation, judgment, and comparison do not bring the experience of understanding; on the contrary, they will stop experience. Be aware of identification and condemnation, justification and comparison; be aware of them and they will come to an end. Be silently aware of becoming; experience this silent awareness. Being still and becoming still are two different states. The becoming still can never experience the state of being still. It is only in being still that all conflict is transcended.

Question: Will you please talk about death? I do not mean the fear of death, but rather the promise and hope which the thought of death must always hold for those who are aware throughout life that they do not belong.

KRISHNAMURTI: Why are we concerned more with death than with living? Why do we look to death as a release, as a promise of hope? Why should there be more happiness, more joy in death, than in life? Why need we look to death as a renewal, rather than to life? We want to escape from the pain of existence into a promise and hope that the unknown holds. Living is conflict and misery and as we educate ourselves to inevitable death, we look to death for reward. Death is glorified or shunned depending on the travail of life; life is a thing to be endured and death to be welcomed. Again we are caught in the conflict of the opposites. There is no truth in the opposites. We do not understand life, the present, so we look to the future, to death. Will tomorrow, the future, death, bring understanding? Will time open the door to reality? We are ever concerned with time, the past weaving itself into the present, and into the future, we are the product of time, the past; we escape into the future, into death.

The present is the eternal. Through time the timeless is not experienced. The now is ever existent; even if you escape into the future, the now is ever present. The present is the doorway to the past. If you do not understand the present now, will you understand it in the future? What you are now you will be, if the present is not understood. Understanding comes only through the present; postponement does not yield comprehension. Time is transcended only in the stillness of the present. This tranquillity is not to be gained through time, through becoming tranquil; there must be stillness, not the becoming still. We look to time as a means to become; this becoming is endless, it is not the eternal, the timeless. The becoming is endless conflict, leading to illusion. In the stillness of the present is the eternal.

But thought-feeling is weaving back and forth, like a shuttle, between the past, the present, and the future; it is ever rearranging its memories, ever maneuvering itself into a better position, more advantageous and comforting to itself. It is forever dissipating and formulating, and how can such a mind be still, creatively empty? It is continually causing its own becoming by endless effort, and how can such a mind understand the still being of the present? Right thinking and meditation only can bring about the clarity of understanding, and in this alone is there tranquillity.

The death of someone whom you love brings sorrow. The shock of that sorrow is benumbing, paralyzing, and as you come out of it you seek an escape from that sorrow. The lack of companionship, the habits that are revealed, the void and the loneliness that are uncovered through death cause pain, and you instinctively want to run away from it. You want comfort, a palliative to ease the suffering. Suffering is an indication of ignorance, but in seeking an escape from suffering, you are only nourishing ignorance. Instead of blunting the mind-heart in sorrow through escapes, comforts, rationalizations, beliefs, be intensely aware of its cunning defense and comforting demands, and then there will be the transformation of that emptiness and sorrow. Because you seek to escape, sorrow pursues; because you seek comfort and dependence, loneliness is intensified. Not to escape, not to seek comfort, is extremely difficult, and only intense self-awareness can eradicate the cause of sorrow.

In death we seek immortality; in the movement of birth and death we long for permanency; caught in the flux of time we crave for the timeless; being in shadow we believe in light. Death does not lead to immortality; there is immortality only in life without death. In life we know death for we cling to life. We gather, we become; because we gather, death comes, and knowing death, we cling to life.

The hope and belief in immortality is not the experiencing of immortality. Belief and hope must cease for the immortal to be. You the believer, the maker of desire, must cease for the immortal to be. Your very belief and hope strengthen the self, and you will know only birth and death. With the cessation of craving, the cause of conflict, there comes creative stillness, and in this silence there is that which is birthless and deathless. Then life and death are one.

Question: It is easier to be free from sexual cravings than from subtle ambitions; for individuality wants self-expression with every breath. To be free from one's egotism means complete revolution in thinking. How can one remain in the world with such a reversal of mind?

KRISHNAMURTI: Why do we want to remain in the world, the world that is so ruthless, ignorant, and lustful? We may have to live in it but existence becomes painful only when we are of it. When we are ambitious, when there is enmity, when sensory values become all-important, then we are lost and then the world holds us. Can we not live without greed among the greedy, content with little? Among the unhealthy can we not live in health? The world is not apart from us, we are the world; we have made it what it is. It has acquired its worldliness because of us, and to leave it we must put away from us worldliness. Then only can we live with the world and not be of it.

Freedom from sex and ambition has no meaning without love. Chastity is not the product of the intellect; if the mind plans and plots to be chaste, it is no longer chaste. Love alone is chaste. Without love, the mere freedom from lust is barren and so the cause of endless strife and sorrow.

Once again the desire to be free from ambition is a conflict within the pattern of duality. If in this pattern you have trained yourself not to be ambitious, you are still in the opposites, and so there is no freedom. You have only substituted one label for another and so conflict continues. Cannot we experience directly that state beyond the pattern of duality? Do not let us think in terms of becoming, which indicate, do they not, the conflict of opposites. "I am this and I want to become that" only strengthens conflict and so blunts the mind-heart. We are accustomed to think in terms of the future, to be or to become. Is it not possible to be aware of *what is?* When we think-feel *what is* without comparison, without judgment, with that complete integration of the thinker with his thought, then that which is, is utterly transformed; but this transformation can never take place within the field of duality. So let us be aware, not become aware, of ambition. When we are so aware we are conscious of all its implications; this feeling is important, not the mere intellectual analysis of the cause and effect of ambition. When you are aware of ambition, you are conscious of its assertiveness, of its competitive ruthlessness, of its pleasures and pain; you are also conscious of its effect on society and relationship; of its social and business moralities, which are immoral; of its cunning and hidden ways which ultimately lead to strife. Ambition breeds envy and ill will, the power to dominate and to oppress. Be aware of yourself as you are and of the world which you have created, and without condemnation or justification be silently aware of your feeling ambitious.

If you are silently aware, as we explained, then the thinker and his thought are one, they are not separate but indivisible; then only is

there complete transformation of ambition. But most of us, if we are aware at all, are conscious of the cause and effect of ambition and unfortunately we stop there; but if we looked more closely into this process of choice, we would abandon it, for conflict is not productive of understanding. In abandoning it we would come upon the thinker and his thought. Just as the qualities cannot be separated from the self, so the thinker cannot be separated from his thought. When such integration takes place there is complete transformation of the thinker. This is an arduous task demanding alert pliability and choiceless awareness. Meditation comes from right thinking, and right thinking from self-knowledge. Without self-knowledge there is no understanding.

Question: I understand you to say that creativeness is an intoxication from which it is hard to free oneself. Yet you often speak of the creative person. Who is he if he is not the artist, the poet, the builder?

KRISHNAMURTI: Is the artist, the poet, the builder necessarily the creative person? Is he not also lustful, worldly, seeking personal success? So is he not contributing to the chaos and misery in the world? Is he not responsible for its catastrophes and sorrows? He is responsible when he is seeking fame, is envious, when he is worldly; when his values are sensate; when he is passionate. Because he has a certain talent, does that make the artist a creative person?

Creativeness is something infinitely greater than the mere capacity to express; mere successful expression and its recognition surely does not constitute creativeness. Success in this world implies, does it not, being of this world, the world of oppression and cruelty, ignorance and ill will? Ambition does produce results, but does it not bring with it misery and confusion for him who is successful and for his fellow man? The scientist, the builder, may have brought certain benefits, but have they not brought also destruction and untold misery? Is this creativeness? Is it creativeness to set man against man as the politicians, the rulers, the priests are doing?

Creativeness comes into being when there is freedom from the bondage of craving with its conflict and sorrow. With the abandonment of the self with its assertiveness and ruthlessness and its endless struggles to become, there comes creative reality. In the beauty of a sunset or a still night, have you not felt intense, creative joy? At that moment, the self being temporarily absent, you are vulnerable, open to reality. This is a rare and unsought event, out of your control, but having once felt its intensity, the self demands further enjoyment of it, and so conflict begins.

We all have experienced the temporary absence of the self and have felt at that moment the extraordinary creative ecstasy, but instead of its being rare and accidental, is it not possible to bring about the right state in which reality is eternal being? If you seek that ecstasy then it will be the activity of the self, which will produce certain results, but it will not be that state which comes through right thinking and right meditation. The subtle ways of the self must be known and understood, for with self-knowledge comes right thinking and meditation.

Right thinking comes with the constant flow of self-awareness—awareness of worldly actions as well as of the activities in meditation. Creativeness with its ecstasy comes with the freedom from craving, which is virtue.

Question: During the last few years you seem to have concentrated in your talks, more and more, on the development of right thinking. Formerly you used to speak more about mystic experiences. Are you deliberately avoiding this aspect now?

KRISHNAMURTI: Is it not necessary to lay right foundation for right experience? Without right thinking, is not experience illusory? If you would have a well-built and lasting house, must you not lay it on a firm and right foundation? To experience is comparatively easy, and depending on our conditioning, we experience. We experience according to our beliefs and ideals but do all such experiences bring freedom? Have you not noticed that according to one's tradition and belief experience comes? Tradition and creed mold experience, but to experience reality which is not of any tradition or ideology, must not thought go above and beyond its own conditioning? Is not reality ever the uncreated? And must not the mind cease to create, to formulate, if it would experience the uncreated? Must not the mind-heart be utterly still and silent for the being of the real?

As any experience can be misinterpreted, so any experience can be made to appear as the real. On the interpreter depends the translation and if the translator is biased, ignorant, molded in a pattern of thought, then his understanding will conform to his conditioning. If he is so-called religious, his experiences will be according to his tradition and belief; if he is nonreligious, then his experiences will shape themselves according to his background. On the instrument depends its capacity; the mind-heart must make itself capable. It is capable of either experiencing the real or creating for itself illusion. To experience the real is arduous for it demands infinite pliability and deep, basic stillness. This pliability, this stillness is not the result of desire or of an act of will, for desire and will are the outcome of craving, the dual drive to be and not to be. Pliability and tranquillity are not the outcome of conflict; they come into being with understanding and understanding comes with self-knowledge.

Without self-knowledge you merely live in a state of contradiction and uncertainty; without self-knowledge what you think-feel has no basis; without self-knowledge enlightenment is not possible. You are the world, the neighbor, the friend, the so-called enemy. If you would understand, you must first understand yourself, for in you is the root of all understanding. In you is the beginning and the end. To understand this vast complex entity, mind-heart must be simple.

To understand the past, mind-heart must be aware of its activities in the present, for through the present alone the past may be understood, but you will not understand the present if there is self-identification.

So through the present the past is revealed; through the immediate consciousness the many hidden layers are discovered and understood. Thus through constant awareness there comes deep and wide self-knowledge.

June 10, 1945

Fourth Talk in The Oak Grove

Can each one who is responsible for the conflict and misery in himself, and so in the world, allow his mind-heart to be dulled by erroneous philosophies and ideas? If you who have created this struggle and suffering do not change fundamentally, will systems, conferences, blueprints bring about order and goodwill? Is it not imperative that you transform yourself, for what you are the world is? Your inward conflicts express themselves in outward disasters. Your problem is the world's problem and you alone can solve it, not another; you cannot leave it to others. The politician, the economist, the reformer is like yourself an opportunist, a cunning deviser of plans; but our problem, this human conflict and misery, this empty existence

which produces such agonizing disasters, needs more than cunning devices, more than superficial reforms of the politician and the propagandist. It needs a radical change of the human mind, and no one can bring about this transformation, save yourself. For what you are, your group, your society, your leader is. Without you the world is not; in you is the beginning and end of all things. No group, no leader can establish eternal value save yourself.

Catastrophes and misery come when temporary sensate values dominate over eternal value. The permanent, eternal value is not the result of belief; your belief in God does not mean that you are experiencing eternal value, the way of your life alone will show its reality. Oppression and exploitation, aggressiveness and economic ruthlessness inevitably follow when we have lost reality. You have lost it when, professing the love of God, you condone and justify the murdering of your fellow man, when you justify mass murder in the name of peace and freedom. As long as you give supreme importance to sensory values, there will be conflict, confusion, and sorrow. Killing another can never be justified, and we lose man's immense significance when sensate values remain predominant.

We will have misery and tribulation so long as religion is organized to be part of the state, the handmaiden of the state. It helps to condone organized force as policy of the state; and so encourages oppression, ignorance, and intolerance. How then can religion allied with the state fulfill its only true function—that of revealing and maintaining eternal value? When reality is lost and not sought after, there is disunity and man will be against man. Confusion and misery cannot be banished by the forgetful process of time, by the comforting idea of evolution which only engenders slothfulness, smug acceptance and the continuous drift towards catastrophe; we must not let the course of our lives be directed by others, for others, or for the sake of the future. We are responsible for our life, not another; we are responsible for our conduct, not another; not another can transform us. Each one must discover and experience reality, and in that alone is there joy, serenity, and highest wisdom.

How then can we come to this experience—through the change of outward circumstances or through transformation from within? Outer change implies the control of environment through legislation, through economic and social reform, through knowledge of facts, and through fluctuating improvement, either violent or gradual. But does modification of the outer circumstances ever bring about fundamental inner transformation? Is not inner transformation first necessary to bring about an outward result? You may, through legislation, forbid ambition as ambition breeds ruthlessness, self-assertiveness, competition, and conflict, but can ambition be rooted out from without? Will it not, suppressed in one way, assert itself in another? Does not the inner motive, private thought-feeling, always determine the outer? To bring about an outward peaceful transformation, should there not take place first a deep psychological change? Can the outer, however pleasant, bring about lasting contentment? The inner craving ever modifies the outer. Psychologically what you are your society is, your state is, your religion is; if you are lustful, envious, ignorant, then your environment is what you are. We create the world in which we live. To bring about a radical and peaceful change, there must be voluntary and intelligent inner transformation; this psychological change is surely not to be brought about through compulsion, and if it is, then there will be such inner conflict and confusion as will again precipitate society into disaster. The inner regeneration must be voluntary, in-telligent, not compelled. We must first seek reality and then only can there be peace and order about us.

When you approach the problem of existence from without, there is at once the dual process set going; in duality there is endless conflict and such conflict only dulls the mind-heart. When you approach the problem of existence from within, there is no division between the inner and the outer; the division ceases because the inner is the outer, the thinker and his thoughts are one, inseparable. But we falsely separate the thought from the thinker and so try to deal only with the part, to educate and modify the part, thereby hoping to transform the whole. The part ever becomes more and more divided, and thus there is more and more conflict. So we must be concerned with the thinker from within and not with the modification of the part, his thought.

But unfortunately most of us are caught between the uncertainty of the outer and the uncertainty of the inner. It is this uncertainty that must be understood. It is the uncertainty of value that brings about conflict, confusion, and sorrow and prevents our following a clear course of action, either of the outer or of the inner. If we followed the outer with full awareness, perceiving its full significance, then such a course would inevitably lead to the inner, but unfortunately we get lost in the outer, for we are not sufficiently pliable in our self-inquiry. As you examine sensory values by which our thoughts-feelings are dominated, and become aware of them without choice, you will perceive that the inner becomes clear. This discovery will bring freedom and creative joy. But this discovery and its experience cannot be made for you by another. Will your hunger be satisfied through watching another eat? Through your own self-awareness you must awaken to false values and so discover eternal value. There can be fundamental change within and without only when thought-feeling disentangles itself from those sensate values that cause conflict and sorrow.

Question: In truly great works of art, poetry, music there is expressed and conveyed something indescribable which seems to mirror reality or truth or God. Yet it is a fact that in their private lives most of those who created such works have never succeeded in extricating themselves from the vicious circle of conflict. How can it be explained that an individual who has not liberated himself is able to create something in which the conflict of the opposites is transcended? Or to put the question in reverse, don't you have to conclude that creativeness is born out of conflict?

KRISHNAMURTI: Is conflict necessary for creativeness? What do we mean by conflict? We crave to be, positively or negatively. This constant craving breeds conflict. We consider this conflict inevitable, almost virtuous; we consider it essential for human growth.

What happens when you are in conflict? Through conflict mind-heart is made weary, dull, insensitive. Conflict strengthens self-protective capacities, conflict is the substance on which the self thrives. In its very nature the self is the cause of all conflict, and where the self is, creation is not.

Is conflict necessary for creative being? When do you feel that creative, overpowering ecstasy? Only when all conflict has ceased, only when the self is absent, only when there is complete tranquillity. This stillness cannot take place when the mind-heart is agitated, when it is in conflict; this only strengthens the self-enclosing process. As most of us are in a state of constant struggle within ourselves, we rarely have such moments of high sensibility or stillness, and when they do occur they are accidental. So we try to recapture those accidental moments and only further burden our mind-heart with the dead past.

Does not the poet, the artist, go through the same process that we do? Perhaps he may be more sensitive, more alert and so more vulnerable, open, but surely he, too, experiences creation in moments of self-abnegation, self-forgetfulness, in moments of complete stillness. This experience he tries to express in marble or in music; but does not conflict come into being in expressing the experience, in perfecting the word, and not at the moment of experience itself? Creation can only take place when the mind-heart is still, and not caught in the net of becoming. The open passivity to reality is not the result of craving with its will and conflict.

Like us the artist has moments of stillness in which creation is experienced; then he puts it down in paint, in music, in form. His expression assumes great value for he has painted it, it is his work. Ambition, fame become important and in an endless, stupid struggle he is caught. He thus contributes to the world's misery, envy and bloodshed, passion and ill will. He gets lost in this struggle and the more he is lost, the further recedes his sensibility, his vulnerability to truth. His worldly conflicts dim the joyous clarity even though his technical capacity helps him to carry on with his empty and hardening visions.

But we are not great artists, musicians, or poets; we have no special gifts or talents; we have no release through marble, painting, or through the garland of words. We are in conflict and sorrow but we, too, have occasional moments of the immensity of truth. Then momentarily we forget ourselves, but soon we are back into our daily turmoil, blunting and hardening our mind-heart. The mind-heart is never still; if it is, it is the silence of weariness, but such a state is not the silence of understanding, of wisdom. This creative, expectant emptiness is not brought about by will or by desire; it comes into being when conflict of the self ceases.

Conflict ceases only when there is complete revolution in value, not mere substitution. Through self-awareness alone can the mind-heart free itself from all values; this transcending of all values is not easy, it comes not with practice, but with the deepening of awareness. It is not a gift, a talent of the few, but all who are strenuous and eager can experience creative reality.

Question: The present is an unmitigated tragic horror. Why do you insist that in the present is the eternal?

KRISHNAMURTI: The present is conflict and sorrow, with an occasional flash of passing joy. The present weaves back and forth into the past and into the future, and so the present is restless. The present is the result of the past, our being is founded upon it. How can you understand the past save through its result, the present? You cannot dig into the past by any other instrument than the one you have, which is the present. The present is the doorway to the past and if you wish, to the future. What you are is the result of the past, of yesterday, and to understand yesterday you must begin with today. To understand yourself, you must begin with yourself as you are today.

Without comprehending the present, which is rooted in the past, you will have no understanding. The present misery of man is understood when, through the door of the present, he is able to be aware of the causes that have produced it. You cannot brush aside the present in trying to understand the past, but only through awareness of the present does the past begin to unfold itself. The present is tragic and bloody; surely not by denying it, not by justifying it, will we understand it. We have to face it as it is and uncover the causes that have brought about the present. How you regard the present, how your mind is conditioned to it, will reveal the process of the past; if you are prejudiced, nationalistic, if you hate, what you are now will pervert your understanding of the past; your passion, ill will and ignorance—what you are now—will corrupt your understanding of the causes that have led to the present. In understanding yourself, as you are now, the roll of the past unfolds itself.

The present is of the highest importance; the present, however tragic and painful, is the only door to reality. The future is the continuance of the past through the present; through understanding the present is the future transformed. The present is the only time for understanding for it extends into yesterday and into tomorrow. The present is the whole of time; in the seed of the present are the past and the future; the past is the present and the future is the present. The present is the eternal, the timeless. But we regard the present, the now, as a passage to the past or to the future; in the process of becoming, the present is a means to an end and thereby loses its immense significance. The becoming creates continuity, everlastingness, but it is not the timeless, the eternal. Craving to become weaves the pattern of time. Have you not experienced in moments of great ecstasy, the cessation of time?—there is no past, no future, but an intense awareness, a timeless present. Having experienced such a state, greed begins its activities and recreates time, recalling, reviving, looking to the future for further experience, rearranging the pattern of time to capture the timeless. Thus greed, the becoming, holds thought-feeling in the bondage of time.

So be aware of the present, however sorrowful or pleasant; then it will unfold itself as a time process, and if thought-feeling can follow its subtle and devious ways and transcend them, then that very extensional awareness is the timeless present. Look only to the present, neither to the past nor to the future, for love is the present, the timeless.

Question: You decry war and yet are you not supporting it?

KRISHNAMURTI: Are we not all of us maintaining this terrible mass murder? We are responsible, each one, for war; war is an end result of our daily life; it is brought into being through our daily thought-feeling-action. What we are in our occupational, social, religious relationships, that we project; what we are, the world is.

Unless we understand the primary and secondary issues involved in the responsibility for war, we shall be confused and unable to extricate ourselves from its disaster. We must know where to lay the emphasis, and then only shall we understand the problem. The inevitable end of this society is war; it is geared to war, its industrialization leads to war; its values promote war. Whatever we do within its borders contributes to war. When we buy something, the tax goes towards war; the postage stamps help to support war. We cannot escape from war, go where we will, especially now, as society is organized for total war. The most simple and harmless work contributes to war in one way or another. Whether we like it or not, by our very existence we are helping to maintain war. So what are we to do? We cannot withdraw to an island or to a primitive community, for the present culture is everywhere. So what can we do? Shall we refuse to support war by not paying taxes, not buying stamps? Is that the primary issue? If it is not, and if it is only the secondary, then do not let us be distracted by it.

Is not the primary issue much deeper, that of the cause of war itself? If we can understand the cause of war, then the secondary issue can be approached from a different point of view altogether; if we do not under-

stand, then we shall be lost in it. If we can free ourselves from the causes of war, then perhaps the secondary problem may not arise at all.

So emphasis must be laid upon the discovery within oneself of the cause of war; this discovery must be made by each one and not by an organized group, for group activities tend to make for thoughtlessness, mere propaganda, and slogan, which only breed further intolerance and strife. The cause must be self-discovered, and thus each one, through direct experience, liberates himself from it.

If we consider deeply we are well aware of the causes of war: passion, ill will, and ignorance; sensuality, worldliness, and the craving for personal fame and continuity; greed, envy, and ambition; nationalism with its separate sovereignties, economic frontiers, social divisions, racial prejudices, and organized religion. Cannot each one be aware of his greed, ill will, ignorance, and so free himself from them? We hold to nationalism for it is an outlet to our cruel, criminal instincts; in the name of our country or ideology, we can murder or liquidate with impunity, become heroes, and the more we kill our fellow men, the more honor we receive from our country.

Now is not liberation from the cause of conflict and sorrow the primary issue? If we do not lay emphasis upon this, how will the solution of the secondary problems stop war? If we do not root out the causes of war in ourselves, of what value is it to tinker with the outward results of our inner state? We must, each one, dig deeply and clear away lust, ill will, and ignorance; we must utterly abandon nationalism, racism, and those causes that breed enmity. We must concern ourselves wholly with that which is of primary importance and not be confused with secondary issues.

Question: You are very depressing. I seek inspiration to carry on; you do not cheer us with words of courage and hope. Is it wrong to seek inspiration?

KRISHNAMURTI: Why do you want to be inspired? Is it not because in yourself you are empty, uncreative, lonely? You want to fill this loneliness, this aching void; you must have tried different ways of filling it, and you hope to escape from it again by coming here. This process of covering up the arid loneliness is called inspiration. Inspiration then becomes a mere stimulation, and as with all stimulation, it soon brings its own boredom and insensitivity. So we go from one inspiration, stimulation, to another, each bringing its own disappointment and weariness; thus the mind-heart loses its pliability, its sensitivity; the inner capacity of tension is lost through this constant process of stretching and relaxing. Tension is necessary to discover, but a tension that demands relaxation or a stimulation soon loses its capacity to renew itself, to be pliable, to be alert. This alert pliability cannot be induced from the outside; it comes when it is not dependent upon stimulation, upon inspiration.

Is not all stimulation similar in effect? Whether you take a drink or are stimulated by a picture or an idea, whether you go to a concert or to a religious ceremony, or work yourself up over an act, however noble or ignoble—does not all this blunt the mind-heart? A righteous anger, which is an absurdity, however stimulating and inspiring it may be, makes for insensitivity; and is not the highest form of intelligence, sensitivity, receptivity, necessary to experience reality? Stimulation breeds dependence and dependence, whether worthy or unworthy, causes fear. It is relatively unimportant how one is stimulated or inspired, whether through organized church or politics or through distraction, for the result will be the same—insensitivity caused through fear and dependence.

Distractions become stimulations. Our society primarily encourages distraction, distraction in every form. Our thinking-feeling itself has become a process of wandering away from the center, from reality. So it is extremely difficult to withdraw from all distractions, for we have become almost incapable of being choicelessly aware of *what is*. So conflict arises which further distracts our thought-feeling, and it is only through constant awareness that thought-feeling is able to extricate itself from the net of distractions.

Besides, who can give you cheer, courage, and hope? If we rely on another, however great and noble, we are utterly lost, for dependence breeds possessiveness in which there is endless struggle and pain. Cheer and happiness are not ends in themselves; they are, as courage and hope, incidents in the search of something that is an end in itself. It is this end that must be sought after patiently and diligently, and only through its discovery will our turmoil and pain cease. The journey towards its discovery lies through oneself; every other journey is a distraction leading to ignorance and illusion. The journey within oneself must be undertaken not for a result, not to solve conflict and sorrow; for the search itself is devotion, inspiration. Then the journeying itself is a revealing process, an experience which is constantly liberating and creative. Have you not noticed that inspiration comes when you are not seeking it? It comes when all expectation has ceased, when the mind-heart is still. What is sought after is self-created and so is not the real.

Question: You say that life and death are one and the same thing. Please elaborate this startling statement.

KRISHNAMURTI: We know birth and death, existence and nonexistence; we are aware of this conflict between the opposites, the desire to live, to continue, and the fear of death, of noncontinuance. Our life is held in the pattern of becoming and nonbecoming. We may have theories, beliefs, and accordingly, experience, but they are still within the field of duality, of birth and death.

We think-feel in terms of time, of living, of becoming, or of not becoming, or of death, or of extending this becoming beyond death. The pattern of our thought-feeling moves from the known to the known, from the past to the present to the future; if there is fear of the future, it clings to the past or to the present. We are held in time and how can we, who think-feel in terms of time, experience the reality of timelessness, in which life and death are one?

Have you not experienced in moments of great intensity the cessation of time? Such a cessation is generally forced upon one; it is accidental, but depending upon our pleasure in it, we desire to repeat the experience again. So we become once more prisoners of time. Is it not possible for the mind-heart to stop formulating, to be utterly still and not forced into stillness by an act of will? Will and determination are still self-continuation and so within the field of time. Does not the determination to be, the will to become, imply self-growth, time, which makes for the fear of death?

As the stump of a dead tree in the middle of a stream gathers the floating wreckage, so we gather, we cling to our accumulation; thus we and the deathless stream of life are separate. We sit on the dead stump of our accumulation and consider life and death; we do not let go the ever-accumulating process and be of the living waters. To be free from accumulation there must be deep self-knowledge, not the superficial knowledge of the few layers of our consciousness. The dis-

covery and the experience of all the layers of consciousness is the beginning of true meditation. In the tranquillity of mind-heart are wisdom and reality.

Reality is to be experienced, not speculated upon. This experience can only be when the mind-heart ceases to accumulate. Mind-heart does not cease to accumulate through denial or through determination, but only through self-awareness; through self-knowledge the cause of accumulation is discovered. It is experienced only when the conflict of the opposites ceases. Only right thinking, which comes with self-knowledge and right meditation, can bring about the unity of life and death. It is only by dying each day that there can be eternal renewal.

It is difficult to so die if you are in the process of becoming, if you are gathering, sitting on the stump of dead accumulation. You must abandon it, plunge into the ever-living waters; you must die each day to the day's gathering, die both to the pleasant and the unpleasant. We cling to the pleasant and let the unpleasant go; so we strengthen in gratification and know death. Without seeking reward, let us abandon our gatherings and then only can there be the immortal. Then life is not opposed to death or is death a darkening of life.

June 17, 1945

Fifth Talk in The Oak Grove

This morning I am going to answer questions only. These answers and talks will be of little significance if they remain merely on the verbal level. Most of us seek stimulation and find it in various ways but it soon wears out. Only experience keeps the mind-heart pliable and alert, but experience is beyond and above intellectual and emotional gratification and stimulation. Feeling makes reason pliable and it is this pliability of reason with the vulnerability of feeling that brings experience. It is experience, when rightly understood, that transforms.

At all times, and especially now, there is need for transformation through vital experience; this transformation is essential in a world that has become utterly ruthless, a world whose values are predominantly sensate, a world that is corrupt in its own degradation. Without deeply and widely experiencing eternal value, we shall not find any solution to our problems; any answer other than that of the real will only increase our burden and sorrow. To so experience, each one must stand alone, not dependent on any authority, on any organization, religious or secular, for dependence of any kind creates uncertainty and fear, thus preventing the experiencing of the real. In the outer world there is no hope, no clarity, no creative and renewing understanding, there is only bloodshed and confusion and mounting disaster. Only within is there understanding and this understanding is to be discovered not through example, not through authority. Through self-awareness and self-knowledge only, can come tranquillity and wisdom. There is no tranquillity if you are following another; there is no peace if you are worldly; there is no understanding if there is self-ignorance. Through silent awareness of the outer and in being objectively aware of the events of life, you are inevitably forced to be aware of the inner, the subjective; in comprehending the self the outer becomes clear and significant. The outer has no significance in itself; it has significance only in relation to the inner. To experience and understand the inner you must be prepared to be alone; you must withstand the persuasive weight of the outer, its logical and cunning deceits.

Question: You said last Sunday that each one of us is responsible for these terrible wars. Are we also responsible for the abominable tortures in the concentration camps and for the deliberate extermination of a people in Central Europe?

KRISHNAMURTI: Is it not very evident that each one of us is responsible for war? Wars do not come into being out of unknown causes, they have definite sources, and those who wish to extricate themselves from this periodical madness called war must search out these causes and free themselves. War is one of the greatest calamities that could happen to man who is capable of experiencing the real. He must be concerned with eliminating the cause of war within himself, not with who is less or more degraded and terrible in war. We must not be carried away with secondary issues, but be aware of the primary issue which is organized killing itself. The secondary issues may cause fear and the desire for vengeance, but without understanding the essential reasons for war, conflict and sorrow will not cease.

To kill another is the greatest crime for man is capable of realizing the highest. War, the deliberate organization of murder, is the greatest catastrophe that man can bring upon himself, for with it comes untold misery and destruction, degradation, and corruption; when once you admit such a vast "evil" as the organized murder of others, then you open the door to a host of minor disasters. Each one of us is responsible for war, for each one has brought about the present condition, consciously or unconsciously, by his attitude towards life, by the false values he has given to existence. Having lost the eternal value, the passing sensory values become all-important. There is no end to ever-expanding desire. Things are necessary but have no eternal value, and the mad desire for possessions ever leads to strife and misery.

When acquisitiveness in every form is encouraged, when nationalism and separate sovereign states exist, when religion separates, when there is intolerance and ignorance, then killing your fellow man is inevitable. War is the result of our everyday life. Passion, ill will, and oppression are justified when they are national; to kill for the state, for the country, for an ideology, is considered necessary, noble. Each one indulges in this degrading ruthlessness, for there is in each one the desire to do harm. War becomes a means of releasing one's own brutal instincts and encourages irresponsibility. Such a state is only possible when sensate values predominate.

As each one is responsible for the shaping of this culture, if each one does not radically transform himself, then how can there be an end to this brutal world and its ways? Each one is responsible for these tragedies and disasters, for tortures and bestialities, if he thinks-feels in terms of nations, groups, or thinks of himself as Hindu or Buddhist, Christian or Muslim. If a so-called foreigner in India is killed by a nationalist, then I am responsible for that murder if I am a nationalist; but I am not responsible if I do not think-feel in terms of nations, groups, or classes, if I am not lustful, if I have no ill will, if I am not worldly. Then only is there freedom from responsibility for killing, torturing, oppressing.

We have lost the feeling of humanity; we feel responsible only to the class or group to which we belong; we feel responsible to a name, to a label. We have lost compassion, the love of the whole, and without this quickening flame of life we look to politicians, to priests, to some economic planning for peace and happiness. In these there is no hope. In each one alone is there creative understanding, that compassion which is necessary for the well-being of man. Right means create right ends, wrong means will bring only emptiness and death, not peace and joy.

Question: I feel I cannot reach the other shore without help, without the grace of God.

If I can say, "Thy will be done" and dissolve myself in it, do I not dissolve my limitations? If I can relinquish myself unconditionally, is there not grace to help me bridge the gulf which separates God and me?

KRISHNAMURTI: This abandonment of the self is not an act of will; this crossing over to the other shore is not an activity of purpose or of gain. Reality comes in the fullness of silence and wisdom. You may not invite reality, it must come to you; you may not choose reality, it must choose you.

We must understand effort, unconditional stillness, self-abandonment, for through right awareness alone comes meditative tranquillity.

What is right effort? There is an understanding of right effort when there is an awareness of the process of becoming. Just as long as effort is made to become, so long will duality exist—the thinker separating himself from his thought. This conflict of opposites is considered inevitable and necessary for freedom and growth. When one who is greedy makes an effort to become nongreedy, this effort we consider righteous and spiritual. But is it right effort? Is effort spent in overcoming the opposite productive of understanding? Is one not still greedy in trying to become nongreedy? He may take on a new, gratifying, verbal garb, but the maker of the effort is still the same, he is still greedy. The effort made to become not only creates the conflict of opposites but also is directed along wrong channels, for, to become is still to be in conflict and sorrow; so there is no freedom for experiencing truth in the long corridor of opposites.

Our effort is spent in denying or accepting, and thus thought-feeling is made blunt in this endless conflict. This surely is wrong effort for it is not productive of creative understanding. Right endeavor consists in being choicelessly aware of this conflict, in being silently observant without identification. It is this silent, choiceless awareness of conflict that brings freedom. In this passive awareness that is tranquil, reality comes into being.

Be aware of your conflict, of how you deny, justify, compare, or identify; of how you try to become; be aware of the deep, full significance of the pain of the opposites. Then will come the experience of the inseparability of the thinker and his thought, the stillness of understanding through which alone there can be radical transformation, the crossing over to the other shore without the action of will.

There is a vast difference between becoming still and being still. We must die each day to all experiences and accumulations, fears and hopes, and we can only do this by actively being aware of our conflicts, and then being passively still. We must live each day the four seasons, the spring, summer, autumn, and winter of passivity. As in winter the fields lie fallow, open to the heavens, to revitalize themselves, so the mind-heart must allow itself to be open, creatively empty. Then only can there be the breath of reality.

This creative emptiness, this ardent passivity, is not brought about through an act of will. It is extremely difficult for those who are slaves to distraction, who are incessantly active, who are ever striving to become, to be alertly passive. If you would understand, the mind-heart must be still; there must be heightened sensitivity to receive, and there can be tranquillity only in understanding. This silent awareness is not an act of determination, but it comes into being when thought-feeling is not caught in the net of becoming. You never say to a child become still, but be still. We say to ourselves we will become, and for this becoming we have various excuses and interminable reasons, and so we are never still. The becoming still can never be the being still; only with the death of becoming is there being.

In moments of great creativity, in moments of great beauty, there is utter tranquillity; in these moments there is complete absence of the self with all its conflicts; it is this negation, the highest form of thinking-feeling, that is essential for creative being. But these moments are rare with most of us, the moments when the thinker and his thought are transcended; these occasions happen unexpectedly, but the self soon returns. Having once experienced this living stillness, thought-feeling clings to its memory, thus preventing the further experience of reality. This cultivation of memory is effort directed along wrong channels, resulting in the strengthening of the self with its conflict and pain; but if we are deeply aware of our problems and conflicts and understand them, then this very cultivation of self-knowledge brings about alert passivity and tranquillity. In this living silence is reality. Only in utter simplicity, when all craving has ceased, is the bliss of reality.

Question: I am an inventor and I happen to have invented several things which have been used in this war. I think I am opposed to killing, but what am I to do with my capacity? I cannot suppress it as the power to invent drives me on.

KRISHNAMURTI: Which do you think-feel is the more urgently important problem to understand—the power to kill or the capacity to invent? If you are concerned only with inventing, with the mere expression of your talent, then you must find out why you give so much emphasis to it. Does not your capacity give you a means of escape from life, from reality? Then is not your talent a barrier to relationship? To be is to be related and nothing can exist in isolation. So without self-knowledge your capacity to invent becomes dangerous to your neighbor and to yourself.

Does your occupation aid in destroying your fellow man? Your inventions and activities may temporarily help, but if they lead him to ultimate destruction, then of what use are they? If the end result of this culture is mass murder, then of what significance is your talent? What is the purpose of inventing, improving, rearranging, if it all leads to the destruction of man? If you are only interested in fulfilling your particular capacity, disregarding the wider issues of life and the ultimate end of existence, then your talent is meaningless and worthless. Only in relation to the ultimate reality is your capacity significant.

I feel that all of you are not vitally interested in this question. Is this not also your problem? You may be an artist, a carpenter, or have some other occupation, and this question is as vital to you as to the inventor. If you are an artist or a doctor, your occupation or the expression of your talent must have its foundation in reality, otherwise it becomes merely a form of self-expression and mere expression of the self leads inevitably to sorrow. If you are interested only in self-expression then you are contributing to the conflict, confusion, and antagonism of man. Without first searching out the meaning of life, mere self-expression, however gratifying, will only bring misery and disaster.

Beware of mere talent. With self-knowledge the craving for self-fulfillment is transformed. The craving for fulfillment brings its own frustration and disillusionment, for the desire for self-fulfillment arises from ignorance.

Question: Can I find God in a foxhole?

KRISHNAMURTI: A man who is seeking God will not be in a foxhole. How false are the ways of our thinking! We create a false situation and in that hope to find truth; in the false we try to find the real. Happy is he who sees the false as the false and that which is true as true.

We have become perverted in the ways of our thinking-feeling. In sorrow we wish to find happiness; only in abandoning the cause of sorrow is there joy. You and the soldier have created a culture which forces you to murder and to be murdered, and in the midst of this cruelty you desire to find love. If you are seeking God you will not be in a foxhole, but if you are there and seek Him, you will know how to act. We justify murder and in the very act of murdering we try to find love. We create a society essentially based on sensate value, on worldliness, which necessitates the foxhole. We justify and condone the foxhole and then, in the foxhole or in the bomber, we hope to find God, love. Without fundamentally altering the structure of our thought-feeling, the real is not to be found. Being envious, greedy, and ignorant, we want to be peaceful, tolerant, and wise; with one hand we murder and with the other we pacify. It is this contradiction that must be understood; you cannot have both greed and peace, the foxhole and God; you cannot justify ignorance and yet hope for enlightenment.

The very nature of the self is to be in contradiction; and only when thought-feeling frees itself from its own opposing desires can there be tranquillity and joy. This freedom with its joy comes with deep awareness of the conflict of craving. When you become aware of the dual process of desire and are passively alert, there is the joy of the real, joy which is not the product of will or of time.

You cannot escape from ignorance at any time, it must be dispelled through your own awakening; none can awaken you save yourself. Through your own self-awareness does the problem of your making cease to be.

Question: What is a lasting way to solve a psychological problem?

KRISHNAMURTI: There are three stages of awareness, are there not, in any human problem. First, being aware of the cause and effect of the problem; second, being aware of its dual or contradictory process; and third, being aware of self and experiencing the thinker and his thought as one.

Take any problem that you have—for example, anger. Beware of its cause, physiological and psychological. Anger may arise from nervous tiredness and tension; it may arise from certain conditioning of thought-feeling, from fear, from dependence or from craving for security, and so on; it may arise through bodily and emotional pain. Many of us are aware of the conflict of the opposites; but because of pain or disturbance due to conflict, we instinctively seek to be rid of it violently or in varieties of subtle ways; we are concerned with escaping from the struggle rather than with understanding it. It is this desire to be rid of the conflict that gives strength to its continuity, and so maintains contradiction; it is this desire that must be watched and understood. Yet it is difficult to be alertly passive in the conflict of duality; we condemn or justify, compare or identify; so we are ever choosing sides and thus maintaining the cause of conflict. To be choicelessly aware of the conflict of duality is arduous, but it is essential if you would transcend the problem.

The modification of the outer, of the thought, is a self-protective device of the thinker; he sets his thought in a new frame which safeguards him from radical transformation. It is one of the many cunning ways of the self. Because the thinker sets himself apart from his thought, problems and conflicts continue, and the constant modification of his thought alone, without radically transforming himself, merely continues illusion.

The complete integration of the thinker with his thought cannot be experienced if there is no understanding of the process of becoming and the conflict of opposites. This conflict cannot be transcended through an act of will, it can only be transcended when choice has ceased. No problem can be solved on its own plane; it can be resolved lastingly only when the thinker has ceased to become.

June 24, 1945

Sixth Talk in The Oak Grove

This morning I shall answer as many questions as possible.

Question: If we had not destroyed the evil that was in Central Europe, it would have conquered us. Do you mean to say that we should not have defended ourselves? Aggression must be met. How would you meet it?

KRISHNAMURTI: This wave of aggression, of blood, of organized criminality, seems to arise periodically in one group and pass over to another. This is recurrent in history. No country is free from this aggression. We are all, each in his way, responsible for this wave of mass aggression and destruction.

Is it possible to live without aggression and so without defense? Is all effort a series of attacks and defenses? Can life be lived without this destructive effort? Each one should be aware of his responses to this problem. Does not all effort to become necessitate the self-assertiveness and self-expansion of the individual and so of the group or nation, and lead to conflict, antagonism, and war?

Is it possible to solve this problem of aggression along the lines of defense? Defense implies self-protection, opposition, and conflict, and is antagonism to be dissolved by opposition? Is it possible to live in this world and yet be free from this constant battle between yours and mine, with its ruthless attack and defense? Because we desire to protect our name, our property, our nationality, our religion, our ideals, we cultivate the spirit of attack and defense. We are possessive, acquisitive, and so we have created a social structure which necessitates progressively ruthless exploitation and aggression. This acquisitive becoming breeds its own opposition, and so defense and attack become part of our daily existence. No solution can be found as long as we are thinking-feeling in terms of defense and attack, which only maintain confusion and strife.

Is it possible to think-feel without defense and attack? It is possible only when there is love, when each one abandons greed, ill will, and ignorance, which express themselves through nationalism, craving for power, and other forms of criminality and cruelty. If one wishes to solve this problem permanently, surely thought-feeling must free itself from all acquisitiveness and fear. This attitude of attack and defense is cultivated in our daily life and ends ultimately in war and other catastrophes. The difficulty lies in our own contradictory nature; we want peace and yet we cultivate those causes that bring about war and destruction. We want happiness and freedom and yet we indulge in lust, ill will, and thoughtlessness; we pray for understanding and yet deny it in our daily life; we want to enjoy both opposites and so we are confused and lost.

If you want to put an end to this wave of ruthlessness, of appalling destruction and misery, if you wish to save your son, your husband, your neighbor, you must pay the price. This misery is not the creation of one group or race but of each one of us; each one must thoughtfully abandon the causes that produce these calamities and untold misery. You must completely set aside your nationalism, your greed, and ill will, your craving for power and wealth and your adherence to organized religious prejudices which, while asserting the unity of man, set

man against man. Only then will there be peace and joy.

Why is it that we seem to be incapable of living creatively and happily without destroying each other? Is it not because we so condition ourselves through our own passion, ill will, and stupidity that we are incapable of living joyously and serenely? We must break through our own conditioning and be as nothing. We are afraid of being nothing, so we escape and thus feed our fear with greed, hate, ambition.

The problem is not how to defend but how to transcend the desire for self-expansion, the craving to become. Only those individuals who abandon their passions, their craving for fame and personal immortality, can help to bring about creative peace and joy.

Question: In one's growth is there not a continuous and recurring process of the death of one's cherished hopes and desires; of cruel disillusionment in regard to the past; of transmutation of those negative phenomena into a more positive and vitalizing life— until the same stage is reached again on a higher spiral? Are not conflict and pain therefore indispensable to all growth and at all stages?

KRISHNAMURTI: Are conflict and pain necessary for creative being? Is sorrow necessary for understanding? Is not conflict inevitable in becoming, in self-expanding? Is not the creative state of being the freedom from conflict, from accumulated existence? Does accumulation at any stage on the spiral of becoming bring about the creative being? There is becoming and growth along the horizontal path of existence, but does it lead to the timeless? It is to be experienced only when the horizontal is abandoned. Is the experience of being related to the conflict of the horizontal, the conflict of becoming? Through time the timeless cannot be realized.

What happens when we are in conflict? In the struggle to overcome conflict, we become disillusioned, we enter into darkness or, being in conflict, we try to find escapes in various forms. If thought-feeling is caught neither in disillusionment nor in comforting refuge, then conflict will find the means of its own ending. Conflict produces disillusionment or the desire to escape, for we are unwilling to think out, feel out all the implications involved in it; we are lazy, too conditioned to change, accepting authority and the easy way of life. To understand conflict and to be able to examine it with freedom, there must be a certain disinterested tranquillity. But when we are in conflict or in sorrow, our instinctive response is to escape from it, to run away from its cause, not to face its hidden significance; so we seek various channels of escape—activity, amusement, gods, war. So distractions multiply; they become more important than the cause of sorrow itself; we then become intolerant of the means of escape of others and try to modify or reform them, but conflict and sorrow continue.

Now is conflict necessary for understanding? Is understanding the result of growth? Do we not mean by growth the constant becoming of the self, accumulating and renouncing, being greedy and becoming nongreedy, the endless process of becoming? The very nature of the self is to create contradiction. Is conflict between the opposites growth, bringing with it understanding? Does the struggle in the endless corridor of the opposites lead anywhere except to further conflict and sorrow?

There is no end to conflict and sorrow in becoming. This becoming leads to the conflict of contradiction in which most of us are caught; being caught in it, we think struggle and pain are inevitable, a necessary and evolutionary process. So time becomes an indispensable factor for growth, for further becoming. In this spiral of becoming there is no end to strife and pain. So our problem is how to put an end to them. Thought-feeling must go beyond and above the pattern of duality; that is, when there is conflict and pain, live with it unconditionally without escaping; to escape is to compare, to justify, to condemn; to be aware of sorrow is not to seek a refuge, an alleviation, but to be aware of the ways of thought-feeling. So when there is understanding of the futility of refuge, of escape, then that very sorrow creates the necessary flame that will consume it. Tranquillity of understanding is needed to transcend sorrow, not the conflict and pain of becoming. When the self is not occupied with its own becoming, there is an unpremeditated clarity, a deep ecstasy. This intensity of joy is the outcome of the abandonment of the self.

Question: I have struggled for many, many years with a personal problem. I am still struggling. What am I to do?

KRISHNAMURTI: What is the process of understanding a problem? To understand, mind-heart must unburden itself of its accumulation so that it is capable of right perception. If you would understand a modern painting you must, if you can, put aside your classical training, your prejudices, your trained responses. Similarly if we want to understand a complex psychological problem, we must be capable of examining it without any condemnatory or favorable bias; we must be capable of approaching it with dispassion and freshness.

The questioner says that he has been struggling for many years with his problem. In his struggle he has accumulated what he would call experience, knowledge, and with this increasing burden he tries to solve the problem; thus he has never come face to face with it openly, anew, but has always approached it with the accumulation of many years. It is the accumulated memory that confronts the problem, and so there is no understanding of it. The dead past darkens the ever-living present.

Most of us are driven by some passion and are unaware of it, but if we are, we generally justify or condone it. But if it is a passion which we desire to transcend, we generally struggle with it, try to conquer or suppress it. In trying to overcome it we have not understood it, in trying to suppress it we have not transcended it. The passion still remains or it has taken another form, which is still the cause of conflict and sorrow. This constant and continuous struggle does not bring understanding but only strengthens conflict, burdening the mind-heart with accumulated memory. But if we can delve deeply into it and die to it or come anew to it without the burden of yesterday, then we can comprehend it. Because our mind-heart is alert and keen, deeply aware and still, the problem is transcended.

If we can approach our problem without judging, without identifying, then the causes that lie behind it are revealed. If we would understand a problem we must set aside our desires, our accumulated experiences, our patterns of thought. The difficulty is not in the problem itself but in our approach to it. The scars of yesterday prevent the right approach. Conditioning translates the problem according to its own pattern, which in no way liberates thought-feeling from the struggle and pain of the problem. To translate the problem is not to understand it; to understand it and so transcend it, interpretation must cease. What is fully, completely understood leaves no trace as memory.

Question: I am intensely lonely. I seem to be in constant conflict in my relationships on account of this loneliness. It is a disease and must be healed. Can you help me, please, to heal it?

KRISHNAMURTI: The present chaos, misery, is a product of this aching loneliness, void, for thought itself has become empty, without significance. Wars and increasing confusion are the outcome of our empty lives and activities.

Whether we are conscious of it or not, most of us are lonely; the more we are aware of it, the more intense, burning, and painful it becomes. The immature are easily satisfied in their emptiness, but the more one is aware, the greater is this problem. There is no escape from aching loneliness, nor is it to be overcome by thoughtlessness, by ignorance; ignorance, like superstition, yields a certain gratification, but this only furthers conflict and sorrow. Most of us are intensely lonely, and the anguish is penetrating and dulls the mind-heart. Its engulfing sorrow seems to spread endlessly, and we seek constantly to escape from it, to cover it up, to fill this aching void consciously or unconsciously with hope and faith, with amusement and distraction. We try to cover up its anguish through activity, through the pleasure of knowledge, of belief, and of every form of addiction, religious and worldly. Our search for a refuge, for a comfort from this pain is endless; things, relationships, and knowledge are means of escape from the persistent anguish of loneliness. The movement from one escape to another is considered advancement; we condemn the man who fills this void with drink and amusement, but the man who seeks a permanent escape, calling it noble, we consider worthy, spiritual.

Is there any enduring escape from this emptiness? We try various ways to fill the void, but again and again we become aware of it. Do not all remedies, however noble and gratifying, merely avoid the problem? You may find temporary relief but anguish soon returns.

To find the right and lasting answer to loneliness, we must first cease to run away from it, and this is very difficult, for thought is ever seeking a refuge, an escape. It is only when the mind-heart can accept this void unconditionally, yielding to it without any motive, without any hope or fear, that there can be its transformation.

If you would truly understand the problem of loneliness and its greatness, the values of the world must be set aside, for they are distractions from the real. These distractions and their values are the outcome of your desire to escape from your own emptiness and so they, too, are empty. Only when the mind-heart is stripped of all its pretensions and formulations can this aching emptiness be transcended.

Question: I have had what might be called a spiritual experience, a guidance, or a certain realization. How am I to deal with it?

KRISHNAMURTI: Most of us have had deep experiences, call them by what name you will; we have had experiences of great ecstasy, of great vision, of great love. The experience fills our being with its light, with its breath; but it is not abiding, it passes away, leaving its perfume.

With most of us the mind-heart is not capable of being open to that ecstasy. The experience was accidental, uninvited, too great for the mind-heart. The experience is greater than the experiencer, and so the experiencer sets about to reduce it to his own level, to his sphere of comprehension. His mind is not still; it is active, noisy, rearranging; it must deal with the experience; it must organize it; it must spread it; it must tell others of its beauty. So the mind reduces the inexpressible into a pattern of authority or a direction for conduct. It interprets and translates the experience and so enmeshes it in its own triviality. Because the mind-heart does not know how to sing, it pursues instead the singer.

The interpreter, the translator of the experience, must be as deep and wide as the experience itself if he would understand it; since he is not, he must cease to interpret it; to cease, he must be mature, wise in his understanding. You may have a significant experience, but how you understand it, how you interpret it depends on you, the interpreter; if your mind-heart is small, limited, then you translate the experience according to your own conditioning. It is this conditioning that must be understood and broken down before you can hope to grasp the full significance of the experience.

The maturity of mind-heart comes as it frees itself from its own limitations, and not through clinging to the memory of a spiritual experience. If it clings to memory it abides with death, not with life. Deep experience may open the door to understanding, to self-knowledge and right thinking, but with many it becomes only a stirring stimulation, a memory, and soon loses its vital significance, preventing further experience.

We translate all experience in terms of our own conditioning—the deeper it is, the more alertly aware must we be not to misread it. Deep and spiritual experiences are rare, and if we have such experiences we reduce them to the petty level of our own mind and heart. If you are a Christian or a Hindu or a nonbeliever, you accordingly translate such experiences, reducing them to the level of your own conditioning. If your mind-heart is given over to nationalism and greed, to passion and ill will, then such experiences will be used to further the slaughter of your neighbor; then you seek guidance to bomb your brother; then to worship is to destroy or torture those who are not of your country, of your faith.

It is essential to be aware of your conditioning rather than to try to do something about the experience itself, but mind-heart clings to the experiences of yesterday and so becomes incapable of understanding the living present.

July 1, 1945

Seventh Talk in The Oak Grove

Existence is painful and complex. To understand the sorrow of our existence, we must think-feel anew, we must approach life simply and directly; if we can, we must begin each day anew. We must be able each day to revalue the ideals and patterns that we have brought into being. Life can be deeply and truly understood only as it exists in each one; you are that life and without comprehending it there can be no enduring joy and tranquillity.

Our conflict within and without arises, does it not, from the changing and contradictory values based on pleasure and pain? Our struggle lies in trying to find a value that is wholly satisfying, unvarying, and undisturbing; we are seeking permanent value that will ever gratify without any shadow of doubt or pain. Our constant struggle is based on this demand for lasting security; we crave security in things, in relationship, in thought.

Without understanding the problem of insecurity, there is no security. If we seek security we shall not find it; the search for security brings its own destruction. There must be insecurity for the comprehension of reality, the insecurity that is not the opposite of security. A mind that is well anchored, which feels safe in some refuge, can never understand reality. The craving for security breeds slothfulness; it makes the mind-heart unpliable and insensitive, fearful and dull; it hinders the vulnerability to reality. In deep insecurity is truth realized.

But we need a certain security to live; we need food, clothes, and shelter, without which existence is not possible. It would be a comparatively simple matter to organize and distribute effectively if we were satisfied with our daily fundamental needs only. Then there would be no individual, no national assertiveness, competitive expansion and ruthlessness; there would be no need for separate sovereign governments; there would be no wars if we were wholly satisfied with our daily needs. But we are not.

Yet why is it not possible to organize our needs? It is not possible because of the incessant conflict of our daily life with its greed, cruelty, hatred. It is not possible because we use our needs as a means of gratifying our psychological demands. Being inwardly uncreative, empty, destructive, we use our needs as a means of escape; so needs assume far greater significance than they really have. Psychologically, they become all-important; so sensate values assume great significance; property, name, talent, become the means for position, power, domination. Over things made by hand or by mind we are ever in conflict; hence economic planning for existence becomes the dominating problem. We crave for things which create the illusion of security and comfort but which bring us only conflict, confusion, and antagonism. We lose, in the security of things made by the mind, that joy of creative reality, the very nature of which is insecurity. A mind that is seeking security is ever in fear; it can never be joyous, it can never know creative being. The highest form of thinking-feeling is negative comprehension and its very basis is insecurity.

The more we consider the world without understanding our psychological cravings, demands, and conflicts, the more complex and insoluble the problem of existence becomes. The more we plan and organize our economic existence without understanding and transcending the inner passions, fears, envies, the more conflict and confusion will come into being. Contentment with little comes with the understanding of our psychological problems, not through legislation or the determined effort to possess little. We must eliminate intelligently those psychological demands which find gratification in things, in position, in capacity. If we do not seek power and domination, if we are not self-assertive, there will be peace; but as long as we are using things, relationship, or ideas as a means to gratify our ever-increasing psychological cravings, so long will there be contention and misery. With the freedom from craving there comes right thinking, and right thinking alone can bring tranquillity.

Question: I come from a part of the world which has suffered terribly in this war. I see around me widespread hunger, disease, and a great danger of civil war and bloodshed unless these problems are tackled immediately. I feel it my duty to make my contribution to their solution. On the other hand I see in the world of today the need for a point of view like yours. Is it possible for me to pursue my first objective without neglecting the second? In other words, how can I continue the two?

KRISHNAMURTI: Only in the search of the real can there be an enduring solution to our problems. To separate existence from the real is to continue in ignorance and sorrow. To grapple with the problems of hunger, mass murder, and destruction on their own planes is to further misery and catastrophe. In the search of the real world's problem, which is the individual problem, you will find a lasting answer. But if you are only concerned with the reorganization of greed, ill will, and ignorance, there will be no end to confusion and antagonism.

If the reformer, the contributor to the solution of the world's problems, has not radically transformed himself, if he has had no inner revolution of values, then what he contributes will only add further to conflict and misery. He who is eager to reform the world must first understand himself, for he is the world. The present misery and degradation of man is brought on by man himself, and if he merely plans to reform the pattern of conflict without fundamentally understanding himself, he will only increase ignorance and sorrow. If each one seeks eternal value, then there will be an end to the conflict within, and so peace will come into the world; then only will those causes that perpetuate antagonism, confusion, and misery cease.

If you want to put an end to the conflict, confusion, and misery with which we are confronted everywhere, from where are you to begin? Are you to begin with the world, with the outer, and try to rearrange its values while maintaining your own nationalism, acquisitiveness and hatred, religious dogma and superstition? Or must you begin with yourself to eliminate drastically those causes that produce conflict and sorrow? If you are able to set aside the passion and worldliness on which present culture is built, then you will discover and experience eternal value which is never within any framework; then you might be able to help others free themselves from bondage. We desire, unfortunately, to combine the eternal with a whole series of values which lead to antagonism, conflict, and misery. If you would seek truth you must abandon those values that are based on sensation and gratification, on passion and ill will, possessiveness and greed. You need not let your lives be guided by economists, by politicians and priests with their endless plans for peace; they have led you to death and destruction. You have made them your leaders, but now, with deep awareness, you must become responsible for yourself, for within you is the cause and the solution of all conflict and sorrow. You created it and you alone can free yourself, not another can save you.

Therefore our first duty, if one may use that word, is to search out the real, which alone can bring peace and joy. In it alone is there enduring unity of man; in it alone can conflict and sorrow cease; in it alone is there creative being. Without this inward treasure the outward organization of law and economic planning have little significance. With the awareness of the real the outer and inner cease to be separate.

Question: I have tried to meditate along the lines you suggested last year. I have gone into it fairly deeply. I feel that meditation and dreams have a relationship. What do you think?

KRISHNAMURTI: For those who practice meditation, it is a process of becoming, of building up, of denying, or of imitating, of concentration, of narrowing down thought-feeling. They either cultivate virtue as a means towards a formulated end, or try to focus their wandering attention on a saint, a teacher, or an idea. Many use various techniques to go beyond the reach of the means, but the means shape the mind-heart, and so in the end they become slaves to the means. The means and the end are not different, they are not separate. If you are seeking an end you will find the means for it, but such an end is not the real. The real comes into being, you cannot seek it; it must come, you cannot induce it. But meditation as generally practiced is craving to become or not to become; it is a subtle form of self-expansion, self-assertiveness; and so it becomes merely a series of struggles within the pattern of duality. The effort of becoming, positively or negatively, on different levels does not put

an end to conflict; only with the cessation of craving is there tranquillity.

If the meditator does not know himself, his meditation is of little value and becomes even a hindrance to comprehension. Without self-knowledge meditation is not possible, and without meditative awareness there is no self-knowledge. If I do not understand myself, my cravings, my motives, my contradictions, how can I comprehend truth? If I am not aware of my contradictory states, if I am passionate, ignorant, greedy, envious, meditation only strengthens the self-enclosing process; without self-knowledge there is no foundation for right thinking; without right thinking thought-feeling cannot transcend itself.

A lady once said that she had practiced meditation for a number of years and presently went on to explain that a certain group of people must be destroyed, for they were bringing misery and destruction to man. Yet she practiced brotherhood, love, and peace, which she said had guided her life. Do not many of you who practice meditation talk of love and brotherhood, yet condone or participate in war, which is organized murder? What significance then has your meditation? Your meditation only strengthens your own narrowness, ill will, and ignorance.

Those who would understand the deep significance of meditation must begin first with themselves, for self-knowledge is the foundation of right thinking. Without right thinking how can thought go far? You must begin near to go far. Self-awareness is arduous; to think out, feel out every thought-feeling is strenuous; but this awareness of every thought-feeling will bring to an end the wandering of the mind. When you try to meditate do you not find that your mind wanders and chatters ceaselessly? It is of little use to brush aside every thought but one and try to concentrate upon that one thought which you have chosen. Instead of trying to control these wandering thoughts, become aware of them, think out, feel out every thought, comprehend its significance, however pleasant or unpleasant; try to understand each thought-feeling. Each thought-feeling so pursued will yield its meaning, and thus the mind, as it comprehends its own repetitive and wandering thoughts, becomes emptied of its own formulations.

The mind is the result of the past, it is a storehouse of many interests, of contradictory values; it is ever-gathering, ever-becoming. We must be aware of these accumulations and understand them as they arise. Suppose you have collected letters for many years, now you look into the drawer and read letter after letter, keeping some and discarding others; what you keep you reread, and again you discard until the drawer is empty. Similarly, be aware of every thought-feeling, comprehend its significance, and should it return reconsider it for it has not been fully understood. As a drawer is useful only when empty, so the mind must be free of all its accumulations, for only then can there be that openness to wisdom and the ecstasy of the real. Tranquillity of wisdom is not the result of an act of will, it is not a conclusion, a state to be achieved. It comes into being in the awareness of understanding.

Meditation becomes significant when the mind-heart is aware, thinking out, feeling out every thought-feeling that arises without comparison or identification. For identification and comparison maintain the conflict of duality, and there is no solution within its pattern. I wonder how many of you have really practiced meditation? If you have, you will have noticed how difficult it is to be extensively aware without the narrowing down of thought-feeling. In trying to concentrate, the conflicting thoughts-feelings are suppressed or pushed aside or overcome, and through this process there can be no understanding. Concentration is gained at the expense of deep awareness. If the mind is petty and limited, concentration will not make it any the less small and trivial; on the contrary it will strengthen its own nature. Such narrow concentration does not make the mind-heart vulnerable to reality; it only hardens the mind-heart in its own obstinacy and ignorance and perpetuates the self-enclosing process.

When the mind-heart is extensive, deep, and tranquil, there is the real. If the mind is seeking a result, however noble and worthy, if it is concerned with becoming, it ceases to be extensive and infinitely pliable. It must be as the unknown to receive the unknowable. It must be utterly tranquil for the being of the eternal.

So the mind must understand every value it has accumulated, and in this process the many layers, of consciousness, both the open and the hidden, are uncovered and understood. The more there is an awareness of the conscious layers, the more the hidden layers come to the surface; if the conscious layers are confused and disturbed, then the deeper layers of consciousness cannot project themselves into the conscious, save through dreams.

Awareness is the process of freeing the conscious mind from the bondages which cause conflict and pain, and thus making it open and receptive to the hidden. The hidden layers of consciousness convey their significance through dreams and symbols. If every thought-feeling is thought out, felt out, as fully and deeply as possible, without condemnation or comparison, acceptance or identification, then all the hidden layers of consciousness will reveal themselves. Through constant awareness the dreamer ceases to dream, for through alert and passive awareness, every movement of thought-feeling of the open and hidden layers of consciousness is being understood. But if one is incapable of thinking out, feeling out every thought completely and fully, then one begins to dream. Dreams need interpretation and to interpret there must be free and open intelligence; instead, the dreamer goes to a dream specialist, thus creating for himself other problems. Only in deep extensive awareness can there be an end to dreams and their anxious interpretation.

Right meditation is very effective in freeing the mind-heart from its self-enclosing process. The open and hidden layers of consciousness are the result of the past, of accumulation, of centuries of education, and surely such an educated, conditioned mind cannot be vulnerable to the real. Occasionally, in the still silence after the storm of conflict and pain, there comes inexpressible beauty and joy; it is not the result of the storm but of the cessation of conflict. The mind-heart must be passively still for the creative being of the real.

Question: Will you please explain the idea that one must die each day, or that one must live the four seasons in a day?

KRISHNAMURTI: Is it not essential that there should be a constant renewal, a rebirth? If the present is burdened with the experience of yesterday there can be no renewal. Renewal is not the action of birth and death; it is beyond the opposites; only freedom from the accumulation of memory brings renewal, and there is no understanding save in the present.

The mind can understand the present only if it does not compare, judge; the desire to alter or condemn the present without understanding it gives continuance to the past. Only in comprehending the reflection of the past in the mirror of the present, without distortion, is there renewal.

The accumulation of memory is called knowledge; with this burden, with the scars of experience, thought is ever interpreting the present and so giving continuity to its own scars and conditioning. This continuity is time-binding and so there is no rebirth, no renewal. If you have lived an experience fully, completely, have you not found that it leaves no traces behind? It is only the incomplete experiences that leave their mark, giving continuity to self-identified memory. We consider the present as a means to an end, so the present loses its immense significance. The present is the eternal. But how can a mind that is made up, put together, understand that which is not put together, which is beyond all value, the eternal?

As each experience arises, live it out as fully and deeply as possible; think it out, feel it out extensively and profoundly; be aware of its pain and pleasure, of your judgments and identifications. Only when experience is completed is there a renewal. We must be capable of living the four seasons in a day; to be keenly aware, to experience, to understand and be free of the gatherings of each day. With the end of each day the mind-heart must empty itself of the accumulation of its pleasures and pains. We gather consciously and unconsciously; it is comparatively easy to discard what has been consciously acquired, but it is more difficult for thought to free itself from the unconscious accumulations, the past, the incompleted experiences with their recurring memories. Thought-feeling clings so tenaciously to what it has gathered because it is afraid to be insecure.

Meditation is renewal, the dying each day to the past; it is an intense passive awareness, the burning away of the desire to continue, to become. As long as mind-heart is self-protecting, there will be continuity without renewal. Only when the mind ceases to create is there creation.

Question: How would you cope with an incurable disease?

KRISHNAMURTI: Most of us do not understand ourselves, our various tensions and conflicts, our hopes and fears, which often produce mental and physical disorders.

Of primary importance is psychological understanding and well being of the mind-heart, which then can deal with the accidents of disease. As a tool wears out so does the body, but those who cling to sensory values find this wasting away to be a sorrow beyond measure; they live for sensation and gratification, and the fear of death and pain drives them to delusion. As long as thought-feeling is predominantly sensate, there will be no end to delusion and fear; the world in its very nature being a distraction, it is essential that the problem of delusion and health be approached patiently and wisely.

If we are organically diseased then let us cope with this condition, as with all mechanism, in the best way possible. The psychological delusions, tensions, conflicts, maladjustments produce greater misery than organic disease. We try to eradicate symptoms rather than cause; the cause itself may be sensate value. There is no end to the gratification of the senses, which only creates greater and greater turmoil, tension, fear, and so on; such a living must culminate in mental and physical disorder or in war. Unless there is a radical change in value, there will and must be ever increasing disharmony within, and so, without. This radical change in value must be brought about through understanding the psychological being; if you do not change, your delusions and ill-health will inevitably increase; you will become unbalanced, depressed, giving continuous employment to physicians. If there is no deep revolution of values, then disease and delusion become a distraction, an escape, giving opportunity for self-indulgence. We can unconditionally accept an incurable disease only when thought-feeling is able to transcend the value of time.

The predominance of sensory values cannot bring sanity and health. There must be a cleansing of the mind-heart which cannot be done by any outer agency. There must be self-awareness, a psychological tension. Tension is not necessarily harmful; there must be right exertion of the mind. It is only when tension is not properly utilized that it leads to psychological difficulties and delusions, to ill-health and perversions. Tension of the right kind is essential for understanding; to be alertly and passively aware is to give full attention without the conflict of opposition. Only when this tension is not properly understood does it lead to difficulty; living, relationship, thought demand heightened sensitivity, a right tension. We are conscious of this tension and generally misread or avoid it, thus preventing the understanding that it would bring. Tension or sensitivity can heal or destroy.

Life is complex and painful, a series of inner and outer conflicts. There must be an awareness of the mental and emotional attitudes which cause outward and physical disturbances. To understand them you must have time for quiet reflection; to be aware of your psychological states there must be periods of quiet solitude, a withdrawal from the noise and bustle of daily life and its routine. This active stillness is essential, not only for the well-being of the mind-heart but for the discovery of the real, without which physical or moral well-being is of little significance.

Unfortunately most of us give little time to serious and quiet self-recollectedness. We allow ourselves to become mechanical, thoughtlessly following routine, accepting and being driven by authority; we become mere cogs in the vast machine of the present culture. We have lost creativeness; there is no inward joy. What we are inwardly, that we project outwardly. Mere cultivation of the outer does not bring about inward well-being;

only through constant self-awareness and self-knowledge can there be inward tranquillity. Without the real, existence is conflict and pain.

July 8, 1945

Eighth Talk in The Oak Grove

The problem of relationship is not easily comprehended, it requires patience and pliability of mind-heart; mere adjustment or conformity to a system of conduct does not bring about the understanding of relationship; such adjustment and conformity cloud and intensify the struggle. If we would deeply comprehend relationship it must be approached afresh each day, without the scars or memories of yesterday's experiences. These conflicts in relationship build a wall of continuous resistance, and instead of bringing wider and deeper unity create insurmountable differences and disunity.

As you would read an interesting book without skipping a page, so relationship must be studied and understood; the solution to the problem of relationship is not to be found outside of it but in it; the answer is not at the end of the book but is to be found in the manner of our approach to relationship. How you read the book of relationship is of far greater importance than the answer, or the overcoming of the struggle that exists in it. It must be approached every day anew without the burden of yesterday; it is this liberation from yesterday, from time, that brings creative understanding.

To be is to be related; there is no such thing as isolated being. Relationship is a conflict within and without; the inward conflict extended becomes world conflict. You and the world are not separate; your problem is the world's problem; you bear the world in you; without you it is not. There is no isolation and there is no object that is not related.

This conflict must be understood not as a problem of the part but of the whole.

You are aware, are you not, of conflict in relationship, of the constant struggle between you and another, between you and the world? Why is there conflict in relationship? Does it not arise because of the interaction of dependency and conformity, of domination and possessiveness? We conform, we depend, we possess because of inward insufficiency, which gives rise to fear. Do we not know this fear in intimate, close relationship? Relationship is a tension, and deep awareness is necessary to understand it.

Why do we crave to possess or dominate? Is it not because of the fear of insufficiency? Being fearful, we long to be secure; emotionally and mentally we desire to be safe and well anchored in things, in people, in ideas. Inwardly we crave security, which expresses itself outwardly in dependency, conformity, possessiveness, and so on. It is the burning and seemingly ceaseless void that drives us to find a refuge, a hope, in relationship, and we confuse the urge to avoid our anguish of loneliness with love, duty, responsibility.

But what is the true significance of relationship? Is it not a process of self-revelation? Is not relationship a mirror in which, if we are aware, we can observe without distortion our private thoughts and motives, our inward state? In relationship the subtle process of the self, of the ego, is revealed and through choiceless awareness alone can inward insufficiency be transcended. Conflict ceases in the aloneness of reality. This transcending is love. Love has no motive; it is its own eternity.

Question: How can I become integrated?

KRISHNAMURTI: What do we mean by integration? Does it not mean to be made whole, to be without conflict and sorrow?

Most of us try to be integrated within the superficial layers of our consciousness; we try to integrate ourselves so as to function normally within the pattern of society; we desire to fit into an environment which we accept as being normal; but we do not question the significance or the value of the social structure about us. Conformity to a pattern is considered integration; education and organized religion aid us towards this conformity.

Has not integration a deeper significance than mere adjustment to society and its patterns? Is conformity integration? Is not integration pure being and not just the satisfaction of our desire to be made whole, to become normal? The motive behind the urge for integration is surely of great significance.

The urge for integration may arise from ambition, from the desire for power, from the fear of insufficiency and so on. Coordination is necessary to achieve a result, but consider what is involved in the idea of attainment of desire: self-assertiveness, envy, enmity, the pettiness of success, strife and pain. Some people suppress the craving for worldly success but indulge in the craving to become virtuous, to be a Master, to attain spiritual glory, but the craving to become ever leads to conflict, confusion, and antagonism. This again is not true integration. True integration comes when there is awareness, and so understanding through all layers of consciousness. Our superficial consciousness is the result of education, of influence, and only when thought transcends its own self-created limitation can there be true integration. The many opposing and contradictory parts of our consciousness can be integrated only when the creator of these divisions ceases to be; within the pattern of the self there can be only conflict, there can never be integration, completeness.

Integration comes with the freedom from craving. It is not an end in itself, but if you seek self-knowledge, ever deeply, then integration becomes the way to reality.

Question: You may be wise about some things but why are you, as it has been represented to me, against organization? Would you please explain why you consider it a hindrance in our search for reality?

KRISHNAMURTI: Why do we organize? Is it not for efficiency? We organize our existence in order to live; we can organize our thought-feeling so as to make it efficient, but efficient for what? For killing, oppressing, gaining power?

If certain ideas, beliefs, doctrines appeal to you, you join with others to spread effectively what you believe, and for this you create an organization. But is the understanding of reality the result of propaganda, organized belief, enforced or subtle conformity? Is reality discovered through the doctrines of churches, cults, or sects? Is reality to be found through compulsion, through imitation?

We think, do we not, that through conformity, through formulation of beliefs we shall know the real. Must not thought-feeling transcend all conditioning to discover the real? Thought-feeling now experiences that in which it is educated, in which it believes, but such experience is limited and narrow; such a mind cannot experience the real. Conformity can be organized efficiently; adherence to a formula, to a doctrine can be effectively manipulated, but will that lead to reality? Does not reality come into being when there is complete liberation from all authority, from all compulsion and imitation? This state of being we experience only when thought is utterly still. Only in freedom is there the experience of the real.

Regimentation of thought-feeling in the name of religion, peace, and freedom is made attractive and acceptable; your tendency is to accept authority; you desire to be led; you look to others to direct your conduct. The radio, movies, newspapers, governments, churches are molding your thought and feeling, and because you desire to conform, their task becomes easy. Your craving for security creates fear and it is fear that yields to the oppression of authority; fear forces you not how to think but what to think. Only in freedom from fear is there the discovery of the real.

Group effort, without conforming to authority, could be very significant through the revelation of inward individual motives and purposes; the group could mirror the activities of the self and through relationship awaken self-awareness. But if the group is used for self-assertiveness through propaganda or as a means of escape, then it can become a hindrance to the discovery of truth.

Creativeness comes into being when thought-feeling is not held within any pattern, within any formulation. The self is the result of conformity, of conditioning, of accumulated memory; so the self is never free to discover; it can only expand in its own conditioning and organize itself to be efficient and subtle in its assertiveness, pursuits, and demands, but it can never be free. Only when the self ceases to become is there the real. To be free to discover, the memory of yesterday must cease; it is the burden of the past that gives continuity, and continuity is conformity. Do not conform in order to be free for this does not bring freedom, and in freedom alone is there creative being. Freedom cannot be organized and when it is it ceases to be freedom. We try to enclose the living truth in gratifying patterns of thought-feeling and thereby destroy it.

Question: I would like to ask you if the Masters are not a great source of inspiration to us. As life is unequal there must be Master and pupil, surely?

KRISHNAMURTI: Is not this inequality the result of ignorance? Does not this division of man into the high and low deny the real? Is not this domination and submission of man the outcome of ignorance and thoughtlessness?

Our social structure is built upon division and difference of levels—of the clerk and the executive, the general and the soldier, the bishop and the priest, the one who knows and the one who does not know. This division is based on sensate value, which sets man against man. This social pattern breeds endless opposition and antagonism, and there can be an end to conflict within this pattern only when thought-feeling transcends greed, ill will, and ignorance.

With our acquisitive and competitive mentality we try to grasp reality and build a ladder for achievement; we create the high and the low, the Master and the pupil. We think of reality as an end to be achieved, as a reward for righteousness; we think it is to be attained through time, and so maintain the constant division between Master and pupil, the successful and the ignorant.

The wise, the compassionate do not think of man in terms of division; the foolish are caught up in the social and religious division of man. Those who are conscious of this division and know it to be false and stupid overcome it, but yet they persist in division with regard to those they call Masters. If you perceive the misery in this sensate world caused by the division of man into the high and the low, why then are you not aware of it on all planes of existence? In the sensate world the division of man against man is the result of greed and ignorance, and it is also greed and ignorance that create the follower and the leader, the Master and the pupil, the liberated and the unenlightened. ·

The questioner asks if a Master or a saint is not a source of inspiration. When you draw inspiration from another, it is only a distraction, hence uncreative and illusory. Inspiration is sought in many ways but invariably it breeds dependence and fear. Fear prevents understanding, it puts an end to communion, it is a living death.

Is not the creative being of reality the norm? You look to others for hope and guidance because you are empty and poor; you turn to books, to pictures, to teachers, to gurus, to saviors to inspire and strengthen you, you are ever in hunger, ever seeking but never finding. In the creative being of reality alone is there the cessation of conflict and sorrow. But separation and inequality will be maintained as long as there is a becoming; as long as the pupil craves to become a Master. This craving to become is born of ignorance, for the present is the eternal. Only in the aloneness of reality is there completeness; in that flame of creative being there is no other but the 'one'.

Through right means only can reality be discovered, for the means is the end; the means and the end are inseparable; through self-awareness and self-knowledge there is the flame of reality. It does not lie through another but through your own awakened thought. None can lead you to it; none can deliver you from your own sorrow. The authority of another is blinding; only in utter freedom is the supreme to be found. Let us live in time timelessly.

Question: Do you believe in progress?

KRISHNAMURTI: There is the movement of so-called progression, is there not, from the simple to the complex. There is the process of constant adjustment to environment which brings about modification or change, taking on new forms. There is constant interaction between the outer and the inner, each aiding in modifying and transforming the other. This does not demand belief; we can observe society becoming more and more complex, more and more efficiently organized to survive, to exploit, to oppress, and to kill. Existence which was simple and primitive has become very complex, highly organized and civilized. We have "progressed"; we have radios, movies, quick means of transportation, and all the rest of it. We can kill, instead of a few, thousands upon thousands in a moment; we can wipe out, as the phrase goes, whole cities and their people in a few burning seconds. We are well aware of all this and some call it progress; bigger and better houses, more luxury, more amusements, more distractions. Can this be considered progress? Is the expansion of sensate desire progress? Or does progress lie in compassion?

We mean by progress also, do we not, the constant expanding of desire, of the self. Now in this process of expansion and becoming, can there ever be an end to conflict and sorrow? If not, what is the purpose of becoming? If it is for the continuation of struggle and pain, of what value is progress, the evolution of desire, the expansion of the self? If in the expansion of desire there is the cessation of sorrow, then becoming could have significance, but is it not the very nature of craving to create and continue conflict and sorrow?

The self, the 'I', this bundle of memories, is the result of the past, the product of time, and will this self, however much it may evolve, experience the timeless? Can the 'I', becoming greater, nobler through time, experience the real?

Can the 'I', the accumulated memory, know freedom? Can the self which is craving, and so the cause of ignorance and conflict, know enlightenment? Only in freedom can there be enlightenment, not in the bondage and pain of craving. As long as the 'I' thinks of itself as gaining and losing, becoming and not becoming, thought is time-bound. Thought held in the bondage of yesterday, of time, can never experience the timeless.

We think in terms of yesterday, today, and tomorrow; I was, I am, and I will become. We think-feel in terms of accumulation; we are constantly creating and maintaining the idea of time, of continual becoming. Is not being wholly different from becoming? We can only be when we understand the process and significance of becoming. If we would deeply understand we must be silent, must we not? The very greatness of a problem calls for silence as does beauty. But, you will be asking, how am I to become silent, how am I to stop this incessant chattering of the mind? There is no becoming silent; there is or there is not silence. If you are aware of the immensity of being, then there is silence; its very intensity brings tranquillity.

Character can be modified, changed, made harmonious, but character is not reality. Thought must transcend itself to comprehend the timeless. When we think of progress, growth, are we not thinking-feeling within the pattern of time? There is a becoming, modifying, or changing in the horizontal process; this becoming knows pain and sorrow but will this lead to reality? It cannot for becoming is ever time-binding. It is only when thought frees itself from becoming, liberates itself from the past through diligent self-awareness, is utterly tranquil, that there is the timeless.

This tranquillity of understanding is not produced by an act of will, for will is still a part of becoming, of craving. Mind-heart can be tranquil only when the storm and the conflict of craving have ceased. As a lake is calm when the winds stop, so the mind is tranquil in wisdom when it understands and transcends its own craving and distraction.

This craving is to be understood as it is disclosed in everyday thought-feeling-action; through constant self-awareness are the ways of craving, self-becoming, understood and transcended. Do not depend on time but be arduous in the search of self-knowledge.

Question: In answering the question of how to solve a psychological problem lastingly, you spoke about the three consecutive phases in the process of solving such a problem, the first one being the consideration of its cause and effect; secondly, the understanding of that particular problem as part of the dualistic conflict; and then the discovery that the thinker and the thought are one. It seems to me that the first and second steps are comparatively easy, while the third level cannot be attained in a similar simple, logical progression.

KRISHNAMURTI: I wonder if you have observed for yourself the three phases I suggested in trying to solve a psychological problem? Most of us can be aware of the cause and effect of a problem and also be aware of its dualistic conflict, but the questioner feels that the last step, the discovery that the thinker and the thought are one, is not so easy, nor can it be understood logically. These three states or steps I suggested only for the convenience of verbal communication; they flow from one to the other; they are not fixed within a framework of different levels. It is really important to understand that they are not different stages, one superior to the other; they hang on the same thread of understanding. There is an interrelationship between cause and effect and the dualistic conflict and the discovery that the thinker and his thought are one.

Cause and effect are inseparable; in the cause is the effect. To be aware of the cause-effect of a problem needs certain swift pliability of mind-heart for the cause-effect is constantly being modified, undergoing continual change. What once was cause-effect may have become modified now, and to be aware of this modification or change is surely necessary for true understanding. To follow the ever-changing cause-effect is strenuous, for the mind clings and takes shelter in what was the cause-effect; it holds to conclusions and so conditions itself to the past. There must be an awareness of this cause-effect conditioning; it is not static, but the mind is when it holds fast to a cause-effect that is immediately past. Karma is the bondage to cause-effect. As thought itself is the result of many causes-effects, it must extricate itself from its own bondages. The problem of cause-effect is not to be superficially observed and passed by. It is the continuous chain of conditioning memory that must be observed and understood; to be aware of this chain being created and to follow it through all the layers of consciousness is arduous; yet it must be deeply searched out and understood.

So long as the thinker is concerned with his thought, there must be dualism; as long as he struggles with his thoughts, dualistic conflict will continue. Is there a solution for a problem in the conflict of opposites? Is not the maker of the problem more important than the problem itself? Thought can go above and beyond its dualistic conflict only when the thinker is not separate from his thought. If the thinker is acting upon his thought, he will maintain himself apart and so ever be the cause of opposing conflict. In the conflict of dualism there is no answer to any problem, for in that state the thinker is ever separate from his thought. Craving remains and yet the object of craving is constantly being changed; what is important is to understand craving itself, not the object of craving.

Is the thinker different from his thought? Are they not a joint phenomenon? Why does the thinker separate himself from his thought? Is it not for his own continuity? He is ever seeking security, permanency, and as thoughts are impermanent the thinker thinks of himself as the permanent. The thinker hides behind his thoughts and without transforming himself tries to change the frame of his thought. He conceals himself behind the activity of his thoughts to safeguard himself. He is ever the observer manipulating the observed, but he is the problem and not his thoughts. It is one of the subtle ways of the thinker to be troubled about his thoughts and thereby avoid his own transformation.

If the thinker separates his thought from himself and tries to modify it without radically transforming himself, conflict and delusion inevitably will follow. There is no way out of this conflict and illusion save through the transformation of the thinker himself. This complete integration of the thinker with his thought is not on the verbal level, but is a profound experience which comes only when cause-effect is understood and the thinker is no longer caught in dualistic opposition. Through self-knowledge and right meditation, the integration of the thinker with his thought takes place, and then only can the thinker go above and beyond himself. Then only the thinker ceases to be. In right meditation the concentrator is the concentration; as generally practiced the thinker is the concentrator, concentrating upon something or becoming something. In right meditation the thinker is not separate from this thought. On rare occasions we experience this integration in which the thinker has wholly ceased; then only is there creation, eternal being. Until the thinker is silent he is the maker of problems, of conflict and sorrow.

July 15, 1945

Ninth Talk in The Oak Grove

The desire to be secure in things and in relationship only brings about conflict and sorrow, dependence and fear; the search for happiness in relationship without understanding the cause of conflict leads to misery. When thought lays emphasis on sensate value and is dominated by it, there can be only strife and pain. Without self-knowledge, relationship becomes a source of struggle and antagonism, a device for covering up inward insufficiency, inward poverty.

Does not craving for security in any form indicate inward insufficiency? Does not this inner poverty make us seek, accept, and cling to formulations, hopes, dogmas, beliefs, possessions; is not our action then merely imitative and compulsive? So anchored to ideology, belief, our thinking becomes merely a process of enchainment.

Our thought is conditioned by the past; the 'I', the 'me', and the 'mine' is the result of stored up experience, ever incomplete. The memory of the past is always absorbing the present; the self which is memory of pleasure and pain is ever gathering and discarding, ever forging anew the chains of its own conditioning. It is building and destroying but always within its own self-created prison. To the pleasant memory it clings and the unpleasant it discards. Thought must transcend this conditioning for the being of the real.

Is evaluating right thinking? Choice is conditioned thinking; right thinking comes through understanding the chooser, the censor. As long as thought is anchored in belief, in ideology, it can only function within its own limitation; it can only feel-act within the boundaries of its own prejudices; it can only experience according to its own memories, which give continuity to the self and its bondage. Conditioned thought prevents right thinking which is nonevaluation, nonidentification.

There must be alert self-observation without choice; choice is evaluation and evaluation strengthens the self-identifying memory. If we wish to understand deeply, there must be passive and choiceless awareness which allows experience to unfold itself and reveal its own significance. The mind that seeks security through the real creates only illusion. The real is not a refuge; it is not the reward for righteous action; it is not an end to be gained.

Question: Should we not doubt your experience and what you say? Though certain religions condemn doubt as a fetter is it not, as you have expressed it, a precious ointment, a necessity?

KRISHNAMURTI: Is it not important to find out why doubt ever arises at all? What is the cause of doubt? Does it not arise when there is the following of another? So the problem is not doubt but the cause of acceptance. Why do we accept, why do we follow?

We follow another's authority, another's experience and then doubt it; this search for authority and its sequel, disillusionment, is a painful process for most of us. We blame or criticize the once accepted authority, the leader, the teacher, but we do not examine our own craving for an authority who can direct our conduct. Once we understand this craving we shall comprehend the significance of doubt.

Is there not in us a deep-rooted tendency to seek direction, to accept authority? Wherefrom does this urge in us come? Does it not arise from our own uncertainty, from our own incapacity to know what is true at all times? We want another to chart for us the sea of self-knowledge; we desire to be secure, we desire to find a safe refuge, and so we follow anyone who will direct us. Uncertainty and fear seek guidance and compel obedience and worship of authority; tradition, education create for us many patterns of obedience. If sometimes we do not accept and obey symbols of outward authority, we create our own inner authority, the subtle voice of our self. But through obedience freedom cannot be known; freedom comes with understanding, not through acceptance of authority nor through imitation.

The desire for self-expansion creates obedience and acceptance which in turn give rise to doubt. We conform and obey for we crave self-expansion and thus we become thoughtless. Acceptance leads to thoughtlessness and doubt. Experience, especially that called religious, gives us great joy, and we use it as a guide, a reference; but when that experience ceases to sustain and inspire us, we begin to doubt it. Doubt arises only when we accept. But is it not foolish, thoughtless, to accept an experience of another? It is you who must think out, feel out and be vulnerable to the real, but you cannot be open if you cover yourself with the cloak of authority, whether that of another or of your own creation. It is far more essential to understand the craving for authority, for direction, than to praise or dispel doubt. In comprehending the craving for direction, doubt ceases. Doubt has no place in creative being.

He who clings to the past, to memory, is ever in conflict. Doubt does not put an end to conflict; only when craving is understood can there be the bliss of the real. Beware of the man who says he knows.

Question: I want to understand myself, I want to put an end to my stupid struggles and make a definite effort to live fully and truly.

KRISHNAMURTI: What do you mean when you use the term myself? As you are many and ever changing, is there an enduring moment when you can say that this is the ever 'me'? It is the multiple entity, the bundle of memories that must be understood and not seemingly the one entity that calls itself the 'me'.

We are ever-changing, contradictory thoughts-feelings—love and hate, peace and passion, intelligence and ignorance. Now which is the 'me' in all of this? Shall I choose what is most pleasing and discard the rest? Who is it that must understand these contradictory and conflicting selves? Is there a permanent self, a spiritual entity apart from these? Is not that self also the continuing result of the conflict of many entities? Is there a self that is above and beyond all contradictory selves? The truth of it can be experienced only when the contradictory selves are understood and transcended.

All the conflicting entities which make up the 'me' have also brought into being the other 'me', the observer, the analyzer. To understand myself I must understand the many parts of myself, including the 'I' who has become the watcher, the 'I' who understands. The thinker must not only understand his many contradictory thoughts, but he must understand himself as the creator of these many entities. The 'I', the thinker, the observer, watches his opposing and conflicting thoughts-feelings as though he were not part of them, as though he were above and beyond them, controlling, guiding, shaping. But is not the 'I', the thinker, also these conflicts? Has he not created them? Whatever the level, is the thinker separate from his thoughts? The thinker is the creator of opposing urges, assuming different roles at different times according to his pleasure and pain. To comprehend himself the thinker must come upon himself through his many aspects. A tree is not just the flower and the fruit but is the total process. Similarly, to understand myself I must, without identification and choice, be aware of the total process that is the 'me'.

How can there be understanding when one part is used as a means of comprehending the other? Is it possible to understand one contradiction by another? There is understanding only when contradiction as a whole ceases, when thought is not identifying itself with the part.

So it is important to understand the desire to condemn or approve, to justify or compare, for it is this desire that prevents the full comprehension of the whole being. Who is the judge, who is the entity that is comparing, analyzing? Is he not an aspect only of the total process, an aspect of the self that is ever maintaining conflict? Conflict is not dissolved by introducing another entity who may represent condemnation, justification, or love. In freedom alone can there be understanding, but freedom is denied when the observer, through identification, condemns or justifies. Only in understanding the process as a whole can right thinking open the door to the eternal.

Question: As you are so much against authority, are there any unmistakable signs by which the liberation of another can be objectively recognized, apart from the personal affirmation of the individual regarding his own attainment?

KRISHNAMURTI: It is again the problem of acceptance differently stated, is it not? Suppose one does assert that one is liberated, of what great significance is it to another? Suppose you are free from sorrow, of what importance is it to another? It becomes significant only if one seeks to free oneself from ignorance, for it is ignorance that causes sorrow. So the primary point is not who has attained but how to free thought from its self-enchaining sorrow. Most of us are not concerned with this essential issue, but rather with outward signs by which we may recognize one who is liberated in order

that he may heal our sorrows. We desire gain rather than understanding; our craving for guidance, for comfort, makes us accept authority and so we are ever seeking the expert. You are the cause of your sorrow and you alone can understand and transcend it, none can give you deliverance from ignorance save yourself.

It is not important who has attained but it is important to be aware of your attitude and how you listen to what is being said. We listen with hope and fear; we seek the light of another but are not alertly passive to be able to understand. If the liberated seems to fulfill our desires, we accept him; if not, we continue our search for the one who will; what most of us desire is gratification at different levels. What is important is not how to recognize one who is liberated but how to understand yourself. No authority, here or hereafter, can give you knowledge of yourself; without self-knowledge there is no liberation from ignorance, from sorrow.

You are the creator of misery as you are the creator of ignorance and authority; you bring the leader into being and follow him; your craving fashions the pattern of your religious and worldly life, so it is essential to understand yourself and so transform the way of your life. Be aware of why you follow another, why you search out authority, why you crave direction in conduct; be aware of the ways of craving. The mind-heart has become insensitive through fear and gratification of authority, but through deep awareness of thought-feeling comes the quickening of life. Through choiceless awareness the total process of your being is understood; through passive awareness comes enlightenment.

Question: Though you have answered several questions on meditation, I find that you have not said anything about group meditation. Should one meditate with others or alone?

KRISHNAMURTI: What is meditation? Is it not the understanding of the ways of the self, is it not self-knowledge? Without self-knowledge, without awareness of the total process, that which you build into character, that which you strive for, has no reality. Self-knowledge is the very beginning of true meditation. Now will you understand yourself through being alone or with many? The many can be a hindrance to meditation as can also the being alone. The very weight of ignorance of the many who do not understand themselves can overpower one who is attempting to understand himself through meditation. The group can stimulate one but is stimulation meditation? Dependence on the group creates conformity; congregational worship or prayer is susceptible to suggestion, to influence, to thoughtlessness.

To meditate in isolation can also create hindrances and strengthen one's prejudices and conformities. If there is no pliability, eager awareness, mere living alone strengthens one's tendencies and idiosyncrasies, hardens the habits, and deepens the grooves of thought-feeling. Without understanding the significance of meditation, meditating alone can become a self-enclosing process, the narrowing of mind-heart in self-delusion, and the strengthening of obstinacy and credulity.

So whether you meditate with a group or by yourself will have little meaning if the significance of meditation is not rightly understood. Meditation is not concentration, it is the creative process of self-discovery and understanding; meditation is not a process of self-becoming; beginning with self-knowledge, it brings tranquillity and supreme wisdom, it opens the door to the eternal. The purpose of meditation is to be aware of the total process of the self. The self is the result of the past and does not exist in isolation; it is made up. The many causes that have brought it into being must be understood and transcended; only through deep awareness and meditation can there be liberation from craving, from self. Then only is there true aloneness. But when you meditate by yourself, you are not alone for you are the result of innumerable influences, or conflicting forces. You are a result, a product, and that which is made up, selected, put together, cannot understand that which is not. When the thinker and his thought are one, having gone above and beyond all formulation, there is that tranquillity in which alone is the real. To meditate is to penetrate the many conditioned, educated layers of consciousness.

Since we are self-enclosed, in conflict and pain, it is essential to be keenly aware, for through self-knowledge, thought-feeling frees itself from its own self-created impediments of ill will and ignorance, worldliness and craving. It is this meditative understanding that is creative; this understanding brings about not withdrawal, not exclusion, but spontaneous solitude.

The more we are meditatively aware during the so-called waking hours, the less there are dreams, and less is the anxious fear of their interpretation; for if there is self-awareness during waking hours, the different layers of consciousness are being uncovered and understood and in sleep there is the continuation of awareness. Meditation is not for a set period only but is to be continued during the waking hours and hours of sleep as well. In sleep, because of right meditative awareness during waking hours, thought can penetrate depths that have great significance. Even in sleep meditation continues.

Meditation is not a practice; it is not the cultivation of habit; meditation is heightened awareness. Mere practice dulls the mind-heart for habit denotes thoughtlessness and causes insensitivity. Right meditation is a liberative process, a creative self-discovery which frees thought-feeling from bondage. In freedom alone is there the real.

Question: In discussing the problem of illness, you introduced the concept of psychological tension. If I remember correctly you stated that the nonuse or abuse of psychological tension is the cause of illness. Modern psychology on the other hand mostly stresses relaxation, release from nervous tension and so forth. What do you think?

KRISHNAMURTI: Must we not be strenuous if we would understand? As you are listening to this talk is there not attention, a tension? Is not all awareness an intensity of right tension? Awareness is necessary for comprehension; a strenuous attention is needed if we would grasp the full significance of a problem. Relaxation is necessary, sometimes beneficial; but is not awareness, right tension, necessary for deep understanding? Must not the strings of a violin be tuned or stretched to produce the right tone? If they are stretched too much they break, and if they are not stretched or tuned just rightly, they do not give the correct tone. Likewise we break down when our nerves are strained too much; tension beyond endurance causes various forms of mental and physical disorders.

But is not awareness, the widening and stretching of the mind-heart, necessary for understanding? Is understanding the result of relaxation, inattention, or does it come with awareness in which there is not that tension caused by the desire to grasp, to gain? Is not alert stillness necessary for deep understanding?

Tension can either mend or mar. In all relationship is there not tension? This tension becomes harmful when relationship becomes an escape from one's own insufficiency, a self-protective shelter from painful self-discovery. Tension becomes harmful when relationship hardens and is no longer a self-revealing process. Most of us use relationship for self-gratification, self-aggrandizement, but when it fails us a harmful tension is created which leads to frustration, jealousy, delusion, and conflict. As long as the craving of the self continues, there will be the harmful psychological tension of inner insufficiency that causes varieties of delusion and misery. But to understand emptiness, aching loneliness, there must be right awareness, right tension. The tension of greed, fear, ambition, hate, is destructive, is productive of psychological and physical ailments, and to transcend that tension there must be choiceless awareness.

Craving, which expresses itself in many ways in the material and so-called spiritual world, is the cause of conflict in all the different layers of consciousness. The tension of becoming is endless conflict and pain. In being aware of craving and so understanding it, thought liberates itself from ignorance and sorrow.

July 22, 1945

Tenth Talk in The Oak Grove

Is there an enduring state of creative tranquillity? Is there an end to the seemingly endless struggle of the opposites? Is there an imperishable ecstasy?

The end to conflict and sorrow is through understanding and transcending the ways of the self and in discovering that imperishable reality which is not the creation of the mind. Self-knowledge is arduous but without it ignorance and pain continue; without self-knowledge there can be no end to strife.

The world is splintered into many fragments, each in contention with the other; it is torn apart by antagonism, greed, and passion; it is broken up by warring ideologies, beliefs, and fears; neither organized religion nor politics can bring peace to man. Man is against man and the many explanations of his sorrow do not take away his pain. We have tried to escape from ourselves in many cunning ways, but escape only dulls and hardens the mind and heart. The outer world is but an expression of our own inner state; as we are inwardly broken up and torn by burning desires, so is the world about us; as there is incessant turmoil within us, so is there endless conflict in the world; as there is no inward tranquillity, the world has become a battlefield. What we are the world is.

Is there a possibility of finding enduring joy? There is, but to experience it there must be freedom. Without freedom truth cannot be discovered, without freedom there can be no experience of the real. Freedom must be sought out—freedom from saviors, teachers, leaders; freedom from the self-enclosing walls of good and bad; freedom from authority and imitation; freedom from self, the cause of conflict and pain.

Just as long as craving in its different forms is not understood, there will be conflict and pain. Conflict is not to be ended through superficial restatement of values nor by change of teachers and leaders. The ultimate solution lies in freedom from craving; not in another but in yourself is the way. The incessant battle within us all, which we call existence, cannot be brought to an end save through understanding and so transcending craving.

The conflict of acquisitiveness appears in knowledge, in relationship, in possessions; acquisitiveness in any form creates inequality and brutality. This division and conflict between man and man is not to be abolished through mere reform of the outer effects and values. Equality in possessions is not the way out of our extended and enveloping misery and stupidity; no revolution can free man from this spirit of exclusiveness. You may dislodge him from possessions through legislation, through revolution, but he will cling to exclusive relationship or belief. This spirit of exclusiveness at different levels cannot be abolished through any outward reform or through compulsion or regimentation. Yet it is this spirit of exclusiveness that breeds inequality and contention. Does not acquisitiveness set man against man? Can equality and compassion be established through any means of the mind? Must they not be sought elsewhere; does not this separativeness cease only in love, in truth?

The unity of man is to be found only in love, in the illumination that truth brings. This oneness of man is not to be established through mere economic and social readjustment. The world is ever occupied with this superficial adjustment; it is ever trying to rearrange values within the pattern of acquisitiveness; it tries to establish security on the insecurity of craving and so brings disaster upon itself. We hope that outward revolution, outward change of values will transform man; they do affect him, but acquisitiveness, finding gratification at other levels continues. This endless and purposeless movement of acquisitiveness cannot at any time bring peace to man, and only when he is free of it can there be creative being.

Acquisitiveness creates division of those ahead and those behind. You must be both pupil and Master in search of truth; you must make the approach directly without the conflict of example and following. There must be persistent self-awareness, and the more earnest and strenuous you are, the more thought will free itself from its own self-created bondages.

In the bliss of the real the experiencer and the experience cease. A mind-heart that is burdened with the memory of yesterday cannot live in the eternal present. Mind-heart must die each day for eternal being.

Question: I feel that at least to me what you are saying is something new and very vitalizing, but the old intrudes and distorts. It seems that the new is overpowered by the past. What is one to do?

KRISHNAMURTI: Thought is the result of the past acting in the present; the past is constantly sweeping over the present. The present, the new, is ever being absorbed by the past, by the known. To live in the eternal present there must be death to the past, to memory; in this death there is timeless renewal.

The present extends into the past and into the future; without the understanding of the present, the door to the past is closed. The perception of the new is so fleeting; no sooner is it felt than the swift current of the past sweeps over it and the new ceases to be. To die to the many yesterdays, to renew each day is only possible if we are capable of being passively aware. In this passive awareness there is no gathering to oneself; in it there is intense stillness in which the new is ever unfolding, in which silence is ever extending without measure.

We try to use the new as a means of breaking down or strengthening the past and so corrupt the living present. The renewing present brings comprehension of the past. It is the new that gives understanding, and in that light the past has a fresh, life-giving significance. When we listen to or experience something new, our instinctive response is to compare it with the old, with a past experience, with a fading memory. This comparing gives strength to the past, distorting the present, and so the new is ever becoming the past, the dead. If thought-feeling were capable of living in the now without distorting it, then the past would be transformed into the eternal present.

To some of you these talks and discussions may have brought a new and vitalizing understanding; what is important is not to put the new into old patterns of thought or phrase. Let it remain new, uncontaminated. If it is true it will cast out the old, the past, by its very abundant and creative light. The desire to make the creative present enduring,

practical, or useful makes it worthless. Let the new live without anchorage in the past, without the distorting influence of fears and hopes.

Die to your experience, to your memory. Die to your prejudice, pleasant or unpleasant. As you die there is the incorruptible; this is not a state of nothingness but of creative being. It is this renewal that will, if allowed, dissolve our problems and sorrows, however intricate and painful. Only in death of the self is there life.

Question: Do you believe in karma?

KRISHNAMURTI: The desire to believe should be understood and put away for it does not bring enlightenment. He who is seeking truth does not believe; he who is approaching truth has no dogma or creed; he who is seeking the timeless must be free of formulation and the time-binding quality of memory. When we believe we do not seek and belief brings doubt and pain. Search to understand, not to know; for in understanding, the dual process of the knower and the known ceases. In the mere search for knowledge, the knower is ever becoming and so is ever in conflict and sorrow. He who asserts he knows does not know.

The root of the Sanskrit word *karma* means to act, to do. Action is the result of a cause. War is the result of our everyday life of stupidity and ill will and greed; conflict and sorrow are the outcome of the inward turmoil of our craving. Is not our existence the product of enchaining conditioning? Cause is ever undergoing a modification, and alert awareness is necessary to follow and understand it. Silent and choiceless awareness not only reveals the cause but also frees thought-feeling from it. Can effect be separated from cause? Is not effect ever present in the cause? We desire to reform, to rearrange the effects without radically altering the cause. This occupation with effect is a form of escape from the basic cause.

As the end is in the means, so the effect is in the cause. It is comparatively easy to discover the superficial cause, but to discover and transcend craving, which is the deep cause of all conditioning, is arduous and demands constant awareness.

Question: Not only is there the fear of life, but great is the fear of death. How am I to conquer it?

KRISHNAMURTI: What is conquerable has to be conquered again and again. Fear comes to an end only through understanding. Fear of death is in the craving for self-fulfillment; we are empty and we crave completeness, so there is fear; we desire to achieve and so we are afraid lest death should call us. We desire time for understanding, the fulfillment of ambition needs time, and so we are afraid of death. We are in the bondage of time; death is the unknown and of the unknown we are afraid. Fear and death are the companions of life. We crave the assurance of self-continuity. Thought-feeling is moving from the known to the known and is always afraid of the unknown. Thought-feeling proceeds from accumulation to accumulation, from memory to memory, and the fear of death is the fear of frustration.

Because we are as the dead we fear death; the living do not. The dead are burdened by the past, by memory, by time, but for the living the present is the eternal. Time is not a means to the end, the timeless, for the end is in the beginning. The self weaves the net of time and thought is caught in it. The insufficiency of the self, its aching emptiness, causes the fear of death and of life. This fear is with us always—in our activities, our pleasures, and pain. Being dead, we seek life, but life is not found through the continuity of

the self. The self, the maker of time, must yield itself to the timeless.

If death is truly a great problem for you, not merely a verbal or emotional issue nor a matter of curiosity which can be appeased by explanations, then in you there is deep silence. In active stillness fear ceases; silence has its own creative quickening. You do not transcend fear through rationalization, through the study of explanations; the fear of death does not come to an end through some belief, for belief is still within the net of the self. The very noise of the self prevents its own dissolution. We consult, analyze, pray, exchange explanations; this incessant activity and noise of the self hinders the bliss of the real. Noise can produce only more noise and in it there is no understanding.

Understanding comes when your whole being is deeply and silently aware. Silent awareness is not to be compelled or induced; in this tranquillity death yields to creation.

Question: It has never occurred to me to think of myself as being able to attain liberation. The ultimate I can conceive of is that perhaps I might be able to hold and strengthen that entirely incomprehensible relation to God, which is the only thing I live by; and I really do not even know what that is.

You talk about being and becoming. I realize that these words mean fundamentally different attitudes and mine has been definitely one of becoming. I now want to transform what has been becoming all along into being. Am I fooling myself? I do not want simply to change words.

KRISHNAMURTI: We must first understand the process of becoming and all its implications before we can comprehend what is being. Is not the structure of our thought-feeling based on time? Do we not think-feel in terms of gain and loss, of becoming and not becoming? We think reality or God is to be reached through time, through becoming. We think that life is an endless ladder for us to climb ever to greater and greater heights. Our thinking-feeling is caught in the horizontal process of becoming; the becomer is ever accumulating, ever gaining, ever expanding. The self, the becomer, the creator of time, can never experience the timeless. The self, the becomer, is the cause of conflict and sorrow.

Does becoming lead to being? Through time can there be the timeless? Through conflict can there be tranquillity? Through war, hate, can there be love? Only when becoming ceases is there being; through the horizontal process of time the eternal is not; conflict does not lead to tranquillity; hate cannot be changed to love. The becomer can never be tranquil. Craving can never lead to that which is beyond and above all craving. The chain of sorrow is broken only when the becomer ceases to become, positively or negatively.

Now the becomer desires to translate his becoming into being. He sees perhaps the futility of becoming and desires to transform that process into being; instead of becoming, now he must be. He sees the pain of greed and now he desires to transform greed into nongreed, which is still a becoming; he has assumed a new attitude, a new garb called nongreed; but still the becomer continues to become. Does not this desire to translate the becoming into being lead to illusion? The becomer perhaps now perceives the endless conflict and sorrow involved in becoming and so craves a different state which he calls being; but craving continues under a new name. The ways of becoming are very subtle, and until the becomer is aware of them, he will continue to become, to be in conflict and sorrow. By changing terms we think we understand, and how easily we pacify ourselves!

Being is only when there is no effort, positive or negative, to become; only when the becomer is self-aware and understands the enchaining sorrow and wasted effort of becoming and no longer uses will, then only can he be silent. His desire and his will have subsided; then only is there the tranquillity of supreme wisdom. To become nongreedy is one thing and being without greed is another; to become implies a process but being does not. Process implies time; the state of being is not a result, not a product of education, discipline, conditioning. You cannot transform noise into silence; silence can only come into being when noise ceases. Result is a time process, a determined end through a determined means; but through a process, through time, the timeless is not. Self-awareness and right meditation will reveal the process of becoming. Meditation is not the cultivation of the becomer, but through self-knowledge the meditator, the becomer ceases.

Question: If we only consider the obvious meaning of your words, memory constitutes one of the mechanisms against which you have warned time and again. And yet you yourself, for instance, sometimes use written notes to aid your memory in reconstructing the introductory remarks which you obviously have thought out previously. Does there exist one necessary and even indispensable kind of memory related to the outside world of facts and figures, and an entirely different kind of memory which might be called psychological memory, which is detrimental because it interferes with the creative attitude which you have hinted at in expressions like "lying fallow"—"dying each day," etc.?

KRISHNAMURTI: Memory is accumulated experience, and what is accumulated is the known, and what is known, is ever the past. With the burden of the known can that which is timeless be discovered? Is not freedom from the past necessary to experience that which is immeasurable? That which is made up, that is, memory, cannot comprehend that which is not. Wisdom is not accumulated memory but is supreme vulnerability to the real.

Should we not, as the questioner points out, be aware of the two kinds of memories—the indispensable, relating to facts and figures, and the psychological memory? Without this indispensable memory we could not communicate with each other. We accumulate and cling to psychological memories and so give continuity to the self; thus the self, the past, is ever increasing, ever adding to itself. It is this accumulating memory, the self, that must come to an end; as long as thought-feeling is identifying itself with the memories of yesterday, it will be ever in conflict and sorrow; as long as thought-feeling is ever becoming, it cannot experience the bliss of the real. That which is real is not the continuation of identifying memory. According to what has been stored up, one experiences; according to one's conditioning and psychological memories and tendencies, are the experiences, but such experiences are ever enclosing, limiting. It is to this accumulation that one must die.

Is the experience of the real based on memory, on accumulation? Is it not possible for thought-feeling to go above and beyond these interrelated layers of memory? Continuance is memory, and is it possible for this memory to cease and a new state come into being? Can the educated and conditioned consciousness comprehend that which is not a result? It cannot and so it must die to itself. Psychological memory, ever striving to become, is creating results, barriers, and so is ever enslaving itself. It is to this becoming that thought-feeling must die; only through constant self-awareness does this self-identifying memory come to an end; it cannot come to an end through an act of will,

for will is craving and craving is the accumulation of identifying memory.

Truth is not to be formulated nor can it be discovered through any formulation or any belief; only when there is freedom from becoming, from self-identifying memory, does it come into being. Our thought is the result of the past, and without understanding its conditioning, it cannot go beyond itself. Thought-feeling becomes a slave to its own creation, to its own power of illusion, if it is unaware of its own ways. Only when thought ceases to formulate can there be creation.

Question: Do not the images of saints, Masters, help us to meditate rightly?

KRISHNAMURTI: If you would go north why look toward the south? If you would be free why become slaves? Must you know sobriety through drunkenness? Must you have tyranny to know freedom?

As meditation is of the highest importance, we ought to approach it rightly from the very beginning. Right means create right ends; the end is in the means. Wrong means produce wrong ends, and at no time will wrong means bring about right ends. By killing another will you bring about tolerance and compassion? Only right meditation can bring about right understanding. It is essential for the meditator to understand himself, not the objects of his meditation, for the meditator and his meditation are one, not separate. Without understanding oneself, meditation becomes a process of self-hypnosis inducing experiences according to one's conditioning, one's belief. The dreamer must understand himself, not his dreams; he must awaken and put an end to them. If the meditator is seeking an end, a result, then he will hypnotize himself by his desire. Meditation is often a self-hypnotic process; it may produce certain desired results, but such meditation does not bring enlightenment.

The questioner wants to know if examples help one to meditate rightly. They may help to concentrate, to focus attention, but such concentration is not meditation. Mere concentration, though troublesome, is comparatively easy, but what then? The concentrator is still what he is, only he has acquired a new faculty, a new means through which he can function, enjoy, and do harm. Of what value is concentration if he who concentrates is lustful, worldly, and stupid? He will still do harm; he will still create enmity and confusion. Mere concentration narrows the mind-heart, which only strengthens its conditioning, thus causing credulity and obstinacy. Before you learn to concentrate, understand the structure of your whole being, not just one part of it. With self-awareness there comes self-knowledge, right thinking. This self-awareness or understanding creates its own discipline and concentration; such pliable discipline is enduring, effective, not the self-imposed discipline of greed and envy. Understanding ever widens and deepens into extensional awareness; this awareness is essential for right meditation. Meditation of the heart is understanding.

We use examples as a means of inspiration. Why do we seek inspiration? As our lives are empty, dull, and mechanical we seek inspiration outside of ourselves. The Master, the saint, the savior then becomes a necessity, a necessity which enslaves us. Being enslaved, you then have to free yourself from your enchainment to discover the real, for the real can only be experienced in freedom.

Because you are not interested in self-knowledge, you seek from others inspiration, which is another form of distraction. Self-knowledge is a process of creative discovery, which is hindered when thought-feeling is concerned with gain. Greed for a result prevents the flowering of self-knowledge. Search itself is devotion, it is in itself inspiration. A mind that is identifying, comparing, judging, soon wearies and needs distraction, so-called inspiration. All distraction, noble or otherwise, is idolatrous.

But if the meditator begins to understand himself, then his meditation has great significance. Through self-awareness and self-knowledge there comes right thinking; only then can thought go above and beyond the conditioned layers of consciousness. Meditation then is being, which has its own eternal movement; it is creation itself for the meditator has ceased to be.

July 29, 1945

Ojai, California, 1946

-- ✳ --

First Talk in The Oak Grove

Though this is not a small group we will try to have a free and serious discussion instead of turning these gatherings into question and answer meetings. Some, no doubt, would prefer uninterrupted talks, but it seems to me to be more advantageous for all of us to join in a purposeful discussion which requires earnestness and sustained interest.

For what are we striving? What is it that each one is seeking? Until we are aware of our separate pursuits, it is not possible to establish right relationship between us. One might be seeking fulfillment and success, another wealth and power, another fame and popularity; some may wish to accumulate and some to renounce; there might be some who are earnestly seeking to dissolve the ego, while others may wish merely to talk about it. Is it not important for us to find out what it is we are seeking? To extricate ourselves from the confusion and misery in and about us, we must be aware of our instinctive and cultivated desires and tendencies. We think and feel in terms of achievement, of gain and loss, and so there is constant strife; but there is a way of living, a state of being, in which conflict and sorrow have no place.

So to make these discussions fruitful it is necessary, is it not, first to understand our own intentions. When we observe what is taking place in our lives and in the world, we perceive that most of us, in subtle or crude ways, are occupied with the expansion of the self. We crave self-expansion now or in the future; for us life is a process of the continuous expansion of the ego through power, wealth, asceticism, or the cultivation of virtue and so on. Not only for the individual but for the group, for the nation, this process signifies fulfilling, becoming, growing and has ever led to great disasters and miseries. We are ever striving within the framework of the self, however much it may be enlarged and glorified. If this be your aim, and mine wholly different, then we will have no relationship though we may meet; then our discussions will be purposeless and confused. So first we must be very clear in our intention. We must be clear and definite as to what we are seeking. Are we craving self-expansion, the constant nourishment of the ego, the 'me' and the 'mine', or are we seeking to understand and so transcend the process of the self? Will self-expansion bring about understanding, enlightenment; or is there illumination, liberation, only when the process of self-expansion has ceased? Can we reveal ourselves sufficiently to discern in which direction our interest lies? You must have come here with serious intent; therefore we will discuss in order to clarify that intent, and consider if our daily life indicates what our pursuits are and whether we are nourishing the ego or not. So these discussions can be a means of self-exposure to each one of us. In this self-exposure we will discover the true significance of life.

Must we not first have freedom to discover? There can be no freedom if our action is ever enclosing. Is not the action of the ego, the sense of the 'me' and the 'mine', ever a process of limitation? We are trying to find out, are we not, if the process of self-expansion leads to reality or if reality comes into being only when the self ceases.

Question: Must one not go through the self-expansive process in order to realize the immeasurable?

KRISHNAMURTI: May I put the same question differently? Must one go through drunkenness to know sobriety? Must one go through the various states of craving only to renounce them?

Question: Can one do anything with regard to this self-expansive process?

KRISHNAMURTI: May I elaborate this question? We are, are we not, positively encouraging through many actions the expansion of the ego. Our tradition, our education, our social conditioning sustain positively the activities of the ego. This positive activity may take a negative form—not to be something. So our action is still a positive or negative activity of the self. Through centuries of tradition and education, thought accepts as natural and inevitable the self-expansive life, positively or negatively. How can thought free itself from this conditioning? How can it be tranquil, silent? If there is that stillness, that is, if it is not caught in self-expansive processes, then there is reality.

Question: If I rightly understand, surely you are reaching way out into the abstract, are you not? You are speaking about reincarnation, I presume?

KRISHNAMURTI: I am not, sir, nor am I reaching out into the abstract. Our social and religious structure is based on the urge to become something, positively or negatively. Such a process is the very nourishment of the ego through name, family, achievement, through identification of the 'me' and 'mine', which is ever causing conflict and sorrow. We perceive the results of this way of life— strife, confusion, and antagonism, ever spreading, ever engulfing. How is one to transcend strife and sorrow? This is what we are attempting to understand during these discussions.

Is not craving the very root of the self? How is thought, which has become the means of self-expansion, to act without giving sustenance to the ego, the cause of conflict and sorrow? Is this not an important question? Do not let me make it important to you. Is this not a vital question to each one? If it is, must we not find the true answer? We are nourishing the ego in many ways, and before we condemn or encourage, we must understand its significance, must we not? We use religion and philosophy as a means of self-expansion; our social structure is based on the aggrandizement of the self; the clerk will become the manager and later the owner, the pupil will become the Master and so on. In this process there is ever conflict, antagonism, sorrow. Is this an intelligent and inevitable process? We can discover truth for ourselves only when we do not depend on another; no specialist can give us the right answer. Each one has to find the right answer directly for himself. For this reason it is important to be earnest.

We vary in our earnestness according to circumstances, our moods and fancies.

Earnestness must be independent of circumstances and moods, of persuasion and hope. We often think that perhaps through shock we shall be made earnest, but dependence is never productive of earnestness. Earnestness comes into being with inquiring awareness, and are we so alertly aware? If you are aware you will realize that your mind is constantly engaged in the activities of the ego and its identification; if you pursue this activity further, you will find the deep-seated self-interest. These thoughts of self-interest arise from the needs of daily life, things you do from moment to moment, your role in society and so on, all of which build up the structure of the ego. This seems so strangely inevitable, but before we accept this inevitability, must we not be aware of our purposive intention, whether we desire to nourish the ego or not? For according to our hidden intentions we will act. We know how the self is built up and strengthened through the pleasure and pain principle, through memory, through identification and so on. This process is the cause of conflict and sorrow. Do we earnestly seek to put an end to the cause of sorrow?

Question: How do we know our intention is right before we understand the truth of the matter? If we do not first comprehend truth, then we shall go off the beam, founding communities, forming groups, having half-baked ideas. Is it not necessary, as you have suggested, to know oneself first? I have tried to write down my thoughts-feelings as has been suggested, but I find myself blocked and unable to follow my thoughts right through.

KRISHNAMURTI: Through being choicelessly aware of your intentions, the truth of the matter is known. We are often blocked because, unconsciously, we are afraid to take action which might lead to further trouble and suffering. But no clear and definite action can take place if we have not uncovered our deep and hidden intention with regard to nourishing and maintaining the self.

Is not this fear which hinders understanding the result of projection, speculation? You imagine that freedom from self-expansion is a state of nothingness, an emptiness, and this creates fear, thus preventing any actual experience. Through speculation, through imagination, you prevent the discovery of *what is*. As the self is in constant flux, we seek, through identification, permanency. Identification brings about the illusion of permanency, and it is the loss of this which causes fear. We recognize that the self is in constant flux, yet we cling to something which we call the permanent in the self, an enduring self which we fabricate out of the impermanent self. If we deeply experienced and understood that the self is ever impermanent, then there would be no identification with any particular form of craving, with any particular country, nation, or with any organized system of thought or religion, for with identification comes the horror of war, the ruthlessness of so-called civilization.

Question: Is the fact of this constant flux not enough to make us identify? It seems to me that we cling to something called the 'me', the self, for it is a pleasant habit of sound. We know a river even when it is dry; similarly we cling to something that is 'me' even though we know its impermanency. The 'me' is shallow or deep, in full flood or dry, but it is always the 'me' to be encouraged, nourished, maintained at any cost. Why must the 'I' process be eliminated?

KRISHNAMURTI: Now why do you ask this question? If the process is pleasurable you will continue in it and not ask such a question; when it is disagreeable, painful, then only will you desire to put an end to it. According to pleasure and pain, thought is shaped, controlled, guided, and upon such a weak, changing foundation we make an attempt to understand truth! Whether the self should be maintained or not is a very vital issue, for on it depends the whole course of our action, and so how we approach this problem is all-important. On our approach depends the answer. If we are not earnest then the answer will be according to our prejudices and passing fancies. So the approach matters more than the problem itself. Upon the seeker depends what he finds; if he is prejudiced, limited, then he will find according to his conditioning. What then is important is for the seeker first to understand himself.

Question: How do we know if there is an abstract truth?

KRISHNAMURTI: Surely, sir, we are not considering now an abstract truth. We are attempting to discover the true and lasting answer to our problem of sorrow, for on that depends the whole course of life.

Question: Can the conditioned mind observe its conditioning?

KRISHNAMURTI: Is it not possible to be aware of our prejudices? Cannot we know when we are dishonest, when we are intolerant, when we are greedy?

Question: Is not the nourishment of the body equally wrong?

KRISHNAMURTI: We are considering the psychological nourishment, the expansion of the self, which causes such strife and misery. One can accept the activity of the self as inevitable and follow that course, or there may be another way of life. If it is an intense problem to each one of us, then we shall find the right answer.

Question: Shall we not know the true answer when the desire for it is greater than for any other thing?

Question: Is the ego always harmful? Is selfishness ever beneficial?

KRISHNAMURTI: Self-centered attention and activity, positively or negatively, is the cause of strife and pain. How seriously is each one considering this problem? How earnest are we about discovering the truth of the nature and activity of the ego, the self? Our meditation and spiritual discipline have no meaning if first we are not clear upon this point. True meditation is not self-expansion in any form. So until we can have a common understanding of our purpose, there will be confusion, and right relationship between us will not be possible.

Question: Is there not a way straight to the problem, to find out the truth?

KRISHNAMURTI: There is, but this demands utter stillness, open receptivity. This requires right understanding; otherwise effort to be open, to be tranquil becomes another means of self-expansion. I am saying that there is a different way of life—a way that is not of self-expansion, in which there is ecstasy—but it has no validity if you merely accept my statement; such acceptance will become another form of egotistic activity. You must know for yourself, directly, the truth of yourself, and you cannot realize it through another, however great. There is no authority that can reveal it. Truth can be uncovered only through self-knowledge. We have a common problem to which we are trying to find the right answer.

Question: Writing a book could be a self-expansive action, could it not?

Question: Should we not establish a purpose in our lives?

KRISHNAMURTI: The ego can choose a noble purpose and so utilize it as a means for its own expansion.

Question: If there is no self-expansion is there a purpose, as we know it now?

KRISHNAMURTI: A man who is asleep dreams that he has a purpose or must choose a purpose, but does he who is awake have a purpose? He is simply awake. Our frames of reference, our purposes are a means, negatively or positively, of measuring the growth of the self.

Question: Is fulfillment self-expansion?

KRISHNAMURTI: If fulfillment is prevented is there not the pain of frustration of the self? Questions of similar kind will find their answer in discovering the truth concerning the self-expansive process; this depends on earnestness and on the open receptivity of the mind-heart.

Question: Must we not know what is the other way of life before we can relinquish self-aggrandizement?

KRISHNAMURTI: How can we know or be aware of another way of life until we can perceive the falseness, the futility of acquisition and self-expansion? In understanding the ways of self-aggrandizement, we shall become aware. To speculate about the way becomes a hindrance to the very understanding of that life which is not one of self-perpetuation. So must we not discover the truth concerning the habitual activities of the self? It is knowledge of the hindrance that is the liberating factor, not the attempt to be free from the hindrance. Effort made to be free without the liberating action of truth is still within the enclosing walls of the self. You can discover truth only if you are willing to give your whole mind and heart to it, not a few moments of your easily spared time. If we are earnest we will find truth; but this earnestness cannot depend on stimulation of any kind. We must give our full and deep attention to the discovery of the truth of our problem, not for a few grudging moments but constantly. It is truth alone that liberates thought from its own enclosing process.

April 7, 1946

Second Talk in The Oak Grove

We have been saying there can be no right relationship between us if we do not understand each other's intentions. The way of self-expansion is the way of strife and sorrow and is not the way of reality. The ecstasy of reality is to be found through awakened, highest intelligence. Intelligence is not the cultivation of memory or reason but an awareness in which identification and choice have ceased.

To think out a thought fully is difficult for it needs patience and extensional awareness. We have been educated in a way of life which furthers the self through achievement, through identification, through organized religion; this way of thought and action has led us to fearful catastrophes and untold misery.

Question: You have said that illumination could never come through self-expansion, but does it not come through the expansion of consciousness?

KRISHNAMURTI: Illumination, understanding, understanding of the real, can never come through the expansion of the self, through the 'I' making an effort to grow, to become, to achieve, and there is no effort apart from the will of the 'I'. How can there be understanding if the self is ever filtering experience, identifying, accumulating memory? Consciousness is the product of the mind, and the mind is the result of conditioning, of craving, and so it is the seat of the self. Only when the activity of the self, of memory, ceases is there a wholly different consciousness, about which any speculation is a hindrance. The effort to expand is still the activity of the self whose consciousness is to grow, to become. Such consciousness, however expanded, is time-binding and so the timeless is not.

If one desires to understand a vital problem, should not one put aside one's tendencies, prejudices, fears, and hopes, one's conditioning, and be aware simply and directly? In thinking over our problems together, we are exposing ourselves to ourselves. This self-exposure is of great importance for it will reveal to us the process of our own thoughts-feelings. We have to dig deeply into ourselves to find truth. We are conditioned, and is it possible for thought to go beyond its own limitation? It is possible only through being aware of our conditioning. We have developed a certain kind of intelligence in the process of self-expansion; through greed, through acquisitiveness, through conflict and pain we have developed a self-protective, self-expansive intelligence. Can this intelligence comprehend the real which alone can resolve all our problems?

Question: Is intelligence the right word to use?

KRISHNAMURTI: If we all understand the meaning of that term as I am using it here, it is applicable. The main point is, can this intelligence which has been cultivated through the expansion of the self, experience or discover truth; or must there be another kind of activity, another kind of awareness to receive truth? To discover truth there must be freedom from the self-expansive intelligence for it is ever enclosing, ever limiting.

Question: Must we not look at this problem of self-expansion from the point of view of what is true?

KRISHNAMURTI: To see the false as the false and the true as the true is difficult. If you saw the truth about self-expansion, then its problems would begin to fade away. To see the truth in the false is to understand yourself first. It is the truth in the false that is liberating.

Question: Do you imply that there is a greater intelligence than ours?

KRISHNAMURTI: We are not trying to discover whether there is a greater intelligence, but what we are considering is whether the particular intelligence we have so sedulously cultivated can experience or understand reality.

Question: Is there a reality?

KRISHNAMURTI: To discover that, there must be a tranquil mind, a mind that is not fabricating thoughts, images, hopes. As the mind is ever seeking to expand through its own creations, it cannot experience reality. If the mind, the instrument, is blurred, it is of little use in the search of truth. It must first cleanse itself and then only will it be possible to know if there is reality. So each one must be aware, recognize the state of his intelligence. By its very limitation is not the mind a hindrance to the discovery of the real? Before thought can free itself it first must recognize its own limitations.

Question: Can you tell us how to go through this process without impairing ourselves?

KRISHNAMURTI: I am afraid we are talking at cross-purposes, and so we are getting confused. What is it that each one of us is seeking? Are we not aware of a common search?

Question: I am trying to solve my problem. I am seeking God. I want love. I want security.

KRISHNAMURTI: Are we not all seeking to transcend conflict and sorrow? Conflict and sorrow come to us in different ways, but the cause common to us all is self-expansion. The cause of conflict and sorrow is craving, the self. Through understanding and so dissolving the cause, our psychological problems will come to an end.

Question: Will the solution of the central problem end for me all problems?

KRISHNAMURTI: Only if you dissolve the cause of all problems, the self; until then each day brings new strife and pain.

Question: My intelligence says that by solving my individual problem I can fit harmoniously into the whole. Are there different purposes for each one of us?

KRISHNAMURTI Out of our self-contradiction and confusion, have we not invented purposes according to our tendencies and desires? Are not our purposes and problems fabricated by the self?

Being in sorrow, we seek to be happy. If this is our chief concern, as it surely is for most of us, then we must know what the causes are that prevent us from being happy or that make us sorrowful.

Question: How am I to eradicate the causes?

KRISHNAMURTI: Before you put that question, you must be aware of the causes of sorrow. Being in sorrow, you say you are seeking happiness; so the search for happiness is an escape from sorrow. There can be happiness only when the cause of sorrow ceases; so happiness is a byproduct and not an end in itself. The cause of sorrow is the self with its craving to expand, to become, to be other than what it is, with its craving for sensation, for power, for happiness and so on.

Question: If there were no discontent there would be no progress, there would be stagnation.

KRISHNAMURTI: You want both "progress" and happiness and that is your difficulty, is it not? You desire self-expansion but not the conflict and sorrow that inevitably come with it. We are afraid to look at ourselves as we are; we want to run away from the actual, and this flight we call "progress" or the search for happiness. We say that we will decay if we do not "progress"; we will become lazy, thoughtless, if we do not struggle to run away from *what is*. Our education and the world that we have created help us to run away; yet to be happy we must know the cause of sorrow. To know the cause of sorrow and transcend it is to face it, not to seek escape through illusory ideals or through further activities of the self. The cause of sorrow is the activity of the expanding self.

Even to crave to be rid of the self is negative action of the self and hence delusive.

Question: Could we take a positive rather than a negative point of view, saying to ourselves that we are the whole?

KRISHNAMURTI: Is not a positive or negative action of the self still the movement of the self? If the self asserts that it is the whole, is not that an activity of the self, seeking to enclose the whole within its own walls? We think that by constantly asserting we are the whole, we will become the whole; such repetition is self-hypnosis, and to be drugged is not to be illumined. We are not yet aware of the cunning deceptions of our minds, of the subtle ways of the self. Without self-knowledge there can be no happiness, no wisdom.

Question: I do not desire self-expansion.

KRISHNAMURTI: Can it be so easily thought and said? The desire for self-expansion is complex and subtle. The structure of our thought is based on this expansion—to grow, to become, to fulfill.

Question: The cause of sorrow is incompleteness. Expansion stimulates and so we crave for it.

KRISHNAMURTI: Can we not experience here and now, directly, for ourselves, the cause of sorrow? If we can experience and understand this urge to expand, to be, then we shall go beyond the verbal state to the root of sorrow.

Question: I want to find truth and that is one of my reasons for self-expansion.

KRISHNAMURTI: Why are you seeking truth? Do you seek it because you are unhappy, and so through its discovery you hope to be happy? Truth is not compensation; it is not a reward for your suffering, for your struggles. Do you hope that it will set you free? The activity of the self is ever binding and does not lead to truth. Without self-awareness and self-knowledge how can there be the understanding of truth? We think we are seeking truth, but perhaps we are only seeking gratifying remedies, comforting answers. We verbally assert the need for brotherhood, for unity, without eradicating in ourselves the causes of conflict and antagonism. We must be aware of the cause of self-expansion and directly experience its full implications.

Question: Self-expansion is a natural instinct and what is wrong with it?

Question: We want to be loved, and if we are frustrated, we seek another form of gratification. We are continually seeking satisfaction.

KRISHNAMURTI: The seemingly natural instinct for self-expansion is the cause of discontent and pain; it is the cause of our recurrent disasters, civilized ruthlessness, and mounting misery. It may be "natural," but surely it must be transcended for the timeless to be. The craving for gratification is without end.

Question: Why is there the urge to be superior?

Question: I do not know why, but there is in me the urge to be superior. I cannot observe it without being amused or appalled, yet I want to be superior. I know it is wrong to feel superior. It leads to misery, it is antisocial, it is immoral.

KRISHNAMURTI: You are merely condemning the desire to be superior; you are not trying to understand it. To condemn or accept is to create resistance which hinders understanding. Do not all of us desire to be superior in some way or another? If we deny it, if we condemn it, or are blind to it we shall not understand the causes that sustain this desire.

Question: I want to be superior because I want to be loved by people, for it is necessary to be loved.

KRISHNAMURTI: Being inferior, there is the urge to feel superior; not being loved, we desire to be loved. That is, in myself I am insignificant, empty, shallow, so I desire to put on masks for different occasions: the mask of superiority and of nobility, the mask of earnestness, the mask that asserts it is seeking God, and so on. Being inwardly poor, we desire to identify ourselves with the great, with the nation, with the Master, with an ideology, and so on—the form of identification varying with circumstances and moods.

You may pursue virtue and practice spiritual exercises, but by covering up this incompleteness, in denying it consciously or unconsciously, it is not transcended. Until it is transcended all activity is of the self, which is the cause of conflict and sorrow. Being inwardly insufficient, we have developed the cunning art of escape; this escape we call by various pleasant-sounding names. How can this process of the mind comprehend the real? How can it comprehend something not of its own fabrication?

The desire to be superior, to become the Master, to accumulate knowledge, to lose oneself in activities, offers hopeful and gratifying escape from inward poverty, insufficiency. Being incomplete, empty, any activity, however noble, can only be the expansive movement of the self.

Question: Can we not occasionally realize that we are escaping?

KRISHNAMURTI: We may, but our self-expansive urge is so cunning, subtle, that it avoids coming directly in conflict with this aching insufficiency. How to approach this problem is our difficulty, is it not?

Question: When you are free what is the purpose of activity?

KRISHNAMURTI: How can a mind that is the outcome of insufficiency and fear experience an activity which is not of the self? How can a mind that is acquisitive and fearful, bound by dogma and belief, experience reality? It cannot. Speculation of what is beyond its limitation is only a postponement of the realization of its bondage. If I may suggest, can we try during the coming week to be aware of this bondage that has been developed by the process of self-expansion?—for this limitation, this expanding self can never experience or discover the real.

April 14, 1946

Third Talk in The Oak Grove

Without the experience of the real there can never be freedom from conflict and sorrow; the real alone can transform our life, not mere resolution. All activity of the self with its resolutions and negations must cease for the real to be. To understand the activities of the self, there must be earnest endeavor, sustained alertness, and interest. Many of us hold to our beliefs or to our experiences, and this only breeds obstinacy.

Earnestness is not dependent on moods, on circumstances, nor on stimulation. Some who are attempting to live an earnest life are strenuous along some particular groove of thought, belief, or discipline and thus become intolerant and rigid. Such strenuous effort prevents deep understanding and closes the door upon reality. If you will consider this closely, you will see that what is necessary is natural, effortless discernment, the freedom to discover and understand. These ideas, if allowed, will take root and bring about a radical transformation of our daily life. The unforced receptivity is much more significant than the effort made to understand.

Question: I am afraid it is not very clear.

KRISHNAMURTI: Most of us here are making an effort to understand; such effort is the activity of will, which only creates resistance, and resistance is not overcome by another resistance, by another act of will; such effort actually prevents understanding; whereas if we were alertly pliable and aware, we would understand deeply. All effort we now make issues from the desire for self-expansion; only when there is an effortless awareness can there be discovery and understanding, a perception of the true.

When we see a painting we first want to know who the painter is, we then compare and criticize it or try to interpret it according to our conditioning. We do not really see the picture or the scenery but are only concerned with our clever capacity for interpretation, criticism, or admiration; we are generally so full of ourselves that we do not really see the picture or the scenery. If we could banish our judgment and clever analysis, then perhaps the picture might convey its significance. Similarly, these discussions will have meaning only if we are open to the experience of discovery, which is prevented by our clinging obstinately to beliefs, memories, and conditioned prejudices.

Question: Is there anything that one can do to be passively aware? Can I do anything to be open?

KRISHNAMURTI: The very desire to be open can be an effort of the self, which only creates resistance. We can but be aware that we are enclosed, that the activity of will is resistance, and that the very desire itself to gain passive awareness is another hindrance. To make a positive effort to be open is to throw up the barrier of greed. To be aware of the self-enclosing activities is to break them down; to be unaware and yet desire to be open is to create further resistance. Passive awareness comes only when the mind-heart is tranquil. In this stillness the real comes into being. This stillness is not to be induced nor is it the outcome of the activity of will. An intelligence which is the product of desire, of self-expansion, is ever creating resistance, and it can never bring about tranquillity. Such intelligence of self-protectiveness is the product of time, of the impermanent, and so can never experience the timeless.

Question: Is not this intelligence useful in other ways?

KRISHNAMURTI: Its only use is in protecting itself, which has caused untold misery and pain.

Question: From the amoeba to man the intelligence to be secure, to self-expand is inevitable and natural; it is a closed and vicious circle.

KRISHNAMURTI: That may seem so, but the activity to be secure has not led man to security, to happiness, to wisdom. It has led him to ever-increasing confusion, conflict, and, misery. There is a different activity which is not of the self, which must be sought out. A different intelligence is needed to experience the timeless, which alone will free us from incessant strife and sorrow. The intelligence that we now possess is the result of craving gratification, security, in crude or subtle form; it is the result of greed; it is the outcome of self-identification. Such an intelligence can never experience the real.

Question: Do you say that intelligence and self-consciousness are synonymous?

KRISHNAMURTI: Consciousness is the outcome of identified continuity. Sensation, feeling, rationalization, and the continuity of identified memory make up self-consciousness, do they not? Can we say precisely where consciousness ends and intelligence begins? They flow into each other, do they not? Is there consciousness without intelligence?

Question: Does a new intelligence come into being if we are aware of the self-expansive intelligence?

KRISHNAMURTI: We shall know, as experience, the new form of intelligence only when the self-protective and self-expansive intelligence ceases.

Question: How can we go beyond this limited intelligence?

KRISHNAMURTI: Through being passively aware of its complex and interrelated activities. In so being aware the causes that nourish the intelligence of the self come to an end without self-conscious effort.

Question: How can one cultivate the other intelligence?

KRISHNAMURTI: Is that not a wrong question? I wonder if we are paying interested attention to what is being said. The wrong cannot cultivate the right. We are still thinking in terms of self-expanding intelligence, and that is our difficulty. We are unaware of it and so we ask, without thought, "How can the other intelligence be cultivated?" Surely there are certain obvious, essential requirements which will free the mind from this limited intelligence: humility which is related to humor and mercy; to be without greed which is to be without identification; to be unworldly which is to be free from sensate values; to be free from stupidity, from ignorance, which is the lack of self-knowledge, and so on. We must be aware of the cunning and devious ways of the self, and in understanding them virtue comes into being, but virtue is not an end in itself. Self-interest cannot cultivate virtue, it can only perpetuate itself under the mask of virtue; under the cover of virtue there is still the activity of the self. It is as though we were attempting to see the clear, pure light through colored glasses, which we are unaware of wearing. To see the pure light we must first be aware of our colored glasses; this very awareness, if the urge to see the pure light is strong, helps to remove the colored glasses. This removal is not the action of one resistance against another but is an effortless action of understanding. We must be aware of the actual, and the understanding of *what is* will set thought free; this very understanding will bring about open receptivity, transcending the particular intelligence.

Question: How does the intelligence with which we are all familiar come into being?

KRISHNAMURTI: It comes into being through perception, sensation, contact, desire, identification—all of which give continuity to the self through memory. The principle of pleasure, pain, identification is ever sustaining this intelligence which can never open the door to truth.

Question: We do have to make some kind of effort, do we not?

KRISHNAMURTI: The effort that we now make is an activity of the expansion of the self with its particular intelligence. This effort can only strengthen, positively or negatively, the self-protective intelligence or resistance. This intelligence can never experience the real, which alone brings liberation from our conflict, confusion, and sorrow.

Question: How has this intelligence come into being?

KRISHNAMURTI: Has it not been cultivated through specialization? Has it not come into being through imitation, through conditioning? The cultivation of the 'me' and the 'mine' is specialization—the 'me' that is special, all-important: my work, my action, my success, my virtue, my country, my savior—this positive and negative striving to become implies specialization. Specialization is death, the lack of infinite pliability.

Question: I see that, but what am I to do?

KRISHNAMURTI: Be aware, without choice, of this process of specialization, and you will discover that a deep, revolutionary change is taking place within you. Do not say to yourself that you are going to be aware, or that awareness has to be cultivated, or that it is a matter of growth or craftsmanship, which is an indication of postponement, laziness. You

are or you are not aware. Be aware now of this specializing process.

Question: All this implies extensive self-study and self-knowledge, does it not?

KRISHNAMURTI: And that is the very thing we are attempting here; we are exposing to ourselves the ways of our thought-feeling—its cunning, its subtlety, its pride in its so-called intelligence, and so on. This is not book knowledge but actual experience, from moment to moment, in the ways of the self. Thus we are trying to uncover the ways of the self. The desire to expand in the world or to pursue virtue is still the activity of the self; the urge to become, negatively or positively, is the factor in specialization. This desire which prevents infinite pliability must be understood through awareness of the specializing process of the 'me'.

Question: If I am just pliable can't I go wrong, and therefore must I not be anchored in truth?

KRISHNAMURTI: Truth is discovered in the uncharted sea of self-knowledge. But why do you ask this question? Is it not because you are frightened lest you go astray? Does it not imply that you crave to achieve, to succeed, to be ever in the right? We crave security and this craving prevents the freedom of truth. Those who are deep in self-knowledge are pliable. We see that one of the causes of resistance is specialization, and another is imitation. The desire to copy is complex and subtle. The structure of our thought is based on imitation, religious or worldly. Newspapers, radios, magazines, books, education, governments, organized religions—all these and other factors help to make thought conform. Also, each one desires to conform, for it is easier to conform than to be aware. Conformity is the basis of our social existence, and we are afraid to be alone. Fear and thoughtlessness bring about acceptance and conformity, the acceptance of authority. As with the individual so with the group, with the nation.

Conformity is one of the many means through which the self maintains itself. Thought moves from the known to the known, ever fearful of the unknown, of the uncertain, and yet only when there is uncertainty, when the mind is not in the bondage of the known is there the ecstasy of the real. Thought must be alone for the comprehension of the real. Through self-knowledge the imitative process comes to an end.

Question: Must we always face the unknown?

KRISHNAMURTI: The eternal is ever the unknown for a mind that accumulates; what is accumulated is memory and memory is ever the past, the time-binder. That which is the result of time cannot experience the timeless, the unknown.

We shall always be faced with the unknown until we understand the knowable, which is ourselves. This understanding cannot be given to you by the specialist, the psychologist, or the priest; you must seek it for yourself, in yourself, through self-awareness. Memory, the past, is shaping the present according to the pattern of pleasure and pain. Memory becomes the guide, the path towards safety, security; it is this identifying memory that gives continuity to the self.

The search for self-knowledge demands constant alertness, an awareness without choice, which is difficult and arduous.

Question: Are we worms which must turn into butterflies?

KRISHNAMURTI: Again how easily we slip into ignorant ways of thinking! Being evil, we will eventually become good; being mortal, we will become immortal. With these comforting thoughts we drug ourselves. Evil can never become good; hate can never become love; greed can never become non-greed. Hate must be abandoned, it cannot be changed into something which it is not. Through growth, through time, evil cannot become good. Time does not make the ignoble noble. We must be aware of this ignorance and its illusions. We are educated to think that the conflict of the opposites produces a hoped-for result, but this is not so. An opposite is the outcome of resistance and resistance is not overcome by opposition. Each resistance must be dissolved not by its opposite, but through understanding the resistance itself.

Conflict exists between various desires, not between light and darkness. There can never be struggle between light and darkness for where there is light, darkness is not, where there is truth the false is not. When the self divides itself into the higher and the lower, this very contradiction begets conflict, confusion, and antagonism. To be aware of *what is* and not escape into fanciful illusion is the beginning of understanding. We should be concerned with *what is,* the craving for self-expansion, and not try to transform it, for the transformer is still craving, which is the action of the self; the very awareness of *what is* brings about understanding. To be aware from moment to moment brings its own clarification. The desire for achievement and recognition prevents awakening; the sleeper dreams that he must awaken and struggles in his dream, but it is only a dream. The sleeper cannot awaken through dreams; he must cease sleeping. Thought itself must be aware of creating the structure of the self and its perpetuation. One who is earnest must discover for himself the truth about self-perpetuation.

Question: What is there to prove that the perpetuation of the self is in itself bad?

KRISHNAMURTI: Nothing at all, if we are satisfied with it and unaware of the issues of life, but we are all in comparative strife and sorrow. Some cover up their pains or escape from them. They have not resolved their confusion and misery.

Realizing our state of self-contradiction and its painful conflicts, we want to find the right way of transcending it; for in incompleteness there is no peace. Is it not the very nature of the self, at all times, to be contradictory? This contradiction breeds conflict, confusion, and enmity. Craving, the very basis of the self, is ever unfulfilled; in trying to overcome incompleteness, man is ever in conflict within and without. Those who are in earnest must discover for themselves the truth about incompleteness. This discovery does not depend on any authority or formula nor on the acquisition of knowledge. To discover truth we must be passively aware. Since we are afraid and enclosed we must be aware of the causes that create resistance, of the desire for self-perpetuation which creates conflict.

Question: What happens to that self-perpetuating intelligence when a soldier in battle throws himself in front of a gun to save another?

KRISHNAMURTI: Probably at the moment of great tension the soldier forgets himself, but is that a recommendation for war?

Question: Do we not hear that war brings out noble, self-sacrificing qualities?

KRISHNAMURTI: Through a wrong act, the killing of another, can a right, worthy end be realized?

Question: Is not self-knowledge a difficult pursuit?

KRISHNAMURTI: It is and yet it is not. It demands effortless discernment, sensitive receptivity. Constant alertness is arduous because we are lazy; we would rather gain through others, through much reading, but information is not self-knowledge. In the meanwhile we continue with greed, wars, and the vain repetition of rituals. All this indicates, does it not, the desire to run away from the real problem, which is you and your inner insufficiency. Without understanding yourself mere outward activity, however worthy and satisfying, only leads to further confusion and conflict. The earnest search for truth through self-knowledge is truly religious. The truly religious individual begins with himself; his self-knowledge and understanding form the basis of all his activity. As he understands he will know what it is to serve and what it is to love.

April 21, 1946

Fourth Talk in The Oak Grove

In the last three talks we have been considering that intelligence which is developed through the activities and habits of the self—that desire which is constantly accumulating and with which thought identifies itself as the 'me' and the 'mine'. This accumulative, identifying habit is called intelligence; the aggressive and self-expanding desire ever seeking security, certainty, is called intelligence. This enchaining habit-memory binds thought, and so intelligence is imprisoned in the self. How can this intelligence, this mind that is petty, narrow, cruel, nationalistic, envious, comprehend the real? How can thought which is the outcome of time, of self-protective activity, comprehend that which is not of time?

We sometimes experience a state of tranquillity, of extraordinary clarity and joy, when the mind is serene and still. These moments come unexpectedly, without invitation. Such experiencing is not the result of calculated, disciplined thought. It occurs when thought is self-forgetful, when thought has ceased to become, when the mind is not in the conflict of its own self-created problems. So our problem is not how such a creative, joyous moment shall come and be maintained, but how to bring about the cessation of self-expansive thought, which does not imply self-immolation but the transcending of the activities of the self. When a machine is revolving very fast, as a fan with several blades, the separate parts are not visible but appear as one. So the self, the 'me', seems to be a unified entity, but if its activities can be slowed down, then we shall perceive that it is not a unified entity, but made up of many separate and contending desires and pursuits. These separate wants and hopes, fears and joys make up the self. The self is a term to cover craving in its different forms. To understand the self there must be an awareness of craving in its multiple aspects. The passive awareness, the choiceless discernment, reveal the ways of the self, bringing freedom from bondage. Thus when the mind is tranquil and free of its own activity and chatter, there is supreme wisdom.

Our problem then is how to free thought from its accumulated experiences, memories. How can this self cease to be? Deep and true experience takes place only when the activity of this intelligence ceases. We see that unless there is an experience of truth, none of our problems can be solved, whether sociological, religious, or personal. Conflict cannot come to an end by merely rearranging frontiers or reorganizing economic values or imposing a new ideology; throughout the centuries we have tried these many ways, but conflict and sorrow have continued. Until

there is a comprehension of the real, merely pruning the branches of our self-expansive activity is of little use, for the central problem remains unsolved. Until we discover truth there is no way out of our sorrows and problems. The solution is the direct experience of truth when the mind is still, in the tranquillity of awareness, in the openness of receptivity.

Question: Would you please explain again what you mean.

KRISHNAMURTI: We often have religious experiences, sometimes vague, sometimes definite—experiences of intense devotion or joy, of being deeply vulnerable, of fleeting unity with all things—we try to utilize these experiences in meeting our difficulties and sorrows. These experiences are numerous, but our thought—caught in time, turmoil, and pain—tries to use them as stimulants to overcome our conflicts. So we say God, or truth, will help us in our difficulties, but these experiences do not actually resolve our sorrow and confusion. Such moments of deep experience come when thought is not active in its self-protective memories; these experiences are independent of our striving, and when we try to use them as stimulants for strength in our struggles, they only further the expansion of the self and its peculiar intelligence. So we come back to our question: "How can this intelligence, so sedulously cultivated, cease?" It can cease only through passive awareness.

Awareness is from moment to moment, it is not the cumulative effect of self-protective memories. Awareness is not determination nor is it the action of will. Awareness is the complete and unconditional surrender to *what is,* without rationalization, without the division of the observer and the observed. As awareness is nonaccumulative, nonresidual, it does not build up the self, positively or negatively. Awareness is ever in the present and so, nonidentifying and nonrepetitive; nor does it create habit.

Take, for instance, the habit of smoking and experiment with it in awareness. Be aware of smoking, do not condemn, rationalize, or accept—simply be aware. If you are so aware, there is the cessation of the habit; if you are so aware, there will be no recurrence of it; but if you are not aware, the habit will persist. This awareness is not the determination to cease or to indulge.

Be aware; there is a fundamental difference between being and becoming. To become aware you make effort, and effort implies resistance and time and leads to conflict. If you are aware in the moment, there is no effort, no continuance of the self-protective intelligence. You are aware or you are not; the desire to be aware is only the activity of the sleeper, the dreamer. Awareness reveals the problem completely, fully, without denial or acceptance, justification or identification, and it is freedom which quickens understanding. Awareness is a unitary process of the observer and the observed.

Question: Can open, still receptivity of the mind come with the action of will or desire?

KRISHNAMURTI: You may succeed in forcibly stilling the mind, but what is the outcome of such effort? Death, is it not? You may succeed in silencing the mind, but thought still remains petty, envious, contradictory, does it not? Through exertion, through an act of will, we think an effortless state can be achieved in which we may experience the ecstasy of the real. The experience of inexplicable joy or intense devotion or profound understanding comes only when there is effortless being.

Question: Are there not two kinds of intelligence, the one with which we function daily

and the other which is higher, which guides, controls, and is beneficial?

KRISHNAMURTI: Does not the self, for the sake of its own permanency, divide itself into the high and the low, the controller and the controlled? Does not this division arise from the desire for continued self-expansion? However cunningly it might divide itself, the self is still the result of craving, it is still seeking different objectives through which to fulfill itself. A petty mind cannot possibly formulate something which is not also petty. The mind is essentially limited and whatever it creates is of itself. Its gods, its values, its objectives and activities are narrow and measurable, and so it cannot understand that which is not of itself—the immeasurable.

Question: Can a petty thought go beyond itself?

KRISHNAMURTI: How can it? Greed is still greed even if it reaches for heaven. Only when it is aware of its own limitation does the limited thought cease. The limited thought cannot become the free; when limitation ceases there is freedom. If you will experiment with awareness you will discover the truth of this.

It is the petty mind that creates problems for itself, and through awareness of the cause of problems, the self, they are dissolved. To be aware of narrowness and its many results implies deep understanding of it on all the different levels of consciousness—pettiness in things, in relationship, in ideas. When we are conscious of being petty or violent or envious, we make an effort not to be; we condemn it for we desire to be something else. This condemnatory attitude puts an end to the understanding of *what is* and its process. The desire to put an end to greed is another form of self-assertion and so is the cause of continued conflict and pain.

Question: What is wrong with purposeful thinking if it is logical?

KRISHNAMURTI: If the thinker is unaware of himself, though he may be purposeful, his logic will inevitably lead him to misery; if he is in authority, in a position of power, he brings misery and destruction upon others. That is what is happening in the world, is it not? Without self-knowledge thought is not based on reality, it is ever in contradiction and its activities are mischievous and harmful.

To come back to our point: through awareness only can there be cessation of the cause of conflict. Be aware of any habit of thought or action; then you will recognize the rationalizing, condemnatory process which is preventing understanding. Through awareness—the reading of the book of habit page by page—comes self-knowledge. It is truth that frees, not your effort to be free. Awareness is the solution of our problems; we must experiment with it and discover its truth. It would be folly merely to accept; to accept is not to understand. Acceptance or nonacceptance is a positive act which hinders experimentation and understanding. Understanding that comes through experiment and self-knowledge brings confidence.

This confidence may be called faith. It is not the faith of the foolish; it is not faith in something. Ignorance may have faith in wisdom, darkness in light, cruelty in love, but such faith is still ignorance. This confidence, or faith, of which I am speaking comes through experimentation in self-knowledge, not through acceptance and hope. The self-confidence that many have is the outcome of ignorance, of achievement, of self-glory, or of capacity. The confidence of which I speak is understanding, not the 'I understand', but understanding without self-identification. The confidence or faith in something, however noble, breeds only obstinacy, and obstinacy

is another term for credulity. The clever ones have destroyed blind faith, but when they themselves are in serious conflict or sorrow, they accept faith or become cynical. To believe is not to be religious; to have faith in something which is created by the mind is not to be open to the real. Confidence comes into being, it cannot be manufactured by the mind; confidence comes with experiment and discovery; not the experiment with belief, theory, or memory, but experimentation with self-knowledge. This confidence or faith is not self-imposed nor is it identified with belief, formulation, hope. It is not the outcome of self-expanding desire. In experimenting with awareness there is a discovery which is freeing in its understanding. This self-knowledge through passive awareness is from moment to moment, without accumulation; it is endless, truly creative. Through awareness there comes vulnerability to truth.

To be open, vulnerable to the real, thought must cease to be accumulative. It is not that thought-feeling must become nongreedy—which is still accumulative, a negative form of self-expansion—but it must be nongreedy. A greedy mind is a conflicting mind; a greedy mind is ever fearful, envious in its self-growth and fulfillment. Such a mind is ever changing the objects of its desire, and this changing is considered growth; a greedy mind which renounces the world in order to seek reality, God, is still greedy; greed is ever restless, ever seeking growth, fulfillment, and this restless activity creates self-assertive intelligence but is not capable of understanding the real.

Greed is a complex problem! To live in the world of greed without greed needs deep understanding; to live simply—earning a right livelihood in a world organized on economic aggression and expansion—is possible only for those who are discovering inward riches.

Question: In the very act of coming here are we not seeking some spark to enlighten us?

KRISHNAMURTI: What is it that you are seeking?

Question: Wisdom and knowledge.

KRISHNAMURTI: Why do you seek?

Question: We are seeking to fill the deep, hidden inner void.

KRISHNAMURTI: We are then seeking something to fill our emptiness; the filler we call knowledge, wisdom, truth, and so on. So we are not seeking truth, wisdom, but something to fill our aching loneliness. If we can find that which can enrich our inward poverty, we think our search will end. Now can anything fill this void? Some are painfully conscious of it and others are not; some have sought to escape through activity, through stimulation, through mysterious rituals, through ideologies, and so on; others are conscious of this void but have not found a way of covering it up. Most of us know this fear, this panic of nothingness. We are seeking to overcome this fear, this emptiness; we are seeking something that can heal the aching agony of inner insufficiency. As long as you are convinced that you can find some escape, you will go on seeking, but is it not part of wisdom to see that all escape, no matter how alluring, is useless? When the truth about escape dawns on you, will you persist in your search? Obviously not. Then we accept inevitably *what is;* this complete surrender to *what is* is the liberating truth, not the attainment of the objects of search.

Our life is conflict, pain; we crave security, permanency, but are caught in the net of the impermanent. We are the imper-

manent. Can the impermanent find the eternal, the timeless? Can illusion find reality? Can ignorance find wisdom? Only with the cessation of the impermanent is there the permanent; with the cessation of ignorance is there wisdom. We are concerned with the cessation of the impermanent, the self.

Question: One of our great teachers has said, "Seek and ye shall find." Is it not advantageous to seek?

KRISHNAMURTI: By this question we betray ourselves and how little we are aware of the ways of our thought. We are forever thinking of what is advantageous for us and that we desire. Do you think a mind that is seeking profit can find truth? If it is seeking truth as an advantage, then it is no longer seeking truth. Truth is beyond and above all personal advantage and gain. A mind that is seeking gain, achievement, can never find truth. The search for gain is for security, for refuge; and truth is not a security, a refuge. Truth is the liberator, sweeping away all refuge and security.

Besides, why do you seek? Is it not because you are in confusion and pain? Instead of seeking an escape through activity, through psychologists, through priests, through rituals, must you not search out the cause of conflict and sorrow in yourself? The cause is the self, craving. The deliverance from confusion and pain is in yourself, and not another can free you.

Question: If we can open our consciousness to truth, is that not sufficient?

KRISHNAMURTI: We revert to this question in different ways over and over again. Can the mind, the self-consciousness, which is the product of time, understand or experience the timeless? When the mind seeks will it find reality, God? When the mind asserts that it must be open to reality, is it capable of being so?

If thought is aware that it is the product of ignorance, of the limited self, then there is a possibility for it to cease formulating, imagining, being occupied with itself. Only through awareness can thought transcend itself, not through will, which is another form of self-expansive desire. When are we joyous? Is it the result of calculation, of an act of will? It happens when conflicting problems and demands of desire are absent. As a lake is calm when the winds stop, so the mind is still when craving with its problems ceases. The mind cannot induce itself to be quiet, to be still; the lake is not calm until the winds cease. Until the problems the self creates cease, there can be no tranquillity. The mind has to understand itself and not try to escape into illusion, or seek something that it is incapable of experiencing or understanding.

Question: Is there a technique for being aware?

KRISHNAMURTI: What does this question imply? You seek a method by which you may learn to be aware. Awareness is not the result of practice, habit, or time. As a tooth that causes intense pain has to be attended to immediately, so sorrow, if intense, demands urgent alleviation. But instead we seek an escape or explain it away; we avoid the real issue which is the self. Because we are not facing our conflict, our sorrow, we assure ourselves lazily that we must make an effort to be aware, and so we demand a technique for becoming aware.

So it is not by an act of will that truth is uncovered but through tranquil vulnerability the real comes into being.

April 28, 1946

Fifth Talk in The Oak Grove

We have been considering the problem of intelligence, that intelligence which has been developed during the course of self-assertive struggles and self-protective pursuits, of acquisitive demands and imitative conformities; we saw that with that intelligence we hoped to solve our conflicts and discover or experience truth or God. Can that intelligence ever experience the real? If it cannot then how can it come to an end or be transformed? We saw that this is possible only through passive awareness, and that we can at any time be aware without the will to become aware. To understand what is implied in awareness, we examined greed and tried to understand its activities—greed not only for the tangible but also for power, for authority, greed for affection, for knowledge, for service, and so on—we saw that we either condemn or justify greed, thereby identifying ourselves with it. We saw, too, that awareness is a process of discovery which becomes blocked through identification. When we are rightly aware of greed, in its complexity, there is no struggle against it, no negative assertion of nongreed, which is only another form of self-assertiveness; and in that awareness we will find that greed has ceased.

Awareness is not the result of practice for practice implies the formation of habit; habit is the denial of awareness. Awareness is of the moment and not a cumulative result. To say to ourselves that we shall become aware is not to be aware. To say that we are going to be nongreedy is merely to continue to be greedy, to be unaware of it.

How do we approach a complex problem? We do not, surely, meet complexity with complexity; we must approach it simply, and the greater our simplicity, the greater will be the clarification. To understand and experience reality, there must be utter simplicity and tranquillity. When we suddenly see magnificent scenery or come upon a great thought, or listen to great music, we are utterly still. Our minds are not simple, but to recognize complexity is to be simple. If you would understand yourself, your complexity, there must be open receptivity, the simplicity of nonidentification. But we are not aware of beauty or complexity, and so we chatter endlessly.

Question: We must not criticize then if we are to be aware?

KRISHNAMURTI: Without probing deeply into oneself, self-knowledge is not possible. What do we mean by self-criticism? The function of the mind is to probe and to comprehend. Without this probing into ourselves, without this deep awareness, there can be no understanding. We often indulge in the stupidity of criticizing others, but few are capable of probing deeply into themselves. The function of the mind is not only to probe, to delve, but also to be silent. In silence there is comprehension. We are ever probing but we are rarely silent; in us rarely are there alert, passive intervals of tranquillity; we probe and are soon weary of it without the creative silence. But self-probing is as essential for the clarity of understanding as is stillness. As the earth is allowed to lie fallow during the winter, so must thought be still after deep searching. This very fallowness is its renewal. If we delve deeply into ourselves and are still, then in this stillness, in this openness, there is understanding.

Question: This complexity is so deep that one does not seem to have an opportunity for quietness.

KRISHNAMURTI: Must there be an opportunity to be still, to be quiet? Must you create the occasion, the right environment to be peaceful? Is it then peace? With right prob-

ing there comes right stillness. When do you look into yourself? When the problem demands it, when it is urgent, surely. But if you are seeking an opportunity to be silent, then you are not aware. Self-probing comes with conflict and sorrow, and there must be passive receptivity to understand. Surely self-probing, stillness, and understanding are in awareness a single process and not three separate states.

Question: Would you enlarge that point?

KRISHNAMURTI: Let us take envy. Any resolution not to be envious is neither simple nor effective, it is even stupid. To determine not to be envious is to build walls of conclusions around oneself, and these walls prevent understanding. But if you are aware you will discover the ways of envy; if there is interested alertness, you will find its ramifications at different levels of the self. Each probing brings with it silence and understanding; as one cannot continuously probe deeply, which would only result in exhaustion, there must be spaces of alert inactivity. This watchful stillness is not the outcome of weariness; with self-probing there come easily and naturally moments of passive alertness. The more complex the problem, the more intense is the probing and the silence. There need be no specially created occasion or opportunity for silence; the very perception of the complexity of a problem brings with it deep silence.

Our difficulty lies in that we have built around ourselves conclusions which we call understanding. These conclusions are hindrances to understanding. If you go into this more deeply, you will see that there must be complete abandonment of all that has been accumulated for the being of understanding and wisdom. To be simple is not a conclusion, an intellectual concept for which you strive. There can be simplicity only when the self with its accumulation ceases. It is comparatively easy to renounce family, property, fame, things of the world; that is only a beginning; but it is extremely difficult to put away all knowledge, all conditioned memory. In this freedom, this aloneness, there is experience which is beyond and above all creations of the mind. Do not let us ask whether the mind ever can be free from conditioning, from influence; we shall find this out as we proceed in self-knowledge and understanding. Thought which is a result cannot understand the causeless.

The ways of accumulation are subtle; accumulation is self-assertiveness, as is imitation. To come to a conclusion is to build a wall around oneself, a protective security which prevents understanding. Accumulated conclusions do not make for wisdom but only sustain the self. Without accumulation there is no self. A mind weighed down with accumulations is incapable of following the swift movement of life, incapable of deep and pliable awareness.

Question: Are you not encouraging separateness, individualism?

KRISHNAMURTI: He who is influenced is separate, knowing the division of the high and the low, of merit and demerit. Aloneness in the sense of being free from influence is not separative, not antagonizing. It is a state to be experienced, not speculated upon. The self is ever separative, it is the cause of division, conflict, and sorrow. Do you not feel separate; are not your activities those of a self-assertive, self-expansive individual? Obviously your thoughts and activities are now individualistic, narrow; it is your work, your achievement, your country, your belief, even your God. You are separate and so your social structure is based on self-assertiveness, which causes untold misery and destruction;

you may assert we are all one, but in actual daily life your activities are separative, individualistic, competitive, ruthless, leading ultimately to war and misery.

If we are aware of this self-aggressive process in ourselves and understand its implications, then there is a possibility of bringing about a peaceful and happy relationship between man and man. The very awareness of *what is* is a liberative process. So long as we are unaware of what we are and are trying to become something else, so long will there be distortion and pain. The very awareness of what I am brings about transformation and the freedom of understanding.

Question: Cannot one think about the uncreated, about reality, God?

KRISHNAMURTI: The created cannot think about the uncreated. It can think only about its own projection which is not the real. Can thought which is the result of time, of influence, of imitation, think about that which is not measurable? It can only think about that which is known. What is knowable is not the real, what is known is ever receding into the past, and what is past is not the eternal. You may speculate upon the unknown but you cannot think about it. When you think about something you are probing into it, subjecting it to different moods and influences. But such thinking is not meditation. Creativeness is a state of being which is not the outcome of thinking. Right meditation opens the door to the real.

But let us go back to what we were considering. Are we aware that our so-called thinking is the result of influence, of conditioning, of imitation? Are you not influenced by propaganda, religious or secular, by the politician and the priest, by the economist and the advertiser? Collective worship and regimentation of thought are alike, and both hinder the discovery and experience of reality. Propaganda is not the instrument of truth, whether of organized religion or politics or business. If we would discover truth we must be aware of the subtleties of influence, of challenge, and of our response. Learning a technique, a method, does not lead to creative being. When the past ceases to influence the present, when time ceases, there is creative being which can be experienced only in deep meditation.

Question: Is not thinking the initial step to creativeness?

KRISHNAMURTI: The initial step is to be self-aware. Our thinking, as we said, is the result of the past; it is the result of conditioning, of imitation; that being so, all effort it makes to free itself is vain. All it can do and must do is be aware of its own conditioning and cause; through the understanding of the cause there comes freedom from it. If we were aware of our stupidity, ignorance, then there would be a possibility of wisdom; but to consider stupidity as a necessary beginning for intelligence is wrong thinking. If we recognize that we are stupid, then that very recognition is the beginning of thoughtfulness; but recognizing it, if we try to become clever, then that very becoming is another form of stupidity.

Any definite pattern of thought prevents understanding. Understanding is not substitution; mere change of patterns, of conclusions, does not yield understanding. Understanding comes with self-awareness and self-knowledge. There is no substitute for self-knowledge. Is it not important first to understand oneself, to be aware of one's own conditioning rather than seek understanding outside of oneself? Understanding comes with the awareness of *what is.*

Question: Being imitative, what shall we do?

KRISHNAMURTI: Be self-aware, which will reveal the hidden motives of imitation, envy, fear, the craving for security, for power, and so on. This awareness when free of self-identification brings understanding and tranquillity, which lead to the realization of supreme wisdom.

Question: Is not this process of awareness, of self-unfoldment, another form of acquisition? Is not probing another means of self-expansive acquisitiveness?

KRISHNAMURTI: If the questioner experimented with awareness, he would discover the truth about his question. Understanding is never accumulative; understanding comes only when there is stillness, when there is passive alertness. There is no stillness, no passivity when the mind is acquisitive; acquisitiveness is ever restless, envious. As we said, awareness is not cumulative; through identification, accumulation is built up, giving continuity to the self through memory. To be aware without self-identification, without condemnation or justification is extremely arduous, for our response is based on pleasure and pain, reward and punishment. How few are aware of constant identification; if we were we would not ask these questions which indicate unawareness. As a sleeper dreams that he must awaken but does not, for it is only a dream, so we are asking these questions without actually experimenting with awareness.

Question: Is there anything that one can do to be aware?

KRISHNAMURTI: Are you not in conflict, in sorrow? If you are, do you not search out its cause? The cause is the self, its torturing desires. To struggle with these desires only creates resistance, further pain, but if you are choicelessly aware of your craving, then there comes creative understanding. It is the truth of this understanding that liberates, not your struggle against resistance to envy, anger, pride, and so on. So awareness is not an act of will for will is resistance, the effort made by the self through desire to acquire, to grow, whether positively or negatively. Be aware of acquisitiveness, passively observing its ways on different levels; you will find this rather arduous, for thought-feeling sustains itself on identification, and it is this which prevents the understanding of accumulation.

Be aware; take the journey of self-discovery. Do not ask what is going to happen on this journey, which only betrays anxiety, fear, indicating your desire for security, for certainty. This desire for refuge prevents self-knowledge, self-unfoldment, and so, understanding. Be aware of this inward anxiety and directly experience it; then you will discover what this awareness reveals. But unfortunately most of you only desire to talk about the journey without undertaking it.

Question: What happens to us at the end of the journey?

KRISHNAMURTI: Is it not important for the questioner to be aware of why he is asking this question? Is it not because of the fear of the unknown, the desire to gain an end, or the assurance of self-continuity? Being in sorrow, we seek happiness; being impermanent, we search after the permanent; being in darkness, we look for light. But if we were aware of *what is,* then the truth of sorrow, of impermanency, of imprisonment would liberate thought from its own ignorance.

Question: Is there no such thing as creative thinking?

KRISHNAMURTI: It would be rather vain to consider what is creativeness. If we were aware of our conditioning, then the truth of this would bring about creative being. To speculate upon creative being is a hindrance; all speculation is a hindrance to understanding. Only when the mind is simple—purged of all self-deception and cunning, cleansed of all accumulation—is there the real. The purgation of the mind is not an act of will nor the outcome of imitative compulsion. Awareness of *what is* is liberating.

May 5, 1946

Sixth Talk in The Oak Grove

As this is the last talk of this series, perhaps it might be well to make a brief summary of what we have been considering during the past five Sundays. We have been discussing whether the process of what we call intelligence can resolve any of our problems and sorrows; whether the ant like activity which has developed self-protective intelligence can bring about enlightenment and peace.

This activity on the surface, called intelligence, cannot resolve our many difficulties, for within there is still confusion, turmoil, and darkness. This intelligence has been developed through the expansion of the self, the ego, the 'me' and the 'mine'; this activity is the outcome of inner insufficiency, incompleteness. Outwardly thought is active, building and destroying, contradicting and modifying, renewing and suppressing; but within there is void and despair. The outer activity of plastic and steel, reform and counter-reform, is ever lost in the inward emptiness and confusion. You may build wonderful structures or organize spaciously over a smoldering volcano, but what you construct is soon smothered by ashes and destroyed. So this expansive activity of the self, this intelligence—however alert, capable and industrious—cannot penetrate through its own darkness to reality. This intelligence cannot at any time resolve its own conflicts and miseries, for they are the outcome of its own activity. This intelligence is incapable of discovering truth, and only truth can free us from ever-increasing conflicts and sorrows.

We further considered how this self-expansive intelligence is to cease reshaping itself negatively. Whether positive or negative, the activity of craving is still within the framework of the self, and can this activity ever come to an end? We said that only through self-awareness can this accumulative intelligence of the self cease. We saw this awareness to be from moment to moment, without cumulative power; that in this awareness self-identification-condemnation-modification cannot take place, and so there is deep and full understanding. We said that this awareness is not progressive but an instantaneous perception, and that the thought of progressive becoming prevents immediate clarification.

This morning we shall consider meditation. In understanding it we can perhaps comprehend the full and deep significance of passive awareness. Awareness is right meditation and without meditation there can be no self-knowledge. Earnestness in the discovery of one's motives is more important than to seek out a method of meditation. The more earnest one is, the more capacity one has to probe and to perceive. So it is essential to be earnest rather than to form and pursue a conclusion, to be earnest rather than arbitrarily hold to an intention. If we merely hold to an intention, a conclusion, a resolution, thought becomes narrow, obstinate, fixed, but if there is earnestness this very quality is capable of deep penetration. The

difficulty is in being constantly earnest. Spiritual windowshopping is not an indication of seriousness. If you have the capacity to allow thought to unroll itself fully, then you will perceive that one thought contains, or is related to, all thought. There is no need to go from teacher to teacher, from guru to guru, from leader to leader, for all things are contained in you, the beginning and the end. None can help you to discover the real; no ritual, no collective worship, no authority can help you. Another may point out the direction, but to make of him an authority, a gateway to the real, a necessity, is to be ignorant, which breeds fear and superstition.

To delve deeply within oneself and discover needs earnestness. This probing we consider tedious, uninspiring, so we depend upon stimulants, Masters, saviors, leaders, to encourage us to understand ourselves. This encouragement or stimulation becomes a necessity, an addiction, and weakens the quality of earnestness. Being in contradiction and sorrow, we think we are incapable of finding a solution, so we look to another or try to find the answer in a book. To look within demands earnest application which is not brought about through the practice of any method. It comes through serious interest and awareness. If one is interested in something, thought pursues it, consciously or unconsciously, in spite of fatigue and distraction. If you are interested in painting, then every light, every shade has meaning; you do not have to exert to be interested, you do not have to force yourself to observe, but through the very intensity of interest, even unconsciously, you are observing, discovering, experiencing. Similarly if there is an interest in the comprehension and dissolution of sorrow, then that very interest turns the pages of the book of self-knowledge.

To have a goal, an end to be achieved, prevents self-knowledge; earnest awareness reveals the ways of the self. Without self-knowledge there can be no understanding; self-knowledge is the beginning of wisdom. Our thought is the result of the past; our thinking is based on the past, upon conditioning. Without comprehending this past there is no understanding of the real. The comprehension of the past lies through the present. The real is not the reward for self-knowledge. The real is causeless and thought that has cause cannot experience it. Without a foundation there can be no lasting structure, and the right foundation for understanding is self-knowledge. So all right thinking is the outcome of self-knowledge. If I do not know myself, how can I understand anything else? For without self-knowledge all knowledge is in vain. Without self-knowledge incessant activity is of ignorance; this incessant activity, inner or outer, only causes destruction and misery.

Understanding of the ways of the self leads to freedom. Virtue is freedom, orderliness; without order, freedom, there can be no experiencing of the real. In virtue there is freedom, not in the becoming virtuous. The desire to become, negatively or positively, is self-expansive, and in the expansion of the self, there can be no freedom.

Question: You said the real should not be an incentive. It seems to me that if I try to think of the real, I am better able to understand myself and my difficulties.

KRISHNAMURTI: Is it possible to think about the real? We may be able to formulate, imagine, speculate upon what we consider the real to be, but is it the real? Can we think about the unknowable? Can we think, meditate, upon the timeless when our thought is the result of the past, of time? The past is ever the known, and thought which is based on it can only create the known. So to think about truth is to be caught in the net of ignorance. If thought is able to think about

truth, then it will not be truth. Truth is a state of being in which the so-called activity of thought has ceased. Thinking, as we know it, is the result of the self-expansive process of time, of the past; it is the result of the movement of the known to the known. Thought which is the outcome of a cause can never formulate the causeless. It can only think about the known for it is the product of the known.

What is known is not the real. Our thought is occupied with the constant search for security, for certainty. Self-expansive intelligence by its very nature craves a refuge, either through negation or assertion. How can a mind that is ever seeking certainty, stimulation, encouragement, possibly think of that which is illimitable? You may read about it, which is unfortunate, you may verbalize it, which is a waste of time, but it is not the real. When you say that by thinking about truth you can better solve your difficulties and sorrows, you are using the supposed truth as a palliative; as with all drugs, sleep and dullness soon follow. Why seek external stimulants when the problem demands an understanding of its maker?

As I was saying, virtue gives freedom but there is no freedom in becoming virtuous. There is a vast and unbridgeable difference between being and becoming.

Question: Is there a difference between truth and virtue?

KRISHNAMURTI: Virtue gives freedom for thought to be tranquil, to experience the real. So virtue is not an end in itself, only truth is. To be a slave to passion is to be without freedom, and in freedom alone can there be discovery and experience of the real. Greed, like anger, is a disturbing factor, is it not? Envy is ever restless, never still. Craving is ever changing the object of its fulfillment, from things to passion, to virtue, to the idea of God. The greed for reality is the same as the greed for possessions.

Craving comes through perception, contact, sensation; desire seeks fulfillment, so there is identification, the 'me' and the 'mine'. Being satiated with things, desire pursues other forms of gratification, more subtle forms of fulfillment in relationship, in knowledge, in virtue, in the realization of God. Craving is the root cause of all conflict and sorrow. All forms of becoming, negative or positive, cause conflict, resistance.

Question: Is there any difference between awareness and that of which we are aware? Is the observer different from his thoughts?

KRISHNAMURTI: The observer and the observed are one; the thinker and his thoughts are one. To experience the thinker and his thought as one is very arduous, for the thinker is ever taking shelter behind his thought; he separates himself from his thoughts to safeguard himself, to give himself continuity, permanency; he modifies or changes his thoughts, but he remains. This pursuit of thought apart from himself—this changing, transforming it—leads to illusion. The thinker is his thought; the thinker and his thoughts are not two separate processes.

The questioner asks if awareness is different from the object of awareness. We generally regard our thoughts as being apart from ourselves; we are not aware of the thinker and his thought as one. This is precisely the difficulty. After all, the qualities of the self are not separate from the self; the self is not something apart from its thoughts, from its attributes. The self is put together, made up, and the self is not when the parts are dissolved. But in illusion the self separates itself from its qualities in order to protect itself, to give itself continuity, permanency. It takes refuge in its qualities through separating itself from them. The self

asserts that it is this and it is that; the self, the 'I', modifies, changes, transforms its thoughts, its qualities; but this change only gives strength to the self, to its protective walls. But if you are aware deeply, you will perceive that the thinker and his thoughts are one; the observer is the observed. To experience this actual integrated fact is extremely difficult, and right meditation is the way to this integration.

Question: How can I be on the defense against aggression without action? Morality demands that we should do something against evil.

KRISHNAMURTI: To defend is to be aggressive. Should you fight evil by evil? Through wrong means can right be established? Can there be peace in the world by murdering those who are murderers? As long as we divide ourselves into groups, nations, different religions and ideologies, there will be the aggressor and the defender. To be without virtue is to be without freedom, which is evil. This evil cannot be overcome by another evil, by another opposing desire.

Question: Experiencing is not necessarily a becoming, is it?

KRISHNAMURTI: Additive process prevents the experiencing of the real. Where there is accumulation there is a becoming of the self, which is the cause of conflict and pain. The accumulative desire for pleasure and the avoidance of pain is a becoming. Awareness is nonaccumulative for it is ever discovering truth, and truth can only be when there is no accumulation, when there is no imitation. Effort of the self can never bring about freedom for effort implies resistance, and resistance can be dissolved only through choiceless awareness, effortless discernment.

It is truth alone that frees, not the activity of will. The awareness of truth is liberating; the awareness of greed and of the truth about it brings liberation from greed.

Meditation is the purgation from the mind of all its accumulations; the purgation of the power to gather, to identify, to become; the purgation of self-growth, of self-fulfillment; meditation is the freeing of the mind from memory, from time. Thought is the product of the past, it is rooted in the past; thought is the continuation of accumulative becoming, and that which is a result cannot understand or experience that which is without a cause. What can be formulated is not the real, and the word is not the experience. Memory, the maker of time, is an impediment to the timeless.

Question: Why is memory an impediment?

KRISHNAMURTI: Memory, as the identifying process, gives continuity to the self. Memory then is an enclosing, hindering activity. On it the whole structure of the ego, the 'I', is built. We are considering psychological memory, not the memory for speech, facts, for the development of technique, and so on. Any activity of the self is an impediment to truth; any activity or education that conditions the mind through nationalism, through identification with a group, an ideology, a dogma, is an impediment to truth.

Conditioned knowledge is a hindrance to reality. Understanding comes with the cessation of all activity of the mind—when the mind is utterly free, silent, tranquil. Craving is ever accumulative and time-binding; desire for a goal, knowledge, experience, growth, fulfillment, and even the desire for God or truth is an impediment. The mind must purge itself of all its self-created impediments for supreme wisdom to be.

Meditation as it is generally understood and practiced is a process of the expansion of the self; often meditation is a form of self-hypnosis. In so-called meditation, effort very often is directed towards becoming like a Master, which is imitation. All such meditation leads to illusion.

The craving for achievement demands a technique, a method, practice of which is considered meditation. Through compulsion, imitation, and through the formation of new habits and disciplines, there will be no freedom, no understanding; through the means of time, the timeless is not experienced. The change of the objects of desire does not bring release from conflict and sorrow. Will is self-expansive intelligence, and the activity of will to be or not to be, to gather or renounce, is still of the self. To be aware of the process of craving with its accumulative memory is to experience truth, which is the only liberator.

Awareness flows into meditation; in meditation, being, the eternal, is experienced. Becoming can never transform itself into being. Becoming, the expansive and enclosing activity of the self, must cease; then there is being. This being cannot be thought about, cannot be imagined; the very thought about it is a hindrance; all that thought can do is to be aware of its own complex and subtle becoming, its own cunning intelligence and will. Through self-knowledge there comes right thinking which is the foundation for right meditation. Meditation should not be confused with prayer. Supplicatory prayer does not lead to supreme wisdom, for it ever maintains the division between self and the other.

In silence, in supreme tranquillity when the restless activity of memory has ceased, there is the immeasurable, the eternal.

May 12, 1946

Madras, India, 1947

✳

First Talk in Madras

The present world crisis is of an extraordinary nature; there have been probably few such catastrophes in the past. This present crisis is not the usual kind of disaster that occurs so often in the life of man. This chaos is worldwide; it is not Indian nor European but stretching into every corner of the world. Physiologically and psychologically, morally and spiritually, economically and socially, there is disintegration and confusion. We are standing on the edge of a precipice and wrangling over our petty affairs. Few seem to realize the extraordinary character of this world crisis, how profound and how vastly disturbing. Some, realizing the confusion, are active in rearranging the pattern of life on the edge of the precipice, and being themselves confused, are only bringing more confusion. Others try to solve the problem through a particular formula or a system of the extreme left or of the right, or through formulas that lie between the extremes.

These inevitably fail, for a problem, a human problem, is never static, whereas formulas, systems are. Revolution according to a formula ceases to be a revolution. The intellectual professionals, specialists, will never save the world; and the intellect, which is only a part of the total process of man, will always fail as its answers are ever partial and

so not true. Systems, formulas, organized thought, can never save man.

As the crisis, the problem, is ever new, a new approach is essential—a living, dynamic approach that is not anchored to any organization, to any system. A human problem is ever undergoing transformation; it is not static, and a mind that is burdened with a conclusion, with a formula, can never comprehend a living problem. To such a mind, the problem, the complex human entity is not significant; but the system, the formula forces the living into the static, so creates more confusion, more misery for man.

This catastrophic disaster has not come into being through some action of chance; it has been created by each one of us—by our everyday activities of envy and passion, of greed and the craving for power and domination, of competition and ruthlessness, of sensate and immediate values. We are responsible for this appalling misery and confusion, not another, but you and I. Because you are thoughtless, unaware, wrapped up in your own ambitions, sensations, and pursuits, wrapped up in those values that are immediately gratifying, you have created this immense, engulfing disaster. War is a spectacular and bloody expression of our daily life, our life of competition, ill will, social and national division, and so on. You are responsible for this chaos, not any particular group, not any individuals, but you; you are the mass, you are the world. Your problem is the world's problem.

As the problem is new you must approach it anew; there must be revolution in thinking. This revolution is not based on any formula but on self-knowledge, knowledge of the total process of your whole being. Neither the specialization of the part nor the study of the part can lead to the whole. Through self-knowledge there is right thinking which is revolutionary and creative. Individual and individualistic action are two different and opposing things. Individualistic action is action based on greed, envy, ill will, and so on, action of the part; and individual action is action based on the understanding of this total process. Individualistic action is anti-social, antagonistic, or opposed to another. Individualistic activities have brought man to this present chaos and misery. In reaction to individualistic activities, collectivism of many varieties has sprung up. In understanding the total process of our being—only in self-knowledge is there salvation.

To understand the total process there must be no condemnation, judgment, nor identification. If you would understand your son, you must observe him, study him without comparison, without condemnation; similarly if you would understand yourself, you must be aware of your activities, emotions, and thought without condemnation. This is very difficult and arduous, for our education and training have conditioned us to condemn, to judge. This condemnation puts an end to understanding, so we have to be aware of this conditioning. Freedom does not come through effort, but it is the perception of truth that liberates. Truth is liberating, not your effort to be free. Creative thinking which comes through self-knowledge is the solution for our miseries, for it reveals truth, which is the breath of happiness. Right thinking based on self-knowledge leads to meditation in

which creation, truth, God, or what you will takes place. Meditation is not self-hypnosis, as is the general case, but that in which the uninvited comes into being. What is invited is self-projected, so transitory and illusory. Reality or God must come to you and you cannot go to it. Without this reality, life is full of misery, chaotic and destructive. During these talks, with those who are earnest, we shall experiment and cultivate right thinking, which alone can solve our problems permanently. Earnestness is not dependent on moods and circumstances. The problem itself demands earnestness for in the problem itself is its solution.

Question: The communist believes that by guaranteeing food, clothing, shelter to every individual, and abolishing private property, a state can be created in which man can live happily. What do you say about it?

KRISHNAMURTI: The end is the means; they are not separate; through right means the right end is established. To create the right state, right means must be employed. Right means is not separate from right thinking. Right thinking comes with the understanding of the total process of man, of yourself. The cultivation of the part is not the comprehension of the whole. Obviously food, clothing, shelter should and must be available for everyone; there should be a world pool of man's essential needs and right organization for distribution. There is sufficient scientific knowledge to produce the essential needs of man, but greed, nationalistic spirit, craving for prestige and power, prevent the production of the essentials for all human beings. We are not concerned with feeding, clothing, and sheltering man but are engrossed in a particular system which will guarantee food, clothing, and shelter for all. The extreme left or the right are wrangling over the formula that will assure man security; so they are not concerned with man's happiness, but with which formula will guarantee him happiness.

It is these formulas and systems of the intellect, the nationalistic spirit and greed, the craving for power and position that are preventing the organization of a world pool so that every human being has food, clothes, and shelter. Instead of spending the necessary money to find ways and means to feed, clothe, and shelter man, vast sums are spent in armaments, in blasting each other, in atomic bombs, preparing for the inevitable war that is coming. All this indicates that those who are dedicated to conclusions, to particular countries, to property, are not concerned with man's happiness.

Besides, does man live by bread alone? Does his happiness lie in the sensate alone? Surely in giving overemphasis to that which is of secondary importance, we bring confusion and misery. The psychological factors are destroying the organization of bread, and without understanding these factors, merely to lay emphasis on bread is to prevent physical security for man. The more we seek security in the physical, the more insecurity there will be, for where there should be insecurity—psychologically, spiritually—there we seek permanency, security.

So in order to assure man of food, clothing, shelter, we must lay emphasis on the psychological values that man has established for himself. In freeing man from his psychological, spiritual conditioning, he will inevitably organize a society that will assure for every man food, clothing, and shelter.

What is the state but that which we create in our daily relationship; if we are possessive, envious, ruthless, then we will create a state that will represent us. Man is a very complex entity, and to emphasize one part of him, however much that part may need attention, is to jeopardize man himself.

Question: Mahatma Gandhi and others believe that the time has come when men of goodwill, the sages, the wise men, should join together and organize to fight the present crisis. Are you not escaping from this duty, like most of our spiritual leaders are doing?

KRISHNAMURTI: It seems an obvious necessity that men of goodwill should come together, but unfortunately men of goodwill are also human beings with their passions, with their vested interests, with their formulas and plans. The pure of heart are few. Again in organizing the means to overcome the crisis, the men of goodwill seem to lose their goodness. The means seem to become the all-important, and not goodness.

Spiritual leadership is contrary to spirituality. Reality, in which alone there is happiness, is pathless and no one can lead you to it. If any leads, he does not know truth. You have to liberate yourself from all those bondages that cause antisocial actions, that prevent the visitation of truth. You are your own savior and not another. You have to fundamentally and radically transform yourself to go beyond and above the present crisis. No organization, no leader, spiritual or political, can save you from the abyss of catastrophe. You must be your own light. The leader is as confused as the led, and there is no hope in the things made by the hand or by the mind. We are not escaping; we are pointing out that any activity on the edge of the precipice can only precipitate the fall, and there is only safety and happiness away from the precipice. The few who realize this must form centers of enlightenment, away from the abyss.

There is a way out of our present crisis and from all human problems—a way that is not an escape, a way that leads to eternal bliss.

Question: Young men have asked me again and again, "We are frustrated; we do not know what we are to do in the present crisis—our leaders are unable to give us a lead because they themselves are confused. We expected so much from political independence and from the settlement with the Muslim League."

KRISHNAMURTI: As there are several questions involved, let us take them one by one. What do we mean by frustration? To be frustrated is to be psychologically prevented from gaining or achieving that upon which our mind and heart are set. We want something—an ideal, a success, a position, the gratification of an urge, and so on—and when we are thwarted we feel frustrated, a despair, a feeling of being nothing, a miserable failure, and so on. The desire to be has in it, inherently, the seed of frustration. We do not like the ache of loneliness, that peculiar fear of being nothing, that void that is hidden under all our activities. Being aware of it, consciously or unconsciously, we try to cover it or avoid it or run away from it through social activities, through the search for personal happiness or through asceticism or through the search for God and so on. When the activities or the search is questioned, or they fail to achieve their desired result, this void, this emptiness shows itself. The awareness of the void we call frustration.

Now can you ever fill or find a substitution for the void? Having failed to fill it in one direction, are not all attempts to fill it futile? Can it ever be filled? To find out, stop filling it, stop running away from it and understand what this emptiness is; to understand there must be no condemnation nor identification. We have never asked ourselves if this void can ever be filled through any means; we are only concerned with the means of filling it. You may escape from it but you have not understood it, so the void is

still there. What would you think of a man who is trying to fill with water a bucket with a hole in it? So, similarly, this void may be without a bottom, and the more you fill it, the more empty it appears.

The despair of frustration we all know, and instead of understanding and so transcending the cause, we pursue one object of hope after another, ever failing, ever in misery. The other issue raised in the question is that "our leaders are unable to give us a lead as they themselves are confused." The leader is created by the follower, by you, and since you yourself are confused, you can only create a confused leader. Circumstances, forces, help to bring about the leader, but you are responsible for the forces, for the circumstances; a man who is enlightened, clear, does not need a leader, he does not create him, but he who is confused demands a leader and so creates him out of his own confusion. Why do you want a leader? Does he not come into being to tell you what you should or should not do, to direct your conduct? Because you cannot understand the confusion, you look to another to lead you out of it. Being confused, you can only hear the voice of confusion. Confusion is bred by you, you are responsible for it, within and so without, and you alone can clear it up, not another, political or religious. There is confusion, there is misery, and instead of facing it we want someone to direct us. This desire for authority arises when you seek an easy way of life, when you are lazy, when you are thoughtless. It is this very thoughtlessness that has brought about this aching confusion, and you only perpetuate it by seeking authority, by following. What you are, that you project, and not another can save you. No formula nor the embodiment of a formula, the so-called leader, can save you. You need a revolution in thinking, and so in action, and not a revolution to change the leaders. Right thinking comes from self-knowledge and not from a book, not from a system, and right thinking alone can save you from this crisis.

And then there is the third part of this question: "We expected so much from political independence and from the settlement with the Muslim League."

The forces of greed and exploitation do not cease because you have gained self-government; freedom from envy, ill will, and worldliness does not come through change of governments. Greed and exploitation may by legislation and compulsion be stopped at one level, but will show themselves at another; through compulsion and legislation, psychological facts are not abolished, and if we do not take them into account, we shall reap greater misery and disaster. Exploitation of man by man is not only on the economic level, but has its roots in deeper psychological facts which must be understood and transcended to live sanely and happily in this world. Possessiveness and dependence arise out of psychological insufficiency, incompleteness which manifests itself in so many antisocial actions. The cause is in us, and it cannot be abolished through compulsion or legislation, save through self-knowledge and right thinking.

When once you admit division between man and man, then you open the door to a host of evils; war is a major evil, and once a country indulges in it, it has opened the door to every kind of secondary evil and misfortune. This communal difference, this class and racial division—the Brahmin and the non-Brahmin and all the absurdities of the high and the low, the powerful and the weak, and so on—have caused misery for man. Organized religions with their dogmas and beliefs are responsible for the untold misery of man. Political divisions, the conflict of the left and the right systems—in all these divisions and bloody wrangles, man, you, is forgotten. Systems become more important than man. Until you are free from class and

racial, political and national divisions, and from the separation that organized religions bring about, there is no happiness; there will be chaos and misery.

October 22, 1947

Second Talk in Madras

Life is a complex problem, and to understand it there must be patient analysis of the problem and not jumping to a comforting conclusion; there must be a sane detachment to understand the actual, the existing problem. So let us take the journey of understanding. In making this journey do not let us jump to any conclusion and action; we shall act, not based upon any conclusion but upon truth. If we are attached, committed to any form of action, we shall not be capable of understanding the complex process of living; if we are too close to the problem, we are incapable of right observation and comprehension. If we are to understand life, there must be no conclusion, for conclusion puts an end to right thinking. As living is a vast process, any conclusion would be petty and biased. So let us discuss together, if we can, seriously and earnestly, the problem of living and not merely listen superficially to a series of talks; though I may talk, it is your life that is concerned, your joys and pains, your sorrows and strifes.

As every phase of life is interrelated, we must not approach it through any exclusive, specialized path; the merely intellectual or merely the emotional, the psychological or the merely physiological, prevents the understanding of the total process, which is life. In emphasizing the one path, the one phase, we only create conclusions which prevent the understanding of the whole. If we only study or specialize in one corner of the picture, we shall not comprehend the significance of the whole. If you specialize in economics and try to comprehend life from that limited point of view, you will inevitably miss the deeper and wider significance of life and so bring about greater confusion. For the time being put aside your specializations and look at life as a whole. The more we specialize, the more limited, destructive, we shall become. Our human problems are not to be solved by specialists, by experts, the few that can comprehend the entire picture, the whole process of life—they will be the saviors and not the specialists, not the experts.

Life, living and action, is a very complex problem which, if you would understand, must be approached very simply. If you would understand a child, a complex entity, you must not impose upon it your conditioning; you must observe without condemnation. If you see a lovely sunset and you compare it with other sunsets you have seen, then the present sunset has no joy. To understand, there must be a mind that is simple, not an innocent mind, but that which perceives directly, and not translates it according to its conditioning. This is one of our major difficulties in the right approach to the comprehension of life.

What is your relationship to the present degradation and chaos, to the prevailing despair? Perhaps you are not deeply aware of this degradation and despair. Everywhere, here and Europe, we see the utter failure of religion and education, the collapse of systems, either of the left or of the right. What is your relationship to this frightful confusion, to this destructive chaos? If you would bring order out of this chaos, where would you begin? Obviously with yourself, for your relationship with this crisis, with this degradation is direct. Let us not put the blame of this disaster on the few unbalanced leaders or on the systems, for you have created this confusion, and to bring order and peace out of it, you must begin with yourself; you must put order in your own house. Do

not let us consider the rightness or wrongness of systems and formulas which promise hope; do not let us consider theories nor outer revolutions; we must begin with ourselves, for we, you and I, are responsible for this disaster, for this confusion. Without you there is no world; you are the world, you are the problem. This assertion is not an intellectual formulation but an actual fact. Do not set it aside, which only indicates your desire to escape from it. When you recognize your obvious responsibility for the strife and sorrow, what you think, feel, and do, what you are becomes vitally significant, and because you are unwilling to face it, you look to systems, to formulas, to comforting escapes. It is a fact that you are the world, and you are responsible for this aching confusion, and our talks must be based on this fact. Because you are the problem and there is no independent problem apart from you, you have to understand yourself if you would bring peace and order. When you are aware of this fact, you have to act positively and vigorously, and because you are afraid of such an action, you look to systems and to leaders. The only essential and starting point is you. Your individual responsibility is denied, smothered, by giving importance to systems, whether the left or the right or whether it be religious. Systems or formulas to save man become more important than man himself, than you. Organized society takes away individual responsibility; it makes him conform. And society, the state, becomes more important than the individual; through bureaucracy, the boredom of office and routine, the individual creative responsibility is slowly destroyed. The organized religion of dogma and belief saps away individual responsibility and freedom; through belief and dogma, the individual, you, feel secure, so you bring into being organized religion, the state, the system. Man, you, becomes unimportant through the efficiency of the machine, political or mechanical; the industry, the party, assume great significance, and you become merely a tool to be made efficient, to be a unit of a doctrine. This is happening to you, you are responsible for this death and irresponsibility, and yet you are not realizing this fact. Education, instead of awakening you to creative responsibility, is turning you out to be specialists along different lines: lawyers, police, army, and so on. You are educated and you cease to be an individual with deep significance. The more you are educated, the more you are conditioned; the more you read, the more you repeat, and so the less you are capable of revolutionary thinking. Regimentation, through the activities of society and state, education, army, and so on, is imposed upon you. So these and other factors make you a repetitive machine, unaware of your responsibility and significance.

To bring order and peace out of this darkness and misery, you have to start with yourself and not with the system, for psychologically, you are always the master of the machine, of the system. You are of the greatest significance and not the society nor the state, for your relationship with another is society; what you think, what you feel, what you do is of the utmost importance, for you create the environment, the state. Before answering questions, I wish to say that questions will have the right answers if the questioner is earnest in his intentions. If you merely ask an intellectual, superficial question, you may trap me but you will be the loser.

Question: What is the kind of thing that is needed today to live in peace? At the same time, could you show a way by which millions of people can be fed?

KRISHNAMURTI: To have peace you must live peacefully. There are many causes which bring about strife between man and man. Property is one of the causes of contention. Possession of things made by the hand or by the mind leads to strife; the use of things as an instrument for personal gain causes enmity between man and man. So if you want peace you must live without greed; envy is one of the factors that makes for nationalism, setting man against man. Competition and the desire for success, ambition, cause conflict between man and man. Organized religion divides man from man; one dogma, one belief invariably breeds opposing dogma and belief; belief and dogma antagonize man with his fellow man. Conversion is not the way of peace. To have peace you must be free from the causes of antagonism, you must be peaceful. Communalism and the adherence to a particular system, whether economic or religious, does not lead to peace. To have peace you must cease to be a Muslim or a Hindu, a Christian or a Buddhist, for all racial and religious divisions are false, breeding conflict, confusion, and antagonism.

When there is peace in your heart, then it is comparatively easy to organize food, clothing, shelter for all. If you are not free from ambition, from the craving for position and power, then the organization of man's necessities is made impossible; then systems become all-important and not man. There is enough knowledge to feed, clothe, and shelter man, but the men of knowledge are petty and nationalistic, like you, ambitious and greedy. Separatism is a poison that is corrupting the world, you, and if you were aware of this, you would not hesitate to put an end to it. But you are not aware of it; you are vaguely concerned about the starving millions; it is not an immediate and insistent problem. The crisis is far away for most of us, at least you think it is far away, and so you are concerned verbally over it.

Nobody is going to give you peace, not God, because you are not worthy of it. You have made this sorrowful confusion, and hope lies in you alone, not in a system, not in a leader but in yourself alone.

Question: More things are wrought by prayer than this world dreams of! Mahatma Gandhi has wonderfully exemplified its efficacy in his daily life. If individuals without distraction and materialistic aggrandizement lift their hearts to God in penitent prayer, then the mercy of God will dispel the catastrophe that has overtaken the world. Is it not the right attitude to develop?

KRISHNAMURTI: You alone are responsible for this catastrophe and you alone can dispel it, not an outside agency, however great.

We must differentiate between prayer and meditation. What do we mean by prayer? As it is generally understood and practiced, it is a form of supplication or petition; you are in need and you pray; you are in confusion, in sorrow, and you pray. To whom are you praying? To God, you say. But God or truth is the unknown; that which cannot be formulated, cannot be created. It must come to you, you cannot go to it; you may not beg of it, petition it; it must seek you out. When you seek it, when you pray to it, you create it and what you create is not truth, God. The peace of truth shatters the peace that you crave.

God cannot give you peace for the god that you seek is fabricated out of your own mind, and when you pray to it, it does produce certain results; what you ask you receive, but you have to pay for it as in the fairy tales. If you pray for peace you will have it, but it will be the peace of decay, of death. Peace is creative, dynamic, and it does not come into being through supplication. Prayer is wholly different from meditation. He who prays cannot comprehend what is meditation, for he is concerned with gain. Meditation is understanding; understanding does not come through books, through following an example, but through self-knowledge which is a process of self-discovery. Meditation is an awareness of the whole process of living, not merely of any one part of existence; to be aware of every thought, feeling, and action.

Meditation is not concentration; meditation is all-inclusive whereas concentration is exclusive. Focusing your attention on images made by the hand or by the mind, excluding all other thoughts, images, feelings, is not meditation. The excluding process of concentration is comparatively easy and futile. Meditation is an awareness extending everdeeply and widely through the clear perception of the many layers of consciousness.

Prayer, concentration, and meditation are different processes, each having a different end. Prayer and concentration do not open the door of reality; meditation born of self-knowledge opens the door to the immeasurable, to the eternal. Those who are caught in the gratification of prayer and in the concentrated interest of exclusiveness cannot know the purifying significance of meditation. Spontaneity is essential for self-knowledge; spontaneous response reveals the ways of the mind and the heart. When there is no condemnation, no judgment, no identification, awareness reveals the significance of every thought and feeling. Awareness flows into meditation, in which the thinker and the thought are one, without the division between the thinker and his thought. Right meditation brings about stillness, absolute stillness of the mind, uninduced and free. Only then can reality come into being.

Question: You deride the Brahmins. Have they not played an important part in the culture of India?

KRISHNAMURTI: They have, but what of it? Surely the question reveals hereditary pride in the questioner, does it not? This hereditary ownership and pride has done a great deal of harm to society, to the relationship of man and man. What is of the greatest importance is what you are now, not what you were in the past. There were people in every country who were not driven by ambition, unconcerned with power and position, with property and systems, but vitally occupied in the pursuit of the real; they were above and beyond the clamor of society and the state and so were the teachers and helpers of man in strife, in sorrow. They were the guides of mankind, the Brahmins of old. But what has happened to them, who being free, were able to help man to think rightly? They have become merchants, lawyers, politicians, soldiers. Can there be true culture when man is solely occupied with sensate values?

So what matters is not the past but the result of the past, which is the present, you. To understand the past, the present is of the highest significance; the present is the door to the past. If the present is used as a mere passage to the future, then you are preparing for catastrophe, for untold misery and degradation.

Because in ancient days there were a group of people who were free from ambition and authority, from the bondages of greed and ill will, it helped to guide society away from spiritual and moral degradation. The larger the group, the greater the security of the society, of the state, and for this reason only one or two countries, like India, have survived. Because there are very few who are not caught up in the turmoil of the world, the world, you, are in an extraordinary crisis. To bring order and peace out of this mad confusion and misery, you must go above and beyond the causes that have produced this decay. You must be that one who is above all caste and creed, who is free from ambition and ill will, from authority and greed, from intrigue and worldliness.

You alone, enlightened, can lay the foundation for a new culture—a culture that is freed from geographic and racial, national and organized religious bondages, a culture that is not of the East nor of the West, Hindu or Buddhist, Christian or Mohammedan.

To seek the eternal is to be freed from the bondages of time and misery. A very grave responsibility lies upon those who are not immediately concerned with food, clothing, and shelter. To bring about a new culture based on eternal values, there must be revolution in your mind and heart. Mere intellectual formulations, pride of hereditary distinctions and possessions are utterly useless, harmful; they cannot solve the world chaos and misery. In you is the only hope.

Question: You have attained illumination but what about us, the millions?

KRISHNAMURTI: It is not at all important who has attained, but it is very essential to be aware of your own state. The mass is you; the millions are you and I. Despair and confusion, conflict and sorrow surround us; you and I have contributed towards this despair and decay, and none can solve the problems of the world except yourself. Not the illumined, not the leader, neither the temple nor the church; neither a guru nor a system can deliver you, the world, from conflict and sorrow. You alone can solve the problem; it cannot be solved for you by another.

Be aware of the causes of sorrow and strife in yourself and resolve them. Do not talk of saving the mass or safeguarding the millions, for the mass is yourself. Be aware of your sorrow, of your emptiness, of your own confusion, for what you are, the world is. Your problem is the world's problem. To bring about happiness and peace in the world, there must be fundamental transformation of your mind and heart.

You are life and action, and without understanding yourself, to attempt to solve the problems of another or of the world is to bring more confusion, more misery. The regeneration of the world lies in your own hands, for you are the world.

October 26, 1947

Third Talk in Madras

The reformation of society can come only through the regeneration of the individual. There is hope in the individual, in you, not in a system, not in the blueprint of a planned society, not in any religious organization, but in you, the individual. Your relationship with another is society, which brings into being the state. The state is not a separate and uncontrollable entity; it is the outcome of individual thought and action. Though we constantly assert, verbally, that we must love each other, that life is one, that we must strive for brotherhood, actually this relationship between man and man is based on sensate value. This relationship of sensory values has produced wars, ruthlessness, conflict, chaos. This relationship has given birth to individual enterprise and to its opposite, collective action; both individual enterprise and collective action are based on sensory values.

Man, the individual, you, has not found lasting happiness either through the activities of the right or of the left; man is in despair, confused and in sorrow. Does man's happiness lie in sensate values? That is, does your happiness lie in things made by the hand or by the mind? Through self-knowledge alone, the truth of this question can be discovered. A truth is not a truth when repeated; it must be felt, experienced. Self-knowledge is self-discovery. Through self-knowledge alone can you discover truth and lasting happiness. Self-knowledge is the choiceless awareness of the actual process of your whole being. This self-knowledge cannot be learned through a book nor through another. To be aware of the total entity that you are, to be aware of the conscious and unconscious process of your thoughts, feelings, and activities is self-knowledge. The beginning of self-knowledge is to be aware of your mental and emotional activities.

Without self-knowledge there is no basis for thought and action. Self-knowledge is the foundation for all thought and action. If you do not know yourself, there cannot be right thinking and right action. There can be no revolution in values if there is no self-knowledge; this revolution in values alone will solve the world's problems. Since you are the world, since your relationship with another is society, without a revolutionary change of values, which you bring about through self-knowledge, there can be no peace and order, no hope from this confusion and mounting sorrow. So to understand yourself is of the highest importance. To talk of transforming society is utterly vain without self-knowledge. We assert that the problems of the world must be solved as though the world were different from us. Each one of us has contributed towards this conflict, this confusion, this antagonism, this mounting insanity, and we cannot put an end to it if we do not know how to think of the problem, how to approach it, how to examine it. The approach is of greater importance than the problem itself. The problem is not the world but you; you cannot rightly think of the problem until you are aware of it as your most pressing and immediate problem. You may not be aware of it as though it were outside of you. You have created the problem, so you have to be aware of yourself as the problem. The confusion in you has to be cleared away, for to act in confusion is to breed more confusion.

The transformation, the regeneration must begin with you and not with another; this is the right approach. Be aware of your mental and emotional activities, of your daily habits and ideas, of your repetitive fears, of class and communal divisions, of national and racial antagonisms. Before there can be peace in the world, there must be peace and order in you.

We are confronted with one of the most extraordinary catastrophes and with a confusion that is very profound; we are meeting it with systems, with ready-made formulations, with conclusions of this or that group. To bring peace and order out of this chaos, there must be revolution in values; the confusion has arisen because we are dominated by sensate values; we have to rediscover eternal values. The discovery of eternal values must be made by each one; the reformation must begin with each one. Be aware of every thought and feeling and so of every action; for truth is near and not far away.

Question: In a recent article by a famous correspondent, it was stated that wisdom and personal example are not enough to solve the problems of the world. What do you think?

KRISHNAMURTI: As there are many implications in this question, we must analyze them. By correspondents, who have axes to grind, we are persuaded not how to think but what to think; generally, we unfortunately accept what we read. The so-called education has stopped us from thinking, from being aware; writers and correspondents become very important in our lives. We have to be aware of this tendency to accept what is printed. This correspondent and many others demand a political action and personal example. Personal example and political action are not enough to solve the world's problems. Something much more fundamental is needed.

Imitation and conformity are inherent in personal example; the conformity to an ideal can never diminish the burden of sorrow. Personal example in a great crisis is of little significance. Wisdom does not come through imitation, through regimentation of thought; wisdom has no fixed abode; wisdom does not lie in much reading. Political action must ever be partial, incomplete action and so untrue, causing further confusion and misery. What is necessary is a revolution in thinking and feeling. This creative revolution cannot be brought about by a few leaders, by a political action or through a personal example. It is only possible through individual awakening. Personal example or political action according to any formula will not save the world from the catastrophe. Man puts faith in a system, in a party, in leaders, and they have invariably failed. In you alone is there hope, not in another.

It is a human crisis, not an economic or political catastrophe; man's entire being is involved and not any one of his activities. The problem is not the world but you are the problem. Because you are thinking in terms of conclusions and formulations, of systems and patterns, you have brought to yourself, and so to the world, this confusion and misery. Personal examples will not deliver you from conflict and pain. Revolution in values, which creative thinking brings, is very arduous, and so we look to others, to leaders, to examples. The thinking that we do is a response to a conditioning, and so it is not thinking at all. Because you are a Hindu, you are conditioned to a certain pattern of thought and behavior—as the Muslim, as the Christian, and so on. Surely this is not thinking. There can be creative revolution in thinking and feeling only when there is freedom from conditioning, not only from the conscious, but also from the hidden conditioning. You have ceased to be of any nationality, of any system, religious or political; you have to transcend the fallacies of social and economic divisions to think creatively. You agree with what I am saying and probably will come here Sunday after Sunday, but you will unfortunately continue in the set pattern of thought and behavior. So your assent is very superficial and so has no significance. If you begin to question the pattern and to act, you will undoubtedly create more trouble and pain for yourself; so, being aware of this, you give your assent superficially, verbally stating that the world is in a confusion and something must be done about it.

So the problem is you; for you are the world, the mass, the state. If you are aware of the conflict and sorrow within you, the confusion and the ache, in transcending them you are solving the world's problems. Organizational and political problems are comparatively easy to solve; mere theories and book knowledge are not going to deliver you, and so the world, from confusion and misery. Book knowledge becomes a hindrance to direct understanding and action. You must break through your conditioning and those degenerative values which you yourself have created about you. There is no hope in systems, in political actions, impersonal examples, in the leaders, but there is hope only in yourself.

Question: What do you mean when you say that we use the present as a passage to the past or to the future?

KRISHNAMURTI: Last Sunday I said that in using the present as a passage to the past or the future, you are breeding disaster and misery. We use the present as a means to an end, psychologically or physiologically; the present is used only as a passage to the past or to the future. The present is the result of the past; what you now think is based on the past; your being is founded on the past. The past is ever weaving through the present to the future; the future is the past conditioned through the present. The past can only be understood through the present; the door to the past lies through the present. To understand the significance of the past, the present must be comprehended and not be sacrificed for the future. The political and religious groups that sacrifice the present for the future utopia and hope bring disaster and misery to man. The disastrous implications in sacrificing the present for the future are fairly clear. The means are the end; the end is in the means; the means and the end cannot be separated.

The eternal is the present; the timeless is the now. It cannot be approached through time. Yet you are using time—the past, the present, and the future—as a means to realize the immeasurable, the timeless. One has to be aware of the fallacy of sacrificing the present for the future and of the fallacy that the future is going to be different from the present. If you have no understanding now, you will not have understanding in the future; wisdom is ever in the present and does not abide in the future.

Thought is the result of the past, and to understand and so free thought from the past, be aware of what you are now, your thoughts, feelings, and actions; then you will perceive that you are using the present as a mere passage. The time process will not lead to the timeless for the means is the end. If you are using wrong means, you will create wrong ends; only right means will create the right end. War is a wrong means to peace. The means is the end and the end is not disassociated from the means. If there is to be understanding of the timeless, that which is bound to time, thought, must free itself from the past which through the present becomes the future.

Question: The communists say that the rulers of Indian States, the zamindars and the capitalists are the chief exploiters of the nation and that they should be liquidated in order to secure food, clothing, and shelter for all. Gandhi says that the rulers, the zamindars, and the capitalists are the trustees of the persons under their control and influence, and therefore they may be allowed to remain and function. What do you say?

KRISHNAMURTI: It is very odd that everywhere in the world people are acquainted with what their leaders and groups, either of the left or of the right, think, but they themselves do not seem to know what they think. They attach great significance to what others, so-called prominent people, say and very little significance to their own thoughts. What is important is what you think and feel, for it is your life, your misery and conflict that is concerned. Let us regard this question as though we had never read a book nor read any speeches of your so-called leaders. The question is concerned with exploitation and how to be rid of it. How do you become a zamindar or a maharajah? Surely by exploiting the people. To pursue more than what you need becomes exploitation. You need food, clothes, and shelter, but when they become the means of personal aggrandizement, then exploitation begins. To use another to gain power and position, authority and domination is exploitation. Exploitation is the problem and not who exploits. The capitalist, the ruler, the zamindar are like you; if you had the chance you would become like them. You would lose your generosity, your love, the moment you climb the ladder of success, of gain.

Are the capitalists, the zamindars, the Indian state rulers, trustees? To trust there must be love, but love ceases with greed, with the desire to dominate, to influence. Love ceases when you give importance to yourself as a leader or as a zamindar. Both the leader and the led exploit, as well as the maharaja and

the capitalist. Do not be persuaded by any what to think, but be thoughtful.

The problem is exploitation. Does the exploitation cease through collective action and is it increased through individual enterprise? We know that individual greed and the craving for power has plunged the world into confusion and sorrow; we also see that an all-powerful state can and does exploit and bring about other forms of conflict and misery. We see that greed and the craving for power in the individual and in the state or in the collective are destructive, ruthless. In organizing collectively man's necessities, the exploitation of man's being and what he thinks and feels is also being carried on. With acquisition there must ever be exploitation; the craving for acquisition must inevitably bring about exploitation. Acquisition is always psychological. When emphasis is laid on you as an acquiring entity, the individual or the collective, there will be always exploitation. This does not mean that we should not organize for the physical welfare of man, but if the organizer uses the organization as a means of acquisition, then he and the organization will become the means of exploitation.

Can man live in relationship with another without acquisition, which is without exploitation? Can you live in a society without acquisitiveness? Can you live without more and more, without more and more property, which represents power, position, and psychological security? Because you are unwilling not to acquire and not to use human needs as a means to self-aggrandizement, both the movements of the right and the left are liquidating you in their own way. But liquidation, murder, is not, surely, the way.

So can acquisitiveness be relinquished voluntarily? Can you let go freely the craving for power—power gained through the things made by the hand or by the mind? If you do not, society, the others, in their acquisitiveness, are going to compel you, and then you will become a mere cog, as you are now, in another vast social machine. This voluntary abandonment of acquisitiveness is the way out of this suffocating confusion. Acquisitiveness comes with the desire to be secure; the more there is confusion, the greater the desire to be secure. But is there security? Because we have sought security, psychological security, we have created confusion and misery about us. Unless you voluntarily relinquish acquisitiveness, the state will control and regiment you; you will be exploited then by the collective instead of by individuals or by groups. If you voluntarily and intelligently put aside this craving to possess, then you will create a society not based on compulsion and exploitation.

To create a new society you must radically transform your present values, which demands pliable alertness and an extending awareness; but being apathetic, indifferent, you will be directed and compelled, and the world's problems, which are your own, are not dissolved through compulsion. It is arduous to understand the deeper, psychological significance of exploitation, and without understanding it, to merely substitute one exploiter for another is to continue in strife and misery. Because psychologically, inwardly, you are poor, aching with loneliness, with emptiness, possessions made by the hand or by the mind assume predominating significance. This constant companion, this aching void must be faced and understood; then exploitation which is psychological, will cease.

Question: Are your teachings intended only for the sannyasis or for all of us with families and responsibilities?

KRISHNAMURTI: These teachings are meant for all, for those who have renounced the world and for those who are in it. The renouncer is still in the world of his burning desires, as the man of the world. They are both held in bondage, the bondage of sensate values or the bondage of the mind. These teachings bring freedom to both. Reality is not found either in things made by the hand or by the mind; truth is the liberator, the truth of *what is*. One has to understand *what is*—the passions and the envies, the ill will and the acquisitiveness—and the understanding of *what is* is its own liberation. One realizes at rare moments, when the mind is not occupied with itself, when the self is absent, that truth which liberates.

The man of family is caught in the world of his own responsibilities. The more there is confusion about him, the more he is concerned with his family, with himself, and so seeks security, which only adds further confusion. Instead of understanding the significance of confusion himself, he looks to the security of his family, which he calls responsibility. He must bring peace and order within himself and not escape from this fact through the apprehensive search for security. The man who has renounced the world—he too is caught in the desire for security; he is not different for he is burdened with the formulations of his own mind; they too bring him confusion and sorrow. Creation, reality, is when the mind ceases to create.

Is it possible to live in the world without greed and ill will, without stupidity and those passions that destroy man? Yes, it is possible. You may laugh but it is possible. Try and see if it is not possible. To live without greed and ill will, you must be very alert, aware of every thought and feeling; following a leader, accepting conclusions and formulas indicate the lack of awareness which alone can free you from conflict and misery. Without love, family has no significance, and love alone can bring about regeneration and a happy world.

Question: You may have heard of the awful tragedy that has taken place and is even now taking place in the Punjab. Will the individual action based on self-knowledge and right thinking by the few who are capable of such action be significant to the solution of this Punjab problem?

KRISHNAMURTI: What is happening in the Punjab is happening the world over; it is not peculiarly an Indian problem—man's inhumanity to man. Who is responsible for this tragedy? Each one of us; each one is bound to some religious or racial or national stupidity. Do you not think in terms of Hindus and Muslims, of the Germans and the English? We are not human beings; we are mere labels; as nationalistic and patriotic spirit is on the increase everywhere in the world, there is bound to be conflict, confusion, and antagonism. A disease has a cause, and until the cause is removed there cannot be good health. For generations we have lived on wrong thinking and naturally it must result in conflict and misery. This chaos and misery is the outcome of the cultivation of sensate values; through awareness of the cause, the cause ceases to be. The dissolution of the cause is not a matter of time, not of growth, but of immediate perception. We do not immediately perceive for various reasons, one of them being the fear and the consequence of immediate action. So though we are capable of immediate perception, we carry on in our old stupid ways as it is more convenient, not demanding exertion. You must awaken to the causes of misery and disaster, not tomorrow but now. Do not build your philosophy on time, but be aware of *what is,* which will lead thought to the infinite.

Question: You say discipline is opposed to freedom. But is not discipline necessary for freedom?

KRISHNAMURTI: A wrong means can only produce a wrong end, a right means brings about the right end. The means and the end are not separate; they are interrelated, they are one.

If thought is disciplined, regimented, held in a groove of habit, it can only perceive or understand that which is conditioned, limited. If you discipline your mind according to a pattern, then you are bound to produce an end carved out of the means. You discipline yourself either out of fear or out of greed, and the end will be fashioned out of your motives. But where there is greed and fear, reality is not.

But you will say, "I must organize my daily life, otherwise I can do nothing, and is not this organization a kind of discipline?" You organize your daily activities in order to be efficient, to do the many things that have to be done; in order to achieve a result, you discipline or organize yourself. Even such an organized existence becomes a hindrance to pliability, for that which is pliable is enduring. Now, is truth a result? If it is a result it can be achieved through a means, and a result has a cause. But that which has a cause is no longer reality. Truth gives freedom, not discipline, and through discipline truth is not.

To put the problem differently: need you become a drunkard in order to know sobriety? There must be an understanding of the causes which necessitate discipline and their full implication. The desire to gain, to succeed, to be directed, and fear are some of the causes that bring about imitation, the practice of a discipline; in being aware of the causes, the effect, discipline, conformity, cease to be. Then the problem is shifted to the dissolution of the cause, which is not a maker of time.

With awareness there comes freedom, not only of the causes of discipline, but of the whole process of living. Freedom can only come when the mind frees itself from its own self-created conditioning, when it is not conditioned to any pattern of thought. When do you discover or understand? Only when there is freedom, when your thought and feeling is not bound or trained to any pattern of desire. A mind that is in bondage is vagrant, restless, disorderly. When the mind is aware of the causes of its own wandering, then there is already freedom.

Thought cannot understand or formulate what is truth; truth must come to you, you cannot go to it. To receive, there must be freedom. There must be choiceless awareness, not condemnatory and identifying awareness, which brings freedom. In freedom alone can there be the real, the immeasurable.

November 2, 1947

Fourth Talk in Madras

It is important to be aware of the art of listening. Most of us listen with a bias or with a mind stuffed with conclusions, with beliefs and with so-called knowledge; we listen through the noisy mutterings of our own minds, or we listen so inattentively that we hardly understand what is being said. The right relationship between the listener and the speaker is always difficult, for the relationship is temporary and superficial, a brief contact and separation. But I hope these gatherings will not be of that nature, for during these talks each one is gathering knowledge about himself and so able to think rightly. You are not merely listening to a talk and going back to your old form of existence, but awakening to your whole being, you will be able to shatter your old forms of thoughtlessness and habits.

I would request you not to listen to these talks with the idea of learning but let what I am saying take root. If what is being said is true, then it will stand firmly and take root

deeply, but if it is false it will fall off and wither away. So what is important is to listen with alert and yet easeful attention to these talks which should be a part of our daily life, and not merely a thing which you attend once a week. These talks are meant to awaken and to quicken intelligence and not to give you conclusions; for conclusions, like belief, prevent the fruition of thought and intelligence.

We were saying: Why is it that each one of us, and so the world, has given an all-consuming significance to property and psychological separation? Why is it that each one gives such enormous importance to acquisitiveness and to social, national, and racial divisions? Why is it that almost all our problems revolve around possessions and name? I do not know if you are aware of this issue in your daily life, but if you are, have you not asked yourself why is it that property with its many complexities—name, nationality, and other forms of divisions and exclusions—fill your mind? There must be some reason why your mind and heart are so occupied with these things, must there not be? Why is it that man goes to war, murdering each other over property and name? Why is it that he tries to solve the problems that property and name create through the same means? Is it not because he is seeking security? Food, clothing, and shelter are essential, but yet we seem to be incapable of giving man these essentials.

Because we have no greater value than acquisitiveness and class, these have become of extraordinary significance. The interest in something greater frees thought from the lesser, and then the lesser would not assume dominating value. Secondary values, when given dominating importance, bring disaster and misery, which is what is taking place now in the world. So why is there no greater value, though all the so-called sacred books assert that there is? You must seek the answer, must you not? Have you sought it?

You say you have but where has it led you? To greater division, to greater possessiveness. Why is there no greater value?

When the mind and heart seek security, certainty, there can be no greater value than the sensate. Acquisitiveness and the name and class are psychological; they are the result of psychological demands. When the mind is seeking security, it can only create values either made by the hand or by itself. So there can be no greater value than the values of the mind; hence sensate values become the all-important. Legislation to curb acquisitiveness, with its results, is necessary, but that does not solve the problem; revolutions have come and gone, but we are still confronted with the same problem—acquisitiveness and class division. Confusion and misery are still here, and the pursuit of sensate value, either by the left or the right, will not give man order and peace.

How is the greater value to be found? For if you are interested in discovering something greater, then you will not give all-consuming importance to the secondary, to the less. As long as you have not found the greater, the secondary, the lesser becomes dominatingly significant. There is the discovery of the greater through understanding the psychological demand for security. The problem is not food, clothes, and shelter and their effective organization, but the psychological demand; for security, food, clothes, and shelter, the essentials, are used as a means to fulfill the psychological craving. Now, we have assumed that there is security, but is there such a thing as psychological security? We all seek it through different mediums, through things, through relationship, through ideas; the mind is in constant pursuit of security, certainty. On the assurance that there is psychological security, we have built our structure of existence. When the mind is seeking security, it must

cling to the lesser values, the sensate values, and they become all-important.

The discovery of the truth of psychological security lies through self-knowledge. To discover what is beyond the known values, the sensory values, there must be self-knowledge. In the true inquiry of security, sensory values become of less importance. The truth of security is not to be found in its positive or negative assertion, but it is to be discovered only through direct perception, through self-knowledge. When truth is uncovered it brings great joy and clarity. Self-knowledge is important, as it reveals the fundamental truth of our problem, the truth of security. Self-knowledge is a creative process as long as the mind is not using self-knowledge as a means of security or as an achievement. All relationship is a process of self-revelation and not a means towards security. If you are aware of your thoughts, feelings, and actions, they will reveal the ways of the self, which is ever seeking security, certainty. If you are aware, you will perceive that in relationship the mind is seeking psychological security. Can relationship exist in insecurity? If there is uncertainty there is fear and deep inquiry. Certainty puts you to sleep. Self-knowledge becomes of great significance in the pursuit of the truth, of certainty, of permanency. The mind is ever seeking security, the known. If the mind is aware of its own ways of thinking, then it will perceive that it is always moving from the known to the known, from the secure to the secure. It creates from the known the unknown and worships it as the ultimate security, but what it has created is not the real. If you observe very diligently your own way of thinking and feeling, you will see that security is the end of its activities.

It is in freedom that the discovery of the real is made, not in security. Property and name become the all-important problem when we pursue security, certainty. The security in sensory values leads man to conflict and misery, but the truth of sensory values, which can be discovered only through self-knowledge, liberates man from sorrow and disaster.

Question: Will you please explain further what you mean by meditation?

KRISHNAMURTI: In perceiving truly what the problem is, understanding comes. The solution is in the problem, not away from it; understanding lies in the problem itself and not in the answer. What do we mean generally by meditation? We are not condemning meditation but examining what generally takes place in so-called meditation, for in perceiving the truth of what our activities are during meditation, we shall be set free to meditate rightly. You meditate because you have been told to, and action based on authority leads to confusion and conflict. Your mind wanders all over the place as you try to meditate; thought is as a shuttle weaving itself from the past through the present to the future and back again, ever restless, ever anxious, ever vagrant. By excluding all other ideas, thought tries to concentrate on the one idea that it has chosen, but swiftly other thoughts come pouring in; again you try to concentrate and again thought wanders off. Again and again you try to concentrate and fail once more. So you spend your time in conflict, in control, and not in so-called meditation. Or in order to concentrate better you sit in front of a picture or repeat a phrase or a word or try to discover the deeper significance of a word. Developing virtue is also considered meditation. If one can fix one's mind on an idea and identify oneself with it completely, then it is considered a great spiritual achievement. This is generally what is considered meditation, is it not? This is what one generally attempts to do in so-called meditation, is it not?

The mind, being vagrant, disorderly, seeking security, orderliness, pursues an exclusiveness; if it can dwell upon it and identify itself with it, then there is gratification, a sense of achievement. The idea, the phrase, is made by man; the word is repeated by man. Repetition of a word, a phrase, or the gaze puts you in a self-induced trance; such a repetition dulls the mind. The identification with a self-projected idea, though intensely gratifying, is not the real. Reality is not to be formulated, cannot be thought about, for what is thought about is the known, and what is known is not the real. You can only think about the known; you cannot think about the unknown. The projection of the known and its worship is not meditation but a form of self-hypnosis. This form of self-hypnosis is a hindrance to the understanding of the real.

Thought is the result of the past, and what it thinks about is still of time. After all, the purpose of meditation is to uncover reality and not to hypnotize oneself about reality. The real is not uncovered through repetition of words and phrases, by dulling the mind through rituals and through concentration, which is an exclusive process. So is it possible for the unknown to manifest itself? It is possible only when time, the known, has ceased. Memory, the records of experience, is the mind; the mind clings to memory, ever increasing and ever expanding. Memory becomes a hindrance for the unknowing. How would you find out that which is not formulatable, the immeasurable, the real? This is the problem of meditation, is it not? But meditation is not prayer, nor does concentration, the process of exclusion, lead to meditation. So how would you approach the understanding of meditation? The mind which is the result of the past, of the known—can it understand the timeless, the eternal? The timeless comes into being only when time has ceased. Truth can exist only when the known, the accumulated memory, has come to an end. Then how can the mind, the result of the past, free itself from the known? It is free only when thought is not caught in its own structure—in the word, in the phrase, in habit, in discipline, in routine, in belief, in dogma, in memory.

So it is not a question of how to meditate, which is a wrong question. The "how" implies a method; the method is the known; the known can only lead to the known; a wrong means leads to a wrong end; the end is in the means. If the means is known, the end is also the known, but the known is not the real. The real is only when thought is free from the known. The known is the accumulated and the power to accumulate knowledge, name, and things. Can thought free itself from accumulation, from its own creation? Yes. Can the mind, which is the result of the past, free itself from time? It can. It can free itself from time through the gateway of the present; the present is the thought, the feeling, the action—being aware of what you are thinking, feeling, doing now, in the immediate present. The present is the gateway to the timeless. By being aware of what you are thinking and feeling, you will perceive their ways only if there is no condemnation, no justification, no identification. For condemnation, justification, identification, prevent thought from completing itself. The constant awareness of your thought, feeling and action, and your trained and spontaneous responses to them is the beginning of self-knowledge. The awareness of the conscious as well as the hidden activities is self-knowledge. The beginning of self-knowledge is the beginning of meditation. There is no meditation without self-knowledge.

Be aware choicelessly, that is, without condemnation, without justification, without pursuing; then there is the highest form of thinking, creative thinking. That which is creative is creation, the real.

Question: I am beginning to realize that I am very lonely. What am I to do? (Laughter)

KRISHNAMURTI: I wonder why you laugh? Do you laugh because you despise loneliness or you consider it as bourgeois or as a thing not important? Because you are so socially occupied, or so concerned with reform that you consider loneliness as something unworthy of you, that you laugh. Can you laugh it away? It would be interesting to find out why you laugh. The awareness of that laughter is the beginning of self-knowledge. Self-knowledge leads to great heights and depths, and if it is pursued ever deeply and widely, there is great tribulation leading to incredible happiness and ecstasy.

Do you know what loneliness means and are you aware of it? I doubt it, for you generally smother that pain of loneliness by every kind of action, by knowledge, by the conflicts of relationship, and by things. So you are not aware of ache, of loneliness. Loneliness is that sense of being as nothing, the frightening void, the state of extraordinary uncertainty, of having no refuge, no anchorage, an aching emptiness, an unfathomable frustration. Everyone has felt this loneliness—the happy and the unhappy, the very active and the addicts after knowledge— the inexhaustible pain, the pain that is ever there. We try to run away from it, try to cover it up, smother it, but it is ever there.

Again let us approach this question not so much as to find an answer but to understand the problem itself. The problem is the realization of loneliness and what should be the action towards it. What happens actually when there is this ache of loneliness? You try to escape from it, you pick up a book, or go to a cinema, or turn on the radio, or discuss politics, lose yourself in various forms of activities; you worship or you pray, you paint or you write a poem about loneliness. Being aware of the pain and the fathomless fear, you escape from it according to your idiosyncracies or temperament. So the means of escape become all-important—your gods, your knowledge, your activities, your radios. When you give predominant significance to secondary values, then there is confusion and misery; secondary values are invariably sensate, and modern civilization is based on secondary values.

Have you tried to be alone? To be alone demands a great deal of intelligence, for the mind is restless, active, caught in the net of its own desires. It is difficult for thought to be alone without escaping, to be aware of itself without conditioned responses. Thought, being aware of its own emptiness, tries to fill itself, this emptiness, with the known. We are attempting to fill that which we do not know, the void, with the known, with knowledge, with the responses of relationship and with things. Have you succeeded in filling this void, have you been successful in covering it? Obviously not. Can this emptiness, this void be filled? Having tried one escape and finding it useless, do we not find that all escapes are vain? Are not all escapes similar, and so is it not useless to seek different escapes? In understanding the uselessness of one escape, do not all escapes become futile?

What then is the right action in understanding this loneliness? There is an understanding of this aching void only when there is no longer any escape. When you are willing to face *what is,* turning your back on all escapes, turning your back on worldly values, then only is there the transformation of *what is.* The understanding of *what is* is the beginning of self-knowledge, of wisdom.

Question: Are you not becoming our leader?

KRISHNAMURTI: I have received several questions of this nature—that I should enter politics to lead India out of this present confusion and so on.

Why is it that you want a leader? Why do you become a leader and why become a follower? It does not matter whether the leader is political or religious, a guru. You are uncertain. You do not know what to think, you are confused, so you desire to be directed, to be protected, guided. This desire creates political tyranny and dictatorship, and religiously, the acceptance of authority, belief, tradition, which dulls the mind and heart. When there is inner and outer confusion, you seek and create leadership. There is confusion and misery, degradation and starvation; there is exploitation by the rich, by the clever, and by those who are possessed by systems, by formulas, and by those who breed different and antagonistic groups and parties. From this vast confusion you desire to be saved. So you create the leader and you become the follower; you hunger after leaders because inwardly and outwardly you want to be secure, protected from confusion. You fear to be uncertain and so you create authority. In doing this, you destroy yourself by becoming the follower. When you follow a party or a discipline, a leader or a guru, are you not destroying your own thought process?

Being confused and sorrowful, can anyone give you clarity and happiness? None can deliver you from confusion and sorrow save yourself, for you yourself have brought about this confusion and this misery. There is the right solution in the problem itself, and not away from it; in the confusion and misery itself, and not away from it. But you will not look at conflict and pain; all that you ask is to be led away from the understanding of *what is.* So you bring forth the leader to exploit and to be exploited. The leader fulfills himself by leading, by guiding, by intriguing, and manipulating, and he feels himself frustrated when thwarted; for he, like you, feeds on power and position. Exploitation exists not only between the worker and the owner, but also between the follower and the leader. You not only breed the leader, but also you become the means of exploitation. The leader depends upon you and you depend upon him, and since you are in confusion and in sorrow, what you bring forth, the leader, must be inevitably confused and miserable.

This desire to follow is a form of self-fulfillment; you fulfill yourself in a leader and in turn he fulfills himself in you. This mutual self-fulfillment and exploitation can lead nowhere. When there is self-fulfillment through an organization, political or religious, through painting, through writing, through any other activity, it must lead to frustration. Being unconsciously aware of this aching failure, you go from one leader to another, from one guru to another. So the leader becomes very important; he is ever the leader and you are ever the follower.

Self-fulfillment leads to misery and is one of the causes of confusion and degradation. As I am not seeking self-fulfillment in the name of God or country, of peace or belief, and not in any way depending psychologically upon another, I cannot possibly become your leader. It does not matter to me whether there is one or many or none to listen to what I teach, and so there is no mutual exploitation. The greed for power and position leads to exploitation, to intrigues and indignities. So neither am I your leader, your guru, nor are you going to make me one, another among your varied collection. I do not want to lead for the very simple reason that reality is not to be understood by following another. Reality comes into being only when the desire for self-fulfillment in any form whatsoever has wholly ceased. When there is freedom from psychological demands, conscious or unconscious, when thought is free from the pursuing desire, then

there is reality. Reality alone can bring peace and happiness.

Question: What is the difference between belief and confidence? Why do you condemn belief?

KRISHNAMURTI: What do we mean by belief? Why do we have to have belief? Belief implies acceptance, trust, faith in something inward or outward. Belief gives assurance, confidence, a sense of security, and the more that you believe in something, the greater the security. To be psychologically without a belief is very disturbing, is it not? Fear and belief ever go together; they are inseparable, they are the two sides of a coin. Belief comes into being when the mind is seeking security, certainty; it creates belief as a means of self-protection or takes on the belief of others; or it projects its hopes and fears into the future, into time, making them as the ideal, and disciplines itself according to its projections in order to achieve security, a refuge where there is no disturbance of any kind. This factor, the desire for security, for refuge, breeds different forms of beliefs according to environmental and psychological influences. You believe in God, another does not; you are a Hindu or a Muslim, a Christian or a nonbeliever, and so on. Thus, belief divides, setting man against man. The desire to be psychologically secure creates divisions, as mine and yours, and thus gives vast significance to secondary values, to sensory values.

See what belief has done to man and so to the world. Politically or religiously, man is torn apart; the belief in many contending schemes and blueprints is causing conflict and enmity; organized religious beliefs in the name of God and peace are setting man against man; man is destroying man because of his belief in his country, in his security, in his God. Belief invariably breeds more belief, more conflict, more confusion, more antagonism. Belief is the result of the hidden demands of self-fulfillment. Happiness is sought through self-fulfillment, which is through belief, and there is no happiness in things made by the hand or by the mind. If you seek happiness through something, then the thing becomes all-important and not happiness.

What do we mean by confidence? Trust or faith in something. Assurance or confidence gives a certain trust in oneself, as practice on an instrument gives. From this continued and sustained assurance there is a kind of self-aggression. Confidence in the self is another form of self-fulfillment.

Now there is another kind of confidence which comes through self-knowledge. I am using *confidence* for the lack of a better word. To be aware of every thought and feeling and to follow them through completely brings joy; in understanding the many layers of consciousness, the superficial and the hidden, there is freedom whose joy is wholly different from the self-expanding assurance. When there is an understanding of the poison of the hindrances, then there is freedom; when the activities of the self are explored and understood, then there is imperishable ecstasy. This exploration is not based on any belief, on any formulation of the mind. Discovery based on belief ceases to be the true; experience based on belief is the self-projected continuation, and so experience is ever binding. When the mind is aware, its cunning tricks are known, then it knows itself as its own creator. Then, when it ceases to create, there is creation.

November 9, 1947

Fifth Talk in Madras

It would be of deep significance if you and I together could make the journey into self-knowledge, into self-exploration. But the difficulty with most of us is that we are merely observers rather than partakers; we would rather watch the play than be the players. It would be highly beneficial if each one could be a player and not be the mere spectator, as one who is thinking, feeling, living. The difficulty with most of us is that we do not know how to share in discovering for ourselves. We are not accustomed to discover for ourselves the process of our own thinking, from which alone right action can take place. Is it possible not to be mere spectators, but actually partake in what is being explored? Only in this manner can you and I establish a full communicable relationship between us. Most of us have a verbal relationship, but the difficulty lies in going beyond it to a deeper level in which alone there can be understanding. Communication can exist only when there is mutual understanding; if you understand and I do not, then communication between us ceases. To establish the right kind of communication on the same level at the same time is arduous. It would be of significant value if you and I together could explore into the ways of the self; and it would be utterly futile to describe to you the results of my journey.

One problem is the search for happiness and the overcoming of sorrow. We crave for happiness and yet sorrow is our constant companion. Though we must have struggled often with this problem, yet let us examine it anew, as though we were considering it for the first time. No problem is old, for every problem is undergoing a constant change. Let us be aware together of this problem of sorrow and happiness, at the same time and on the same level; do not merely listen to me and take on a communication which is not your own, for these talks, if listened to rightly, will bring about deeper and wider awareness.

We seek happiness through things, through relationship, through thoughts, ideas. So things, relationship, and ideas become all-important and not happiness. When we seek happiness through something, then the thing becomes of greater value than happiness itself. When stated in this manner, the problem sounds simple and it is simple. We seek happiness in property, in family, in name; then property, family, idea become all-important, for then happiness is sought through a means, and then the means destroys the end. Can happiness be found through any means, through anything made by the hand or by the mind? Things, relationship, and ideas are so transparently impermanent, we are ever made unhappy by them. We seek happiness through things and we do not find it there; in relationships we search for it and neither do we find happiness there, for there is impermanency in relationship though we try to take refuge in it; again we try to find happiness in thought, in ideas, in belief, and neither is it there, for one set of ideas can be destroyed by another, one belief overcome by another. Things are impermanent, they wear out and are lost; relationship is constant friction and death awaits; ideas and beliefs have no stability, no permanency. We seek happiness in them and yet do not realize their impermanency. So sorrow becomes our constant companion and overcoming it our problem.

We have never asked ourselves if happiness can be found through things made by the hand or by the mind. Is not sorrow inevitable as long as happiness is not the means and the end itself? Can happiness be found at all? Can it exist in itself? There is happiness only when the search for it ceases. To find out the true meaning of happiness, we must explore the river of self-knowledge. Self-knowledge is not an end in itself. Is there a source to a stream? Every drop of water from the beginning to the end makes the river. To imagine that we will find happi-

ness at the source is to be mistaken. It is to be found where you are on the river of self-knowledge.

To follow the river of the conscious and unconscious thoughts and feelings, motives and demands, is very arduous. Those of you who have listened earnestly must have attempted to be aware of every thought and feeling and so perceive their significance. In this manner the conscious mind is cleared of its conflicts, confusions, and antagonisms so as to receive the hidden thoughts and intimations. To follow the deep river of self-knowledge, there must be the clarification of the conscious, the awareness of what is actually happening. By being aware of the conscious activities, the hidden thoughts and pursuits are understood. The conscious is the present, the now, and through the present the hidden is comprehended; the hidden can only be understood through being intensely yet passively aware of the present, thus thought frees itself from its own self-created tribulations and hindrances. The conscious mind is occupied with the immediate problems of existence; without understanding these problems, thought and feeling cannot proceed to deeper and wider issues. The conscious mind is occupied with the daily problems of life: property, class division, relationship, and so on; these problems weave in and out of the conscious mind; the conscious mind is made up of these problems, and if thought does not free itself from its self-imposed travail, it cannot proceed into deeper depths of self-knowledge.

To follow the river of self-knowledge, the first step, which is the most difficult, must be taken, for the beginning of self-knowledge is the beginning of wisdom. Happiness is not to be found through any means, but self-knowledge itself is joy. Love is its own eternity, so self-knowledge is happiness.

Question: I have been told that you do not read any philosophical or religious literature. I can hardly credit this, as when I listen to you I realize that you must have read or have some secret source of knowledge. Please be frank.

KRISHNAMURTI: I have not read any philosophical, psychological, or religious literature, neither the Bhagavad-Gita nor the Upanishads. The secret source is in oneself, for you and I are the repositories of knowledge; we are the reservoir of all thought and wisdom. You and I are the results of the past, of time, and in understanding ourselves we uncover all knowledge and wisdom. Self-knowledge is the beginning of wisdom, and we can and must discover truth through self-knowledge. Wisdom cannot be bought; neither is it to be found through sacrifice nor does it lie in any book, however sacred. Truth does not come by following any system, any leader, any guru. It comes into being when there is passive awareness, when the mind is alertly receptive. There is a delight, there is an ecstasy incomparable, when there is self-knowledge. But most minds are drugged with the thoughts of others, and imitation and repetition are inevitable. When you quote the Bhagavad-Gita, or the Bible, or the Koran, or some so-called sacred book of China, or some modern philosopher or economist, you are merely repetitive. What is true cannot be repeated, and if repeated, quoted, it ceases to be the truth; it becomes a lie. A lie can be propounded, propagated, but not truth; when a truth becomes an instrument of propaganda, then it ceases to be true. Self-knowledge is not a conclusion, an end; it has no beginning and no end. You must begin where you are, reading every word, every phrase, every paragraph of the book of self-knowledge. To understand its contents there must be no condemnation, no justification, for all identifica-

tion and denial put an end to the stream of self-knowledge. To be awake to the movement of the self, there must be a certain freedom, a spontaneity, for a thought that is disciplined, controlled, molded, can never pursue the swift current of the self. A disciplined mind is shaped in a mold, and so cannot follow the subtle promptings of the different layers of consciousness. But there are rare moments when the disciplined mind, the drugged mind, is spontaneous, and in these moments there is a comprehension of conditioned responses, when thought can go beyond its own limitations.

Wisdom is not in a book, it has no secret source. You will find the real very near; it is in yourself. But to discover it there must be the activity of constant alertness. When thought is passively aware, watching and following, then the map of self-knowledge unfolds itself. Self-knowledge is not by the study of the self in isolation, for there is no isolation. To live is to be related and isolation is merely escape. If thought is alertly passive, watching its own movements and flutters, then when sleep comes the conscious mind is capable of receiving the hints and intimations of the hidden consciousness. He who desires to discover the real, the eternal, must put aside every book, every system, every guru, for that which is can be uncovered only through self-knowledge.

Question: In this country, at present, our government is attempting to modify the system of education. May we know your ideas on education and how it can be imparted?

KRISHNAMURTI: This is a complex subject, and to spend a few minutes in trying to understand the problem seems quite absurd, for its implications are vast. There is great joy in perceiving things clearly. Let us not become entangled and confused with the notions and ideas of others, whether it be the governments, the specialists, or the learned.

What has happened to the world after centuries of so-called education? There have been wars, destruction, and misery; two most catastrophic wars have almost destroyed the structure man has built through his education. We see education has failed, as it has produced the most dreadful destruction and misery that the world has ever known. The state, the government, are now controlling education; thus they will be assured of what you think, for if you were taught how to think, then you would become a danger to the government, to the state. When the state controls or guides education, there must be regimentation to produce efficiency, and as the modern world demands machines, not human beings, technical efficiency is essential. This is what is happening in the world, is it not? Education has been controlled by religious organizations, by priests, and now it is the government, the state. The result of this education has been disasters and misery for man, and the exploitation of man. Exploitation of man by organization, religion, or by the state is still exploitation and sorrow for man. Man being stronger than the system, he eventually breaks it up but unfortunately falls into another system. There is no hope for man as long as education is in the hands of the priests, or of the government, or it is in the hands of those who use education as a means of exploiting man for their party or for their profit.

What is the purpose of education, what is the purpose of living? If this is not clear, education has no significance. Education cannot be divorced from life, which is a total process. Does education vary from period to period, depending on the environment, the religious or the industrial? Is education mere adjustment to the immediate demands of environment? If it is, then the job is far more important than man himself, then the machine, the system, is far more significant than man himself. And this is what is happening in the world at the present time. If the significance of man himself is not understood, then education will have no meaning at all; then man will be a thing used by the state, by the religion, by the party for a system and so on. If you do not know what is the purpose of existence, of life, then why bother how you are educated? If you do not know what is your significance, then you become cannon fodder or a target for atomic bombs. If that is the end purpose of man, then we must make ourselves extremely efficient to kill each other. There are more armies than ever before, more money spent on armaments and new ways of destruction than ever before, and there are more technicians and sergeants. Yet there is more education than before. The scientist is caught in his laboratory, the businessman in his markets, the addicts in their specializations, and neither they nor we are aware of the significance of life.

What is the significance of existence? What is the purpose of this strife and confusion, of this misery and ache? If we do not know that, then education has very little meaning. The purpose of existence is to be free from strife and sorrow, to be free so that the real, the eternal, can be, to be free so that there can be happiness. He who is happy ceases to do mischief in the world; he who loves ceases to possess, to divide. A happy man, who loves and has peace in his heart, is free from all systems, political and religious; he is not the cause of misery and exploitation. To find reality there must be freedom from conditioned thinking and responses, freedom from craving which conditions thought and feeling. Does freedom come through any system of education, either of the left or of the right? Can parents, the environment, give freedom? No systems can free thought; a system by its very nature is binding. The means creates the end, a thought trained in a system is not free. Environment, the parent, the teacher, are extraordinarily important; the educator must be educated. If the educator is confused, narrow, stupid, bound by superstitions, ancient or modern, then he will shape the thought of the child according to the pattern of his stupidity. So the education of the educator is far more important than the education of the child. Does the educator seek self-knowledge from which comes right thinking, which alone can bring about a revolution in values? Almost all the parents and educators do not desire the revolution in values based on right thinking; they seek security, they desire the continuance of things as they are, with certain vague modifications. It is much more difficult to educate the educator than the child, for the educator has already grown stupid. He is confused, he seeks systems as a means of educating the child, and he is driven from one system to another; he will not find the best system, for he is the educator, not the system. If he is confused and ignorant, without self-knowledge, he is incapable of cultivating intelligence in another. The child is the result of his parents; he is the product of the past in conjunction with the present. The idea that given freedom, the child will develop naturally, intelligently, seems fallacious, as after all, the child is not wholly free from conditioned responses. How can the educator awaken intelligence in the child, if the educator himself is ignorant of his conditioning?

Most of us have no love for our children, though we use that word frequently. Without love, can you understand another? Without love, can you educate another? Without love, the system becomes all-important, which turns out machines, not human beings. Love is immediate communion and understanding on the same level, at the same time, and because hearts are withered, we turn to systems, governmental or religious, as a means of freeing thought and awakening intelligence. Because we do not love, the educator, the environment become all-important, and as the educator is like us, he too has no love and so he depends on systems, on the mere cultivation of the intellect.

Is not negative thinking the highest form of comprehension? Wisdom is not the positive acquisition of knowledge, nor the accumulation of facts. Wisdom comes with self-knowledge, and without self-knowledge there is no right thinking. Systems and blueprints of education cannot solve the conflict and misery of man. The love of systems destroys love, and without love there can be no right thinking; there can be no creation. The efficacy and the efficiency of love is greater than the efficiency of the machine.

Question: The traditional method of reaching the adepts or the Masters by training given by man, or through their disciples, is still said to be open to humanity. Are your teachings intended for those who are on that path?

KRISHNAMURTI: There is no path to reality. Reality is not to be found through any path; it is to be found through the uncharted sea of self-knowledge; the immeasurable is not to be measured by the path of the known.

What is known is not the true. What is known is caught in the net of time. A path can only lead to the known. The path to your house, to your village, you know—for you know your abode, your destination. But to the immeasurable there is no path, for the real is not to be formulated, and if it is formed, it ceases to be the real. What you have learned from books regarding truth is not the true. A truth that is repeated ceases to be true. It is only a lie that can be repeated, not truth.

You say that all paths lead to truth, but is that so? Do the path of the ignorant and the path of the man of ill will lead to truth? He must abandon ignorance and ill will to find truth.

A man who is concerned with murder in the name of the state—can he find truth unless he abandons his trade? A man who is addicted to knowledge—can he find truth? Must he not put aside his addiction to find it? A man of division will not find truth. All paths do not lead to truth. The part will not lead to the whole. Will the man of action uncover reality? He will not, for his approach is incomplete. Knowledge, devotion, and action, as three separate paths, cannot lead to truth, but only to illusion, destruction, and to restlessness. The very search for reality demands self-knowledge, devotion, and action. The man of mere action can never uncover truth, nor the man of mere devotion, nor the man who is merely pursuing knowledge. The men of action, of devotion, of knowledge, are not free, for their various activities are self-created and so binding; remove the object of their action and they are lost, a devotee is lost without the object of his devotion.

Wisdom does not come along any path; no Master or his pupil can give you wisdom, happiness. The very division of a Master and a disciple is a source of ignorance and conflict. The special few and their path is vanity, and they pay the price for their security. It is the immature that feel that they are the chosen, that cling to their way, to their action. The mature, the integrated, can come to enlightenment. A man who is committed to a particular action, to a way of life, will not be able to receive the eternal, for the part is ever committed to time.

Through misery you can never find happiness; misery must be understood and so set aside for happiness to be. For love to be, there must be no contention and confusion. Where there is darkness, there is no light, and light is when darkness is not. Love is when there are no possessions, when there is no condemnation, no self-fulfillment. You must become a beggar once again, as you were when you began your search. Do not get entangled in any path, nor lost in any organization. To a man who is earnest in his search after truth, the search itself is action, devotion, and knowledge. Through a crack in the wall, you do not see the whole, clear sky; you must be in the open to behold its beauty. There is hope for him who, abandoning all paths, seeks reality.

Question: What profession would you advise me to take?

KRISHNAMURTI: One thought is related to another, and no question, no problem is isolated. To understand this question, right thinking is necessary, and there is no right thinking without self-knowledge. Every action, every feeling and thought is interrelated; to think out one thought completely is to feel out, think out, all thought. What is happening here at present? Can you choose the profession you like? You take what you can get and you are lucky if you can get one. Since we have lost all values save one, the sensate, there is utter confusion in the world. You go through difficult studies to become an automaton in an office; the structure of society is built on mutual destruction. The society is geared to destroy; all professions contribute to war. A society is degenerate when the soldier, the policeman, the lawyer, are in abundance. A soldier's job is to kill, and his very existence is a continuation of war. Can you choose such a profession? The policeman's lot is not happy; he is there to spy, to report, to watch, to intrigue. Can you choose such a profession? The lawyer, a cunning man without substance, by his cleverness sustains division, flourishes in conflict; he becomes the politician, capable in dealing with superficialities. The politician can never bring peace to the world. Can you choose such a profession? Can you choose these professions that live and thrive on disunity and on suffering? They do not live on kindness and love, but on human stupidity, greed, and ill will. Can you join with him who is gathering wealth through exploitation, through cupidity, through ignorance? So you see how limited our choice is. A doctor, a technician, an artist—they too have their troubles, their misery.

Right thinking alone can bring about a good society whose activities will not be harmful to man. There cannot be right thinking without self-knowledge. Are you willing to spend time to know yourself, to think rightly, which will create a new society? Those of you who are not caught in the immediate task of seeking a job can do something, those of you who have leisure can cultivate right thinking, and so bring about a good society. This responsibility lies on such people. But those who can do not search out right thinking. Right thinking alone can bring about right action; self-knowledge yields right thinking.

November 16, 1947

Sixth Talk in Madras

There is an art in listening. Most of us are accustomed to translate what is being said or interpret it according to our conditioning, background, tradition, and so on. Is it not possible to listen to what is being said as though we were listening to music, to a song? Are you interpreting music when you are listening to it? You are listening to the silence between two notes; you are attentive yet sufficiently relaxed, sufficiently focused to follow the swift movement of music.

Right communion exists only when there is love; there is understanding at the same time, on the same level, without translation and interpretation, when there is love; it is rare to find such complete understanding, for such love is equally rare. But we meet on different levels, at different times, and so communication becomes extremely difficult. Here, what we are trying to do is not only to listen rightly, but also to be creative. To listen not merely to the words, but, without denying, to experiment with what is being said as though you were following alertly and yet silently. But we do not know how to listen, how to observe the new, and what we hear we put in the old forms. We put new wine in old bottles, and the old bottles burst. By putting the new into old terminologies, the flavor of the new is destroyed. We do not approach experiences anew; we come to it with the burden of the past, which only strengthens the past. Love is ever new, ever renewing itself. There is a renewal, a newness for a man of understanding, for he is not caught in a pattern of thought, in interpretation. It would be greatly worthwhile if we could listen with that peculiar quality of creative attention, meeting the new without the burden of the past. As I said, a truth that is repeated ceases to be the truth; if you merely hear it, it is a repetition and so ceases to be the truth, even though you guide it along the familiar channels of thought. If you listen with creative understanding, which is not interpretation, then it is truth which you understand, and it is truth that gives freedom, that gives happiness. We shall miss that happiness, that creative joy, if we translate the new according to old formulas. There can be happiness only when the mind is capable of receiving the new; as the mind is the result of the past, it is extremely arduous to be rid of the old. You must have listened to the song of the bird at early dawn; it is new, incomparable, lovely; your mind is fresh, untroubled by the day's activities, and so is capable of receiving the new, though the song is as old as the hills.

Please listen to what is being said as though you were hearing it for the first time, and you will perceive a curious thing taking place in you; happiness is not something that is old, but it is a constant renewal of itself.

As I said last week, when happiness is sought through a thing made by the hand or by the mind, the thing itself becomes far more important than happiness; happiness then is merely gratification, which is always impermanent. There is happiness when the process of becoming happy is understood, which is what each one is trying to do—to become happy. We are trying to become clever, to become happy, to become virtuous. If we can understand being and becoming, which are two different states, then perhaps we will be aware of happiness. Being and becoming are two wholly different states. Becoming is continuous, and that which is continuous is always binding. Relationship is binding if it is merely continuous; what is continuous is repetitive, a mere habit. When it ceases to be continuous, there is a new quality in relationship. If you go into it, there will be seen that where there is continuity, a becoming, thought moving from one continuity to another, there is always bondage and pain. Without understanding continuity, there is no being. You never say to yourself, "I will become happy." Being can only be understood when becoming ceases.

Virtue gives freedom. Have you not observed the unvirtuous? How stupid he is, how miserable, how he is caught in the net of his own making. He is happy who is virtuous, and he is free; he is not becoming, but is. There can be freedom only in virtue; it gives order, it brings clarity and freedom from strife. But a man who is not virtuous is disorderly, confused, and in conflict. Virtue is not an end in itself, but its yield is freedom, in which alone reality can take

place. But when virtue is used as a means of becoming, then virtue ceases. Being and becoming virtuous are two wholly different states. Virtue is understanding, but becoming virtuous is to continue in ignorance. That which you understand brings freedom; that which you do not brings conflict, confusion, antagonism. When you understand, then there is virtue. Does understanding come by effort, or must there be a state in which effort has ceased for understanding to be? If I desire to understand what you are saying, must I make an effort to listen? Effort exists when there are distractions; distractions are more interesting than listening to you. Not being interested in what you are saying, I have to make an effort not to be distracted in order to listen to you. Where there is earnestness there is communion, communication without effort. Effort is distraction. Now you are listening to me without effort; when you make effort you cease to understand. When you see a painting do you make an effort to understand? You have to make an effort to criticize it, to compare it, to find out who painted it. But if you want to understand it, you sit quietly with it; in that quietness, without distraction, you understand its permeating beauty. So virtue is where there is no effort to become. But since our whole existence is based on effort, we must discover its true significance, the incessant conflict to become. Consciously or unconsciously, we are occupied always with becoming and its joys and pains. Is this striving inevitable, and what for? What do we mean by making an effort? Does it not mean to become something other than *what is?* Being stupid, I strive to become clever. Can stupidity ever become intelligence, or must stupidity cease for intelligence to be? If we can understand this question, then we shall understand the significance of making effort, of striving.

We are afraid to face *what is;* we are afraid to understand *what is,* and so we are ever striving to transform, modify, or change *what is*. A rose is not striving to be other than what it is; in this very being there is creation. It has no other conflict than the natural struggle to live. With us there is not only the natural struggle to live—food, clothes and shelter—but there is constant effort to transform *what is*. In understanding *what is,* there is creation. To understand *what is* is very arduous, for thought is distracting itself from *what is;* it is ever transforming *what is* into something. Religion and education are based on this idea that *what is* must be changed, modified. You are this and you must become that; you are greedy and you must become nongreedy, and so strive, strain, and struggle. To understand *what is* needs no striving. Greed ceases only when you understand it, and not when you strive to become nongreedy. But to understand *what is,* greed, you must give your whole undivided attention, be significantly aware of its extensional value. There is no understanding of *what is* if you are concerned with distraction, which is the transformation of *what is*. Greed can never become nongreedy; only when greed ceases is there virtue; stupidity can never become intelligence. Only when stupidity is recognized as stupidity is there the beginning of intelligence, but to strive after intelligence is to be still stupid.

Is effort necessary to understand *what is?* Effort is distraction, distraction from *what is*. As our tendency, spiritually and socially, is based on the transformation of *what is,* this desire to change has in itself become a distraction; we spend our energies in this transformation, which requires effort. We do not understand *what is,* and yet we are attempting to change *what is* through discipline, through compulsion, and so on. How can you transform *what is* without understanding it? To understand *what is* there must be no condemnation, no justification, no suppression or distortion. Suppression and control do not

bring understanding; suppression and discipline are a distraction from *what is*. If we spent the distracting energy of changing *what is* in understanding *what is,* we would find there is a radical transformation of *what is*. Understanding comes only when there is no strife, no distraction; only when there is quietness, only when there is no striving to be other than *what is*.

Question: What is the difference between introspection and awareness?

KRISHNAMURTI: There is introspection when there is the action of the self to change itself, to modify itself, to transform itself. In this process there is always condemnation, justification, identification. I am greedy, which is wrong, and I must become non-greedy; I am angry but I must become peaceful. Introspection is a tyrannical process, leading nowhere. There is a continuity in introspection which becomes a bondage, an impediment to understanding. Every experience is translated according to the pattern of the self, which is ever examining, analyzing, interpreting, putting aside those things which are painful and guarding those which are pleasurable. Introspection is a constant struggle to change *what is*.

Awareness is the complete recognition of *what is* and so the understanding of *what is*. There is no understanding when there is condemnation; there is understanding with passive awareness, with silent observation, then *what is* begins to unfold itself. What is the response of a man of introspection when he is conscious of greed? Either of condemnation or of identification; if it is painful he attempts to change it, and if it is pleasurable, he pursues it. The response is one of justification or of condemnation; he is ever translating *what is* in terms of becoming. In the strife of becoming and not becoming we are confused and weary. The introspective action is residual; the action springs always from the residue, the memory of yesterday. In the man of awareness there is no residual response. He is simply aware; he is not translating, neither condemning nor identifying, and so his responses are nonresidual, spontaneous.

There is a vast difference between residual response and awareness; the one is ever becoming, and so constant strife and pain, and the other is being aware of *what is,* and so understanding it goes above and beyond *what is.* The man of introspection can never transcend the object of his examination. If you go deeply into awareness, you will perceive the creative quality of being aware and the destructive quality of introspection. A man of introspection is concerned with changing *what is* and so can never be creative; he is concerned with his self-improvement and so can never be free. He is only moving within the walls of his own desires and so can never find reality. Reality will shun him, for he is caught in the net of becoming, becoming righteous. A respectable man, a righteous man, is a curse, which does not mean that the sinner is not also a curse. There is a possibility in the sinner to see, feel more, but the man enclosed in his own respectability can never perceive beyond his own walls. A man of awareness understands directly *what is,* and in its understanding there is instant transformation. This understanding is creation.

Question: Do you believe in immortality?

KRISHNAMURTI: What do you mean by belief, why do you believe, and what is there to believe? Do you believe that you are alive, that you see? Does not belief come into being when you are confused and anxious and so give you a sense of well-being, of security? Belief, then, is other than *what is* and a man who is aware of *what is* has no

need for belief, never believes. Belief is based on authority, inner or outer, as it gives him security, physical or psychological. A man who is secure, inwardly or outwardly, can never find the real. Only the man who is inquiring, uncertain, searching, neither accepting nor denying, can find truth. A man who is at ease, secure in his belief, is lost in credulity, in obstinacy; he is not only a prisoner to his belief, which destroys creative thinking, but also he is ever fearful and unhappy.

What do we mean by immortality? We will perhaps gather its significance if we understand what is continuity. If we can understand death, then perhaps we shall be able to perceive the meaning of immortality. If we can understand ending, then the immortal, the imperishable is. Death is the unknown; as reality, the imperishable, is the unknown, so is death. You have given your thought from time immemorial to the understanding of God; volumes have been written upon it, and yet you have avoided death. Why is it? Death, the unknown, you have shunned and put away, and God you have pursued; every temple has an image or an inscription, and you have given life to things made by the hand or by the mind. Why have you pursued God, the unknown? Do you know Him? If you did, it would be a different world, there would be love and goodness. Why do you accept the one, God, and shun the other, death? The one you shun, for you fear the ending of continuity; and you pursue the other for you crave continuity, permanency. You invest in God for the sake of permanency, not knowing what you are investing in. Is this not very odd? And after investing, you ask if there is immortality, for you desire a further guarantee; and you are gratified with him who gives you this assurance.

Surely, the problem is not if there is or if there is not immortality. If I tell you there is, will that assertion transform your life now?

No. If I tell you that there is no immortality, you will go to another until you find comforting assurance. You are caught between the believer and the nonbeliever, which causes pain. To understand the anxious fear of death, you must find out why there is an unbridgeable division between life and death, and why you pursue ceaselessly, generation after generation, what you call God, not knowing Him. Has there been a sacred book dealing with death? Yet there have been and will be book after book on what is called God. What reality is, is one thing, but if you know it as an idea, as a speculation, then it is another, then it is not the real. The unknown cannot be measured by words. The word is not the thing; the real cannot be told to him who is not aware of it. There is immediate communion between those who love. You may write poems concerning love, but you cannot communicate with another if he does not know love.

It is futile to inquire if there is God, but you will discover if there is or if there is not if you search it out. So you will find out the significance of death if you diligently and rightly search. You seek continuity through property, through name, family, and through belief and ideation. So long as you are assured of self-continuity, there is no fear. The man who is seeking psychological continuity invests in property, and finding its impermanency, he seeks it in other forms, in race, in nation, in organization, in activity, in love, and if that is denied, he seeks it in a temple, in church, and ultimately in what he calls God, and that is threatened also by death, the unknown. So you are not really concerned with reality, with God, with death, but with continuity, calling it by a lovely word, immortality. You desire only continuity in some form or another. What happens to anything that continues? It decays, it rots; it is caught in mere function, in routine, in habit. Continuance is an assurance of decay. When

there is no fear, which comes only with the understanding of continuity, then only does the division between life and death cease.

Reality and death are the unknown, and a mind that has its being in the known can never understand the unknown. The known is ever the continuous. The mind clings to the known and gives life to the known, to memory; it is ever active in the house of the known and in that it craves to continue. That which is known is already in the net of time. Only when the mind frees itself from the net of time, is the eternal, the timeless. He who desires continuity is in constant fear of life and death, and the escapes that civilization has bred to pacify his fears have drugged him, made him dull; he is incapable of seeing the immense significance of death. Death is as rich as life, as the real; both are the unknown, and a mind that is caught in the known can never understand the imperishable, the immortal.

Question: Please explain further what you mean by the clarification of the conscious.

KRISHNAMURTI: Last Sunday I said that the superficial layers of consciousness must clarify themselves, free themselves from their entangling problems so that the hidden motives and pursuits, hopes and fears, can be perceived and understood. To understand the immediate, mind must be calm. If you have a problem, you worry over it as a dog worries over a bone; thinking about it, anxious to find a solution, you go to bed with it, worn out by the struggle. When you sleep your conscious mind is relaxed, quiet, and when you wake up the solution to the problem is often perceived. The conscious mind, having thought over the problem, has become calm, has detached itself from it, and so the deeper depths of consciousness can give the significance of the problem. The conscious mind, the upper layers of consciousness, must free themselves from problems, so that they are always tranquil, so that they can receive the hints, the intimations of the hidden. The conscious layers are restless, creating problem after problem, moving from one response to another, from one desire to another, from one distraction to another. Have you not noticed that the superficial layers of the mind are never still, their noisy activity overpowering all other action? They are ever battling and striving, cunning and alert in affairs and in the temple. How can such a mind receive anything? A drawer is useful only when it is empty. The conscious mind that is not empty is a useless mind, it is no good for anything save for modern civilization, which is so degenerate and dark, as this civilization is the product of the upper layers of consciousness. The upper layers of consciousness are mechanical, swift, and cunning, ever safeguarding themselves.

How does one bring about tranquillity in the superficial layers of consciousness? This is an inevitable response, but is it not a wrong question? Is this not a question put by the conscious mind, and so is it not still an activity of the immediate mind? The very action to clarify itself is still an activity of the conscious mind, is it not? And so the conscious mind is still active, only in another direction. What is important, then, is to be aware of *what is,* of the actual restless activity of this superficial mind; to be aware of it without denying it or justifying it; to be aware of its cunning substitutions, its distractions, its cunning. By being, not becoming, aware of the superficial layers of consciousness, there comes tranquillity. The very awareness brings about understanding so long as there is no condemnation or justification. The mind, being aware of its own activities, brings about calmness. Be aware, simply aware, of a habit, and there will be the understanding and the ending of the habit. The mind is extremely active, and that

which is fast cannot be understood unless it is slowed down; for the mind to slow itself down is very arduous. It can be done if every thought and feeling is thought out, felt out completely. To think out, feel out fully, there must not be any identification or condemnation.

Question: You have realized reality. Can you tell us what God is?

KRISHNAMURTI: How do you know, if I may ask, that I have realized? If you are aware that I have realized, then you also must have realized. To know is to be a partaker in knowledge. You also must experience to have an understanding of the experience. Besides, what does it matter if I have or have not realized? Is not what I am saying the truth? Even if I have not realized, as you call it, am I not speaking the truth? A man who worships another, even though he has realized, is worshipping for his gain, and so he will not find reality; he who worships those who have realized is giving himself over to authority, which is ever blinding, and so he will never find reality. It is not at all important, for the purposes of understanding, who has and who has not realized; though tradition says to the contrary. All that you can do is to keep company with good men, which is difficult for the good are rare. The good are those who are not after some personal gain, who are not seeking advantage, who neither possess nor are possessed. You idealize him who has realized in the hope of gain, which creates a false relationship, and communion is only possible where there is love. In all these talks and discussions, we do not love each other; you are on the defensive and so afraid, you want something from me—knowledge, an experience, and so on—which indicates that there is no love. The desire to gain breeds authority, which is not only blinding but becomes the means of exploitation. Where there is love there is understanding; where there is love it is of little significance who has or who has not realized.

Since your heart has withered, God, the idea, has become all-important. You want to know God as you have lost the song in your heart, and you pursue the singer. Can the singer give you the song of your heart? He may teach you how to sing but he cannot give you the song. You may know the steps of a dance, but if there is no dance in your heart, you move mechanically. You do not know love if you are pursuing a gain, if you are searching out a result, an achievement. A man who loves has no ideal, but the man who has an ideal or the desire to achieve an ideal has no love. Beauty is not an ideal, an achievement; it is the reality of the now, not of tomorrow. Love understands the unknown; then the supreme is. But concerning it there is no word, for no word can measure it. Love is its own eternity. Without love, there is no happiness; if there were love, you would not seek happiness in things, in family, in ideals, and then these things would have their right value. Because we do not love, you seek happiness in God. It is an investment in God, in the hope of happy returns. You want me to tell you what reality is. Can the immeasurable be measured by words? Can you catch the wind in your fist? If you formulate that which is the real, is that the real? When the unknown is translated into the known, it ceases to be the eternal. Yet you hunger after it. You crave to know for the continuance of yourself. You do not allow yourself to be aware of *what is*—the turmoil, the strife, the pain, the degradation—but long to escape from *what is*. Why do you not give your whole attention to *what is,* be aware of it, without condemnation or identification? In understanding the knowable, there comes tranquillity, not induced or enforced, but that silence which is creative emptiness in which

alone reality can come into being. The becoming is incapable of receiving the real. In understanding *what is,* there is being. Then reality is not in the distance, the unknown is not far off, it is in *what is.* As the answer is in the problem, the reality is in *what is.* In the awareness of *what is,* there is truth, and it is truth that liberates, and not your striving to be free. Reality is not far, but we give it distance as a means of self-continuity. The timeless is the now, and it cannot be understood by him who is caught in the net of time. Meditation is for thought to free itself from time. Complete action, and not continuous action, is meditation. When the mind understands the process of continuity, memory—memory which is not only the factual but the psychological—there comes into being creative freedom. In continuity there is death, and in ending there is renewal.

November 23, 1947

Seventh Talk in Madras

Must we not understand the relationship between yourself and myself? Is not the relationship of the teacher and the disciple false? The acquisition of knowledge, of technique, establishes a different relationship between the knower and the learner—and is that our relationship? Are you actually learning anything from me? Are we not understanding together the everyday existence in which there is so much pain, strife, and misery? Apart from technical knowledge, do we learn anything? Does not understanding come when there is passive awareness, freedom? Is understanding the result of accumulation? Does understanding come through knowledge, through books? It is important to establish right communication, which is right relationship between yourself and myself. When you approach me with the desire to gain, communication between us ceases. You show respect to me, and does that indicate understanding? Towards your wives, servants, neighbors there is generally indifference, callousness, and disrespect. You show respect to him from whom you expect a gain, a gratification, and to others you are hard and indifferent.

Is mere learning the whole of existence? What have we to learn and is there anything to learn? Do we not lose love if we treat life as a school in which we learn? Then existence is painful, and sorrowful. If we can understand the significance of existence from moment to moment, then there will be joy, happiness. But if you are out merely to learn, to accumulate, through which accumulation you interpret further experience, then life becomes a tragedy, a darkness. To verbally comprehend what I say and use the verbal structure as a pattern for thought will not bring about understanding. Understanding exists where there is no effort. Understanding comes in freedom and it is not born of accumulation, of knowledge. Life is swift and painful, and to understand its significance, effort must be comprehended. We are not happy people; look at the strain, the confusion and the sorrow we go through. There is never a moment of deep, abiding happiness. We are in constant battle within ourselves and so with our neighbors. We will understand the significance of life if we understand the meaning of effort. Does happiness come through effort? Have you made an effort to be happy? Joy does not come through effort nor through suppression, control, or through indulgence. Our life is a long, drawn out strife with regretful indulgences; a constant overcoming with ensuing dullness; passions, envy, and stupidity are consuming our life. Do love and understanding come by strife, by effort? Obviously not, but we do not seem to realize this, and yet we are struggling through every means to be happy, to have understanding. Is there

creation through effort? There is creation only with the cessation of effort. There is creation only when there is no effort, when there is complete integration of all the levels of consciousness; then there is joy, then there is a song in one's heart. There is struggle in expression but not in creation. The moment of creation is not born of strife.

We must understand the problem of striving. If we can understand the significance of effort, then we can translate it into action in our daily life. Does not effort mean a struggle to change *what is* into what it is not, or what it should be, or what it should become? We are constantly escaping from *what is,* to transform or modify it. He who is truly content is he who understands *what is,* who gives the right significance to *what is.* True contentment lies not in little or much possession, but in understanding the whole significance of *what is.* Only in passive awareness is the meaning of *what is* understood. I am not, at the moment, talking of the physical struggle with the earth, with construction or a technical problem, but of psychological striving. The psychological struggles and problems always overshadow the physiological. You may build a careful social structure, but as long as the psychological darkness and strife are not understood, they invariably overturn the carefully built structure.

Effort is distraction from *what is.* In the acceptance of *what is,* striving ceases. There is no acceptance when there is the desire to transform or modify *what is.* Striving, an indication of distraction, must exist so long as there is a desire to change *what is.* The various methods of overcoming anger have not appeased anger, but if instead of making effort to transform anger into nonanger there were alert and passive awareness, or acknowledgement of *what is,* then what would happen? If you were aware that you were angry, then what would happen? Would you indulge in anger? If you were aware that you were angry, aware of *what is,* knowing the folly of the transforming of *what is* into what it is not, would there be still anger? If there is choiceless awareness of anger, complete awareness in which there is no condemnation, justification, or identification, then you will find there is an instantaneous cessation of anger. To be so aware is extremely arduous because our tendency is to modify or deny.

Virtue is not the denial of vice. There is virtue when effort to become has ceased. Maturity or integration comes with complete awareness of *what is.* The awareness of vice is the beginning of virtue. When there is an awareness of anger, anger ceases. Experiment with this awareness and you will discover its efficacy. In being aware of *what is,* there is creative freedom. There can be no freedom without virtue. The stupid man is the unvirtuous man; he is disorderly. By his actions he brings misery upon himself and upon society; because he is stupid he is caught in belief, in deceit, in ill will. Virtue demands the highest form of intelligence. To bring order within oneself requires self-knowledge, not mere conformity nor suppression. When you are aware of the false as the false, there is freedom and understanding, for the truth of the false is perceived. Freedom can be approached only negatively. Virtue lies in understanding, not in becoming virtuous. The process of becoming leads to confusion and misery, for virtue is in being and not in becoming. The I-will-be is an indication of stupidity, for in it is implied a process of becoming, which is to be unvirtuous. Understanding is now and not in the hereafter. Anger cannot be transformed into nonanger, anger ever remains as anger. If there is choiceless awareness of anger—that is being aware of anger without condemnation, justification, or identification—then anger falls away, without effort. Only when there is no awareness of exactly *what is,* then effort to transform takes place. So effort is nonawareness. Awareness reveals the significance of *what is,* and the complete acceptance of the significance brings freedom. So awareness is noneffort; awareness is the perception of *what is* without distortion. Distortion exists whenever there is effort.

As I said, there will be no right answer if the questioner himself is not earnest. To find the right answer to a question, the problem must be studied, and not look for an answer. Life is not a matter of conclusions with ready-made answers of yes and no. Life is a series of challenges and responses, and to understand these challenges and responses, there must be self-knowledge, the awareness of your everyday thoughts, feelings, and actions. You must begin near to go far; you must go through the valley to climb high. Self-knowledge is the beginning of an awareness of everyday thought, feeling, and action, and not the search of the self beyond the mind and its realization. The answers which I give to the many questions are meant to reveal the process of your own thinking and feeling. They are not conclusions for the purpose of guidance. For that which is a conviction, a conclusion, is not the truth.

Question: I am very seriously disturbed by the sexual urge. How am I to overcome it?

KRISHNAMURTI: Let us understand this process of overcoming. In overcoming there is no understanding; what you overcome has to be conquered again and again, like a physical enemy. Overcoming is another form of suppression, and what is suppressed or controlled will come up again in another form. Conquering one country by another is a futile and endless process. Overcoming is a difficult and tedious process, a stupid activity; understanding demands careful and right observation, a tentative approach, intelligence. The thoughtless is always overcoming. The struggle to overcome is real folly, which does not imply indulgence, the opposite which is equally foolish. The problem has to be understood and not to be suppressed or overcome. What has been overcome appears again and again in different ways.

You will have understanding of the problem only when you are not lost in overcoming it, justifying it, or identifying with it; you will have an understanding of the problem only when the problem itself is all-important. By being aware of the problem, it yields its significance. You must accept the problem to understand it. Creativeness is involved in this problem of the questioner. All our thoughts and feelings are uncreative, so sex as pleasure becomes a problem. Pleasures have become sensate and mechanical, and so the sexual urge, in which there is self-forgetfulness and so creative joy, becomes a consuming problem. There is creative joy when the activities of the self are absent. All activities of the self breed boredom and misery. The so-called religious activity of the self has become thoughtless and miserable, mechanical, a vain repetition; authority blinds you; fear cripples you; rituals are vain repetition, a release for sentimentalism. The worship of the image, the inscription, or the idea is uncreative, for it is one of the subtle forms of activities of the self, this self-projected identification. The reading of sacred books and the repetition of words only dulls thought and feeling, which is another form of escape. Joy, happiness which comes with virtue and freedom is the highest form of intelligence, but that is denied with the desire to gain, with belief, with authority, with imitation. Religion is virtue which yields freedom, and only in freedom can the real come into being. The following of authority, going to temples, churches, repeating mantras, chants, attending upon the priest is not religion. In thought and feeling you are starved. Your minds are made dull by conformity, and your hearts are dry by conflict of passion, ill will, and sensate desires. Machines are not creative, habit only dulls the mind and heart. Repetition destroys clarity, the power to think, to feel, to understand.

Education, business, the gathering of money, the tedious routine of office work, the thoughtless entertainments, and so on have destroyed joy and happiness. You are hedged around by stupid society, by uncreative thought, by distorting emotionalism, and what then do you expect? Sexual urge then becomes the all-consuming problem. If you understand what it means to be creative, religiously and emotionally, when you love and when you cry, then sex becomes a secondary problem. When the secondary problems assume primary importance, then conflict, confusion, and misery set in. Passion, though religion and law have forbidden it, has not been understood.

Through strife and regimentation you have lost love. Love is chaste. Without love, to overcome the sexual urge or to indulge in it has no meaning. You and your society are the results of the lack of love, the degradation, the exploitation, the ruthlessness, the wars. How immature, how unformed you are. Passion begets children; possession and jealousy dominate, and what kind of civilization do you expect from such responses? You are told to find God, you must be a *bramacharya*, a celibate. Can you find God without love? That which you achieve through an act of will, through conforming to an ideal, through following a belief, a conclusion, will not lead you to the real. The way to the real lies through self-knowledge, which brings understanding, and not through suppression or indulgence, nor through substitution and distortion. With love is chastity; but to become chaste, the action of craving and self-continuity, is to be ugly, vicious, and immature. We do not know love; your life is a series of aspirations for an ideal or objective position, the continuance of yourself through property, family, or through the ideal. Without love, existence has no significance. Suppression of passion does not solve the problem of existence, the sex passion or the passion to become. You may suppress the sexual urge, but if you are ambitious, that passion becomes another dominating problem which is equally brutal, vicious, and ugly. But to a man who loves, passion does not become a problem. You are caught in the net of habit, of imagination, and of yesterday's memory. Why are you held in it? Again, you are not creative, you do not love. Creation is constant renewal. That which was will never be. You hold to memory for in it there is excitement, stimulation. Inwardly you are starved and empty, fearful and isolated, and so repetition and recollection follow. Love is neither memory nor repetition; it is ever new and full. What is repeated becomes mechanical, without joy. The problem is not sex but creativeness. You are hedged about with anxiety, you are caught in the search for security, physical as well as psychological; you are stimulated by the advertisements, by the cinemas, by the periodicals, and so on. Stimulation without creative release is very destructive. Politics are cunning deceptions, and the structure of society is based on violence, ruthlessness, envy. There must be an inward revolution which only right thinking can bring about. Only through self-knowledge can right thinking and creation come into being. Reality comes into being with the cessation of the self, with its power to accumulate self-enclosing memories. You are enclosed by your own craving and fears, memories and ideals, and the only self-forgetting release you have becomes in its turn an overwhelming problem. Do not condemn it, suppress it, or find substitutions for it, but be aware of it

and its deep and wide significance is soon revealed. Only then, as the full meaning of the problem is understood, does the problem lose its grip on the mind. Seeing the false as the false and the truth in the false is the beginning of wisdom. You cannot see the false if you are not aware of every thought, feeling, and action. Awareness is the door to love and it is love that purifies, that is chaste.

Question: What are your views about the implications of the belief in reincarnation?

KRISHNAMURTI: As a means towards self-knowledge, we will consider this question, but not to find any definite conclusion. Truth is not to be found in any conclusion, belief, conviction, or ideal.

Fear has been used by society to control man's activities. Man is threatened for his present activities by future reward and punishment. There are those who are not intimidated by future reward or punishment, but are immersed in their sensate activities, and there are few whose actions are shaped by this fear. For the present we are not considering either of these two actions, nor are we concerned with belief. Belief to a man who is seeking truth has no significance whatsoever, for belief is merely a source of comfort, security, a refuge, an anchorage. A man who is tethered to a belief can never discover or understand reality. A man who is seeking truth must set out on the uncharted sea, he has no haven, no ideal that can guide him. He must adventure and find.

In this question there are two fundamental issues involved—continuity and cause and effect. First, let us consider continuity. It is said that in each one there is a spiritual essence or entity which continues after the death of the body. You also feel this to be true as it gratifies your craving for continuity. You and I must find the truth of this so please do not be on the defensive nor condemn this idea. Truth is not found either through condemnation or through identification. To accept authority is to be blind, and authority of any kind, inner or outer, never gives clarity and understanding. So do not accept what the sacred books assert or cling to your own feeling, for what you feel—the so-called intuition—is the outcome of your desire for security. Now is there a spiritual essence, a spiritual entity in you apart from the transitory? Spiritual essence must be of the timeless, must it not? So it must be, then, beyond and above birth and death, beyond the reach of time. If the spiritual entity is beyond time and space, as it must be, then it is out of your reach; you cannot think about it nor be concerned with its continuance or noncontinuance. As it is of no time and so not continuous, why then do you hold to it? Why then do you assert that there is or that there is not a spiritual, timeless entity? If it is eternal, then it could not be continuous. But to you it is of time, for you cling to it. If it is real, it is beyond your desire, beyond your grasp. What you know is not the true and you cling to it. You assert that this spiritual essence is the 'me'. Why? The 'me' is the continuous and so of time; then it cannot be the timeless, and yet you cling to it, calling it the eternal. This leads to illusion.

So you have to understand the problem of continuity and of death. What is it that continues? Memory, is it not? Thought in action leaves a residue, memory, and it is memory that continues. Memory as the 'me' and 'mine' continues through property, through family and name, and through idea, belief, physiological and psychological continuity. This continuity is threatened by death, and continuity is caught in another level of existence, in the ideational, in the soul, in the atma, in God. Now what is it that continues? You, that is, your thoughts, memories, your everyday experiences. The identified memories, my achievements, my qualities, my possessions are the 'me', and does this come to an end? You know you, the body, is going to die, but does the 'me', the identified memories, continue? So, the problem is not the discovery of the truth of reincarnation, but the craving to continue. What is the thing that you cling to so despairingly, so anxiously? Are they not your memories? You are your memories and let these memories cease and you cease. These accumulating memories have no substance in themselves, but the constant identifying remembrance gives vitality to them. The 'I remember' is the identifying process with the past. Thought, which is the result of the past, gives continuity through the present to the future. The habit of remembrance, the habit of accumulation, and so on, continues. What happens to that which is continuous? It soon becomes dull, it decays, it is noncreative. This is what is actually taking place in us and about us, in society. You cling to memory for it is very gratifying, comforting. Where there is gratification and its search, there must be continuity. Gratification soon ends, but it is sought again through other means, hoping for permanent gratification through belief and, ultimately, through God.

That which is continuous has no renewal. Only in ending is there renewal. What is continuous is not the immortal; what is continuous is ever in the shadow of death, with its inexhaustible fear. You cling to your memories and are living in death, in decay. Only in ending is there creation.

Then there is the question of cause and effect. Are cause and effect two separate processes, or are they interrelated? The effect is ever becoming the cause. There is never a moment of cause separate from effect. What was the cause has now become the effect. The time interval between cause and effect leads to illusion. Cause and effect are always together; the effect is where the cause is.

When you are aware of *what is,* the cause and effect are also perceived, from which arises transformation, not in the future but now. There is immediate transformation when there is an understanding of *what is.* There is a timeless change, not a change brought about through time. If you perceive the cause which is becoming effect and the effect becoming the cause, then there is immediate understanding and so the cessation of the cause. If you are aware of anger, there is instant perception of its cause and so its dissolution. This action frees thought from the illusion that understanding can come about through time. The cause is in the effect, as the end is in the means.

The believer and the nonbeliever are both caught in their belief, in their stupidities, and so are incapable of finding the true. In becoming aware of the problem itself, there is a beginning of self-knowledge. Self-knowledge is the beginning of wisdom. Seeing the false as the false, and the true in the false, and truth as the truth, is the highest intelligence.

Question: From your talks it seems clear that reason is the chief means of acquiring self-knowledge. Is this so?

KRISHNAMURTI: Can reason be separated from feeling? If it can be, then it ceases to be reason. You have separated it, and so developed the intellect, which prevents integration. The cultivation of the intellect is the cultivation of disharmony. The intellect can never solve any of our human problems, and yet modern civilization is the product of the intellect. To understand the problems which the intellect has bred, there must be reason which is not divorced from feeling. Any overemphasis of the intellect or of the emotion or of the senses prevents integration. Balance, inward order and clarity, can never be brought about by the intellect, and as we have cultivated it at the cost of everything else, we are paying for it through repeated disasters, such as wars, and through the conflict and misery of sensate values. The worship of the intellect is a sign of degeneration.

Reason can come into being only when there is integration, maturity. Reason must go beyond itself for reality to come into being. So long as there is thinking there cannot be the real, for thought is the product of the past; it is the outcome of time, the response of time, and it can never comprehend the timeless. Thinking must come to an end for the being of the timeless. The thinking process can be violated, disciplined, suppressed, but that will not bring understanding. The mind must be aware of itself, of its superficial and hidden activities. From this choiceless awareness there comes silence, stillness. When thought, which is the result of the past in conjunction with the present, is no longer creating, then there is a stillness, a silence which is not self-induced, not a self-hypnotized result. In this tranquillity creation comes into being. Thought must cease to create for creation to be.

Mere intellection has no relationship with reality; mere logical conclusions bar the door to reality. Happiness, ecstasy, is not the product of the intellect, but it comes into being with the creative breath of the real.

November 30, 1947

Eighth Talk in Madras

It would be an orderly and peaceful world if there were neither the teacher, the guru, nor the disciple. Have you ever considered why there must be a guru and a disciple? Why do you have to look to another for guidance, for enlightenment? The desire to gain, to acquire, breeds conflict and misery; this desire for profit, whether spiritual or in this world, breeds antagonism between man and man. If we can understand together this struggle for gain, we shall find peace, and the division between the teacher and the disciple will cease; the fear, called love and respect, between the master and pupil will disappear if we cease to think in terms of becoming.

Being caught in the process of becoming, of acquisition, and realizing its strife and pain, the desire to get out of it gives birth to the conflict of duality. Gain always engenders fear, and fear gives birth to the conflict of opposites—the overcoming of *what is* and transforming it into that which is desired. Does not an opposite contain the germ of its own opposite? Is virtue the opposite of vice? If it is, then it ceases to be virtue. If virtue is the opposite of vice, then virtue is the outcome of vice. Beauty is not the denial of the ugly. Virtue has no opposite. Greed can never become nongreed, any more than ignorance can become enlightenment. If enlightenment is the opposite of ignorance, then it is no longer enlightenment. Greed is still greed when it tries to become nongreed, for the becoming itself is greed. The conflict of the opposites is not the conflict of dissimilars, but of changing and opposing desires. Conflict exists only when *what is* is not understood. If we can understand *what is*, then there is no conflict of its opposite. *What is* can be understood only through choiceless awareness in which there is neither condemnation, justification, nor identification.

Question: You have often talked of relationship. What does it mean to you?

KRISHNAMURTI: There can be no existence in isolation. To be is to be related, and without relationship there is no existence. Relationship is challenge and response. The relationship of one with another is society; society is not independent of you; the mass is not a separate entity by itself, but is the product of you and your relationship with another, the group. Relationship is the awareness of interaction between you and another. Now what is this relationship based on? You say it is based on interdependence, mutual assistance, and so on, but apart from the emotional screen which we throw up against each other, what is it actually founded on? On mutual gratification, is it not? If I do not please you, you get rid of me in different ways, and if I please you, you accept me as your wife, your neighbor, or as your friend or guru. This is the actual fact, is it not? Relationship is sought where there is mutual gratification, satisfaction, and when you do not find it or it is not given to you, you change your relationship, you seek a divorce, or, putting up with *what is*, you try to find gratification elsewhere. You change your guru, your teacher, or join another organization. You move from one relationship to another until you find what you seek, which is gratification, security, comfort, and so on. When you seek gratification in relationship, there is always bound to be conflict. When in relationship security is sought, which is ever evasive, there is the struggle to possess, to dominate, and the pain of jealousy, of uncertainty. Self-assertive demands, possessiveness, the desire for psychological security and comfort, deny love. You may talk about love as responsibility, as duty, and so on, but actually there is no love, which can be seen in the structure of modern society. The manner in which you treat your husbands and wives, your children, neighbors, friends, is an indication of the lack of love in relationship.

What then is the significance of relationship? If you observe yourself in relationship, do you not find that it is a process of self-revelation? Does not your contact with another reveal, if you are aware, your own state of being? Relationship is a process of self-revelation, of self-knowledge. Since it reveals unpleasant, disquieting thoughts and actions, there is a flight from such relationship into a comforting and soothing one. Relationship becomes of very little significance when it is based on mutual gratification, but it becomes very significant when it is self-revealing.

Love has no relationship. It is only when the other becomes more important, then begins relationship of pleasure and pain. When you give yourself over utterly and wholly, when you love, then there is no relationship—relationship as mutual gratification or as a process of self-revelation. There is no gratification in love. Such love is a marvelous thing. In it there is no friction but a state of complete integration, of ecstatic being. There are such moments, such rare, happy, joyous moments when there is love, complete communion. Love recedes when the object of love becomes more important; then the conflict of possession, of fear, of jealousy begins and so love recedes, and the further it recedes, the greater the problem of relationship becomes, losing its worth, its meaning. Love cannot be brought into being through discipline, through any means, through any intellectual urgency. It is a state of being which comes when the activities of the self have ceased. These activities must not be disciplined away, suppressed, or shunned, but understood. There must be an awareness, and so an understanding, of the activities of the self, in all its different layers.

We do have these rare moments of love when there is no thought, no motive, and because they are rare, we cling to them ever hopefully, but this memory is a barrier to the living reality of love. To understand relationship it is important to be aware of what is actually taking place, in all its subtle forms, and this will bring about self-knowledge, it will reveal the activities of the self. Because you do not desire to be revealed to yourself—that you are seeking gratification and hiding yourself in comfort—relationship loses its significance, its depth, and its beauty. Love comes into being only when there is self-forgetfulness, that communion with reality.

Question: The Theosophical Society announced you to be the Messiah and World Teacher. Why did you leave the Society and renounce the Messiahship?

KRISHNAMURTI: Let us examine the question of organizations. There is rather a nice story of a man who was walking along a street and behind him two strangers were following. As he walked along, he saw something very bright, picked it up and put it in his pocket. The two strangers observed his action, and one said to the other, "This is a very bad business for you, isn't it?" The other, who was the Devil, replied, "No, though he picked up truth, I am going to help him organize it." Can truth be organized or through any organization can you find it? Must you not go beyond and above all organization and beliefs to discover truth? Why do these so-called spiritual organizations, churches, exist? They are built around beliefs, dogmas, and so on, are they not? Beliefs and organizations are ever separating people, keeping people apart, as the Hindu and Muslim, as the Buddhist and the Christian. Belief, in any form, political or religious, throws up a barrier between man and man, inevitably bringing conflict and misery. Though the adherents of organizations and beliefs talk of brotherhood and love, they are the very people who will encourage and connive at the destruction of others.

Are such organizations necessary? You understand what I mean by organizations? I am referring to the psychological, so-called spiritual, religious organizations. Are they necessary? They exist on the supposition that they will help man to realize truth or God or what you will. They exist for propagandistic purposes, for conversion, for increase of membership, and so on; you want to tell others what you think or what you have learned or what appears to be the true. And can truth be propagated? If truth is propagated it ceases to be the true. Truth is to be experienced not according to any belief or pattern, and if experience is organized it ceases to be the true, it becomes a lie, so a hindrance to reality. The real, the immeasurable, cannot be formulated, the unknown cannot be measured by the known. When you measure it, it ceases to be the true; it is a lie and only a lie can be propagated. Organizations that are supposed to be based on the search for the real, when they become propagandists' instruments, they cease to be of any significance; not only the organization to which the questioner refers, but all so-called spiritual organizations become the means of exploitation. Such organizations become like any other business corporation, with buildings, investments which become all-important. Truth is not to be found through any organization; truth comes into being when there is freedom. Belief in any form is the craving for security, and he who is seeking security cannot discover truth.

Whether I am a Messiah or not can be answered simply: I have never denied it and I do not think it matters very much what I think about it. What is important is to find out for yourself if my teachings are the truth. Do not judge by labels, do not give importance to the name; and whether I am the World Teacher, or the Messiah, or something else is of the least significance to you. If the name has become important, then you will miss the truth. One will assert that I am, and another that I am not, but your conflict, confusion, and sorrow are not solved by any of these assertions and denials. It is important, very important, to be earnest after the search of truth, for it gives freedom from strife and pain. The truth of my teachings can be discovered in your daily life, and truth is not distant but very near. The intellectual will not find it for he is caught in the net of his own knowledge which prevents his understanding; the man of devotion will not find it for he is caught in the confusion of his own image and emotion. He who is earnest will understand it.

Question: On two or three occasions during the course of the talks I have attended, I have become conscious, if I may venture to describe the experience, of standing in the presence of one vast void of utter silence and solitude for a fraction of a second. It feels as though I am at the entrance but dare not step into it. What feeling is this, please? Is it some hallucination, self-suggestion in the present stormy, turbulent conditions in which our daily life is passed?

KRISHNAMURTI: During these talks and discussions there have been moments when we felt deeply and understood profoundly, when we perceived for ourselves certain states of consciousness, and since we pushed it to a point of great understanding and depth, there was stillness and absolute silence. But when this immeasurable tranquillity is willed or induced, then it is the product of hallucination, of self-hypnosis; if you yourself, during the course of these discussions and discourses, have not been aware and pursued your own thoughts and feelings ever deeper, and understood them fully and so experienced directly for yourself, then the void of utter silence and solitude become fascinating escapes from the turmoil and pain of existence. There is always the danger of being influenced by another for good and for bad. The indication that you can be influenced is significant; if you can be influenced for the good, you can also be influenced for the bad. War, racial hatred, and so on are examples. The problem is not how to enter this silence, this creative state of being, but whether it has come into being through understanding or through persuasion and influence, through your own careful and wise search, or through craving. If this void of silence has come to you through your own understanding, then it has great significance; if it is merely intellectual or verbal, then it has no significance whatsoever. There is no intellectual understanding; there is understanding when the whole being is alert; there is no partial or intellectual understanding. You understand or you do not understand; partial understanding has no meaning.

Passive awareness brings about the cessation of conflict, and when the mind is no longer creating, there is tranquillity, utter silence. You cannot enter it if there is fear. It must come to you uninduced, uninvited; if you attempt to go to it, then you already know it, and what is known is not the real. If you strive after it, you have already formulated it and so it is not the real. Reality must come to you, you cannot go towards it. All great things come to you. Love must come but if you pursue it, it will ever evade. If you are open, undemanding, still, then it comes.

The question of influence is of significance. We desire to be influenced, we want to be encouraged, we crave for security in another. Being confused, we seek the sanction of authority. There lies the danger—to look to another for deliverance, for understanding. Freedom cannot be given by another, salvation is not found through another, no matter who he is. Understanding comes when the mind is single, free, not distracted by effort. You must give your whole being to understand *what is;* in this complete surrender to *what is,* there comes absolute silence. In the void the real is.

Question: You have said that a mind in bondage is vagrant, restless, disorderly. Will you please explain further what you mean?

KRISHNAMURTI: Have you not noticed that a mind held in bondage to an idea, to a problem, is always restless? It is ever seeking an answer, ever seeking to guard the idea, the belief, so it is ever apprehensive, disorderly. A mind in prison, conscious or unconscious, is ever seeking freedom and so ever vagrant. But if the mind is aware of its own prison, of its self-created bondage, then it is pursuing the truth of the bondage and not wandering away from the problem itself. The problem is the mind itself and not the problem the mind fabricates. When you are conscious of a problem, the response is to be free of it, to solve it, to run away from it; this very striving indicates restlessness, disorder. If there were no interest in the search for an answer to the problem but interest in the understanding of the problem itself—in which alone is the answer—then the mind, being free from the search for an answer, for an escape, and so being concentrated, whole, would be capable of pursuing swiftly every movement of the problem; as the problem is ever new, ever undergoing a modification, the mind must also be fresh, unhampered by belief, by conclusion, by conviction, by theory.

For the mind to free itself from creating problems is meditation. Meditation is not mere repetition of words, mantras, japas, chants, or sitting in front of a picture or image, made by the hand or by the mind. Meditation is not prayer or concentration. Meditation is thought freeing itself from time; through the process of time, the timeless cannot be comprehended, and as the mind is the product of time, thought must cease for the real to be. Thought is the product of time, the experience of yesterday; thought is caught in the net of time and so it cannot understand the timeless, the eternal.

The problem then is for the mind to free itself from time. Whatever it formulates, whatever it creates is of time, whether it be the paramatma, the super-soul, or the Brahma, and so on, it is still of time. Meditation is the freeing of thought from time; meditation is the ending of thought.

Is it not extremely arduous for thought to end itself? No sooner does one thought come into being before another sweeps it aside, so thought is never completed. Meditation is completing thought, ending thought by thinking right through, for in ending there is renewal. How can thought complete itself? For, that which is complete has no continuity. Thought can come to an end only when the thinker understands himself. The thinker and his thought are not two separate processes but one. The thinker is the thought, but the thinker separates himself from his thought for his permanency, for his continuance. Take away the thoughts of the thinker and the thinker is not. Remove the qualities of the 'me', the self, his name, his property, his idiosyncracies, his memories, and the thinker is not. To complete every thought that arises, whether they are so-called good or so-called bad, is extremely arduous, for it involves the slowing down of the mind. A motor of high speed cannot be observed. It must be slowed down to study its parts. For the mind to understand itself, it must slow down. To bring order to the confused, disorderly, vagrant mind, follow each thought through. To follow each thought, put it down on paper, write down some thoughts as they arise. As most minds are vagrant, full of thoughts that seem so disconnected, order and clarity can be brought about when each thought is completed. As you are listening to me, you are following a thought through, you are following the thoughts that are being put forward. Your thoughts are not wandering, and as what I am saying is not mere intellection but an actual experience, you are follow-

ing intently, which indicates that you can slow down your thoughts so as to follow one thought through. In writing down thoughts as they arise, you will soon be conscious of your condemnations, identifications, prejudices, and so on. From this there arises choiceless awareness which will free consciousness from its accumulations. A consciousness that is filled with every kind of memory, racial prejudice, national demands, religious and psychological apprehensions, can never be still. As thought frees itself from time, it will not be possible to indulge in certain activities.

The other day a man came to see me. He wanted to find peace, find what he called God. He stated that he was a speculator. He can never have peace, for he is indulging in activities that are not peaceful. You, too, want peace and happiness, love and joy, but you indulge in those activities that are not peaceful, that are vicious, caught in those professions that are destructive, as the army, the police, and the law. Thought, in understanding its own process, will bring about a crisis in its daily activities. You do not have to wait for a crisis which will demand direct action. Thus, in bringing about clarification, there comes joy and peace. As the pool becomes still when the breezes stop, so when the self-created problems come to an end, there is tranquillity, silence, a silence that is not induced nor compelled. In this silence that which is unutterable comes into being.

Question: Does not the belief in reincarnation explain inequality in society?

KRISHNAMURTI: What a callous way of resolving a problem! Does the problem of inequality cease because you have a belief? You may not explain away suffering according to your belief, for suffering continues, there is still inequality. You believe according to the dictates of your gratification, and belief is not a solution to the pain of division. Is inequality, with its fears, explained away by theories, either of the right or of the left, whether it is an economic or religious belief? The theories of the extreme left or of the modified left or of the right surely do not do away with inequality, which is not based on the sensate but on psychological values. Because you believe in reincarnation, a progressive becoming a little higher and more virtuous than the other fellow, you feel gratified and rewarded; because you are economically or socially better off, or because you have suffered and worked in the past, in the past life, you feel a little superior and the other fellow a little bit below you, who in turn will come up the ladder of achievement, so there will always be those above and those below. Surely, this is a most odd way of dealing with life, is it not? The most brutal and callous way of dealing with one of the problems of life, is it not? You want explanations and explanations apparently satisfy you, whether they are of the right or of the left.

Reincarnation, or the belief in it, is not a solvent of the problems of life, is it? Such beliefs help to postpone understanding, which is ever in the present. The fact of inequality—the untouchable, the Brahmin and the non-Brahmin, the callous commissar and the poor fellow who works way down below him—the fact of division and pain remains, and no explanations, however scientific and beautiful, intellectual or romantic, will wipe it away. Those above and often those below seem to be satisfied with words and more words. How is this inequality to be eliminated? Can it be wiped away by any system, economic or religious? Can a system, either of the left or of the right, do away with the actual fact that man likes to divide himself as the superior and the inferior? Bloody revolutions have not produced equality, though in their beginning they tried to maintain freedom and equality, but when the revolution is over,

when the froth and excitement have subsided, again there is inequality—the boss, the tyrant, the dictator, and all the rest of the ugly business of existence. No government, no theory can wipe out the craving of man to be superior, to dominate; and to look to a theory, to a belief, is to be stupid, to be callous.

You look to a system, to a belief when your hearts are dry, when you have no love; then systems become all-important. When there is love, there is no division as the high and the low; then there is neither the prostitute nor the righteous. For the man caught up in righteousness, there is the brutality of division. Belief or system is not the solvent of our problems; you may, perhaps, build a society in which there is complete economic freedom, but as long as the psychological urge to be superior, to achieve, exists, there will be inequality, wiping away the economic structure, however carefully built. The only true and lasting solvent to your problems is love, kindliness, generosity, mercy. To love, to be merciful is not easy, and a man who is caught up in competition, in ruthless activities, who is pursuing gratification and achievement—to him explanations, beliefs, theories are very comforting. He can pursue his ugly ways and yet feel righteous.

Belief is not a substitution for love, and because you do not know love, you indulge in theories and in the search of systems that promise relief. This verbal pursuit is the most stupid activity. When you love there is neither the bright intellectual nor the wearying dull, neither the sinner nor the righteous, neither the rich nor the poor. It is a marvelous thing to be so free, and only love can give it. Love is possible only when beliefs, conclusions, theories, convictions, drop away. Love is possible only when you are human, not mechanical. How little we love in our daily life! You do not love your children, your wives, or your husbands, for you do not know them, you do not know yourself. Through self-knowledge there is love, and it is only love that resolves the human difficulties. Be simple, put away your aggressiveness, your competitive and greedy pursuits, and you will know love. He who loves is not concerned with the superior or the inferior, with the Master and the disciple. He who is content with *what is* has understanding; he has happiness and love.

Question: I have made the rounds of various teachers, gurus, and I would like to know from you what is the purpose of life.

KRISHNAMURTI: Ladies do a great deal of window shopping, in Europe and in America, going from one shop window to another, looking from the outside at the dresses and wishing they had money to buy, or being content with the excitement of seeing so many things. Similarly there seem to be many who indulge in this peculiar game of pleasure and excitement of going from guru to guru, always window shopping. What happens to such people? They are so often emotionally stretched that elasticity is lost. This artificial stimulation soon dulls feeling and its quick response and pliability are gone. Why do you go to a guru, to a teacher? Obviously for self-protection, for comfort, for direction, and where do you find it always? With a guru who gratifies you, with the teacher who gives you comfort. If the teacher tells you to abandon the ways of the world, to be simple, to love and be merciful, you will not go to him. If he gratifies you in that which you crave, then you fall at his feet. This game is for children, for the stupid, not for grown ups, mature men. Again, if you feel comfortable, peaceful in the presence of the teacher, you become his devotee; this devotion is corruption, unworthy of the thoughtful, the earnest. But if the teacher demands something beyond your miserable comforts and securities, you soon find another. This foolish pursuit of gurus makes the mind dull and the heart empty, their pristine vigor and vitality are lost. What has happened to all of you who have followed gurus? You have lost the beauty of sensitivity, the quickness and depth of mind and heart.

The questioner wants to know from me what the purpose of life is. Apparently, he must have been told the purpose of life by the various teachers he has been to, and now he wants to collect mine; probably to choose among his collection the best and most gratifying. Sirs, this is all so infantile, so immature. The questioner, anonymous, explains in his letter that he is a married man, the father of several children, and is most anxious to be informed of the purpose of life. See the tragedy of it and do not laugh. You are all in the same position, are you not? You beget children, you are in responsible positions and yet you are immature in thought, in life. You do not know love. How shall you find out the purpose of life? Shall another tell you? Must you not discover it for yourself? Is the purpose of life the routine of office work, year after year? Is it the pursuit of money, of position and power? Is it the achievement of an ambition? Is it the performance of rituals, those vain repetitions? Is it the acquisition of virtue, to be walled in by barren righteousness? Surely none of these is the end purpose of life; then what is? To find it, must you not go beyond all these? Only then will you find it.

The man of sorrow is not seeking the purpose of life, he wants to be free from sorrow. But you see, you are not aware that you suffer. You suffer, but escape from it, and so do not understand it. This question should reveal to you the ways of your mind and heart. The question is a self-revelation. You are in conflict, in confusion, in misery, which is the result of your own daily activities of thought and feeling. To understand this conflict, confusion, and misery, you have to understand yourself, and as you understand, thought proceeds deeper and deeper until the end purpose is revealed. But to merely stand on the edge of confusion and ask the meaning of life has no meaning. A man who has lost the song of his heart, he is ever seeking, he is enchanted by the voice of others. He will find it again only when he ceases to follow, when his desire is still.

December 7, 1947

Ninth Talk in Madras

There is a difference between listening and hearing. Hearing is subjective and listening is objective. If we merely listen to words and do not hear their significance, then these talks will have little meaning. Communication is on the same level at the same time; communion exists only when there is love. Understanding is denied when prejudice shapes our mind and heart. Compartmental thinking is a barrier to happiness. Happiness is not the denial of sorrow, but the understanding of sorrow. The conflict and pain of suffering dulls the mind and the heart. Suffering does not make for intelligence; suffering does not bring comprehension. It is a sign of ignorance to assume that suffering cultivates thought and intelligence. Does suffering bring about understanding? What actually happens to us when we suffer? What do we mean by suffering? A psychological disturbance, superficial or profound, brought about by various causes, as the loss of someone dear, as when there is frustration, when there is no meaning to life, when the present has no meaning, and so either the past or the future becomes important. A life of confusion and contradiction is sorrow; a life of emptiness and ignorance is sorrow; a life of acquisition and ambition is sorrow; a life of sensory values is sorrow.

Now, actually, what happens when you suffer? The instinctive response to sorrow is to escape from it, to take flight from it. We try to run away from sorrow through belief, through formulation and explanation, through rituals and priests, through music and gurus or teachers. The very inquiry into the cause of suffering becomes an intellectual or verbal escape, for if one is aware, one realizes directly the cause; the cause and effect are not distant, they are not separate. The sufferer becomes capable in escapes, efficient in guarding himself against suffering. This cunning, this capacity to escape, is considered to be the cultivation of intelligence; the change of the object of escapes is considered growth. But suffering continues. How is suffering to be understood? Merely to search out its cause does not do away with suffering. Suffering comes with craving, craving expresses itself in many forms: greed and prejudice, worldliness and the desire for continuance, and so on. Mere information concerning the cause and its effect does not do away with suffering.

The more you are acquainted, familiar, with suffering, the more you "love" it, the more you invite and converse with it, the more it gives you perfume, its significance. If you run away from it through any avenues of escape, religious or scientific, or find substitutions for suffering, suffering invariably continues. Suffering is to be understood and not overcome, for that which is overcome has to be conquered again and again. Suffering can be understood and transcended only through self-knowledge; with self-knowledge comes right thinking. Right thinking does not come into being if there is condemnation or identification. You do not deny beauty and beauty is not the denial of ugliness. If you refuse suffering you also refuse happiness, for happiness is not the opposite of suffering. The understanding of suffering comes with right thinking; through being aware of every thought, feeling, and action, right thinking comes, and only right thinking can dissolve the cause of pain and suffering.

Question: I heard your last Sunday's talk about duality and the pain of it. But as you did not explain how to overcome the opposite, will you please go further into the matter?

KRISHNAMURTI: We know the conflict of the opposites: we are caught in this long corridor of pain, ever attempting to overcome the opposite. This is our existence, the battle of the opposites: I am this and I want to become that; I am not this and I would like to become that; this constant struggle of the clerk to become the manager, the unvirtuous trying to become the virtuous, and so on. With this process each one is familiar.

Now does the opposite exist? Only what exists is the actual; but the opposite is the negative response to *what is;* the opposite is not, but it comes into being with becoming. The opposite is not the actual, but *what is;* the ideal, positive or negative, is nonexistent, but *what is* is the actual. In understanding *what is* is the beginning of freedom. The feeling of arrogance arises which is the actual; the fact and the negative response to this is humility, the ideal, which is not yet in being. Humility, the opposite, is accepted, for arrogance has been condemned morally and socially and religiously, and also from arrogance there is conflict and pain. So there arises the desire to get rid of arrogance, and as it is no longer profitable, humility, the opposite, is sought after. So what is actually taking place is that I am arrogant and I would like to become humble. Humility is an idea and not yet a psychological fact; the actual is arrogance and its opposite is not, but I would like to become humble. So the very desire to become creates the opposite; the opposite is not existent, an ideal to be achieved.

Love is not the opposite of hate; if it is it ceases to be love. An opposite has the seed of its own opposite; humility, the opposite, is the outcome of arrogance, and so humility has the seed of its opposite. If we begin to understand the very significance of arrogance without condemning it, without introducing its opposite as a means of denial, then the conflict of duality wholly ceases. What is existent is arrogance, and if I can understand that, then I need not go into the battle of becoming. To put it differently, the present is the result of the past, and without understanding the present, the future becomes merely the opposite of *what is,* the present. But the future is the past through the passage of the present, and so the future holds the seed of the present; the future as the opposite is still in the net of time. The present is the passage to the future or the past, and in understanding this movement, thought will no longer be caught either in the past or in the future as an opposite to the present. To understand *what is,* which is arrogance, I must give my whole attention, my whole being, and not be distracted by its opposite.

Why do we name a feeling? Why do we term a reaction as anger, as jealousy, as arrogance, as hate, and so on? Do you term it in order to understand it, or as a means of recognizing it, or to communicate it? Is the feeling independent of the term, or do you understand it through the term? If you understand the feeling through the term, through the word, then the term becomes important and not the feeling. Is it possible not to name the feeling? If it is, then what happens to the feeling? By terming, you entangle the feeling within the frame of reference, and so the living is caught in the net of time, which only strengthens memory, the 'me'. What happens to a feeling, to a response if you do not give a name, a term to it? Does it not come to an end, does it not wither away? Please experiment with this and discover for yourself. Any response to a challenge comes to an end when you do not name it, put it within the frame of reference.

So you have learned now how to get rid of a painful, a sorrowful response. But will you give a name to a feeling that is termed pleasant? When a pleasurable feeling arises and you do not give it a name, it too will die away, wither away. So, pleasurable and painful responses wither away when you do not term them, when they are not absorbed into the frame of reference. Experiment with this and discover for yourself. But is love a response not to be named and so let wither away? It will wither if it is an opposite of hate, for then it is merely a conditioned response to a challenge. If it is merely a reaction, then it is not love. Love is a state of being; it is its own eternity. Most of us are trying to become merciful, generous, kind, and becoming is the result of an opposite, positive or negative. Love is not to be cultivated; if you cultivate mercy it ceases to be mercy, for then it contains its own opposite, hate. Love is when there is no becoming which engenders the opposite.

This conflict of duality, with its confusion and sorrow, is born of thoughtlessness, the lack of right thinking. In understanding the significance of *what is,* the opposite ceases. The opposite comes into being only when *what is,* the present, is avoided. Becoming what is not leads to illusion. In understanding *what is*—arrogance, not only superficially but throughout the deeper layers of consciousness, as achievement, as pride, and so on—and not naming, terming the feeling, then it withers away. The pursuit of the pleasant and the denial of the painful only create conflict and sorrow, dulling the mind and the heart.

Question: Gandhi says in a recent article that religion and nationalism are equally dear to man, and one cannot be bartered away in favor of the other. What do you say?

KRISHNAMURTI: I wonder what is your own response to this question? Will you question your so-called leaders? Must you not criticize, inquire to find out the truth? Through self-criticism, tribulation is inevitable, and it is easier and more convenient to follow than to be aware and understand. The acceptance of authority is blinding, putting an end to understanding, which alone brings happiness. If alert and self-critical awareness is lost, then discovery of truth is not possible. Therein lies the insidious danger of breeding leaders, religious or political, and following them. Mutual exploitation exists between the follower and the leader. In India, as elsewhere, it is extraordinary to watch the growth of leaders, the tyrants in the name of religion and of systems, and the more power they have, the more evil they become. To search out truth, there must be an open heart and a uncontaminated mind, a mind that is not in bondage to a system, to a belief, to a person. To discover truth, you must venture into the open, uncharted seas. We are not concerned with any particular leader, but with authority itself. Creation is not possible within the frame of authority. Creativeness withers in the heat of authority. You may produce some mechanical responses, but creativeness ceases. This is one of the tragedies of modern civilization. When you give yourself over to another, to a priest, to a political leader, to a savior, to a system, to a belief, then you cease to feel, to live, and as human beings, you are nonexistent. Through the pursuit of authority, your conflicts and sorrows are not resolved.

Now, it is said that religion and nationalism are both dear to man, and one cannot be bartered away for the other. Let's find the truth of this, neither opposing it nor defending it, for truth alone is the liberator, it alone gives happiness. What do you mean by religion? Religion is not the worship of an image made by the hand or by the mind, nor does it consist in going to a temple or church, nor in reading sacred books, nor in repeating words or chants, and to believe is not to be religious.

Religion is the search for reality as God, or what name you will. Organized religions with their beliefs, with their rituals, with their fears and exploitations, are an impediment to the discovery of reality, for they condition the mind and the heart according to their particular pattern. Religion is the search and the discovery of the real, and not the performance of rituals, not the following of a guru, teacher, or savior. The approach to truth must be negative, for positive action is based on the known, and what is known is not the real. Reality is the unknowable, and you cannot come to it through any path, for all paths are the known. Any positive approach to the unknown is not possible, for the positive is the known; truth is when the known ceases. The eternal cannot be approached through time; the timeless is when time ceases, when thought, which is the result of time, comes to an end.

Nationalism is the craving for identification, the attachment to a group, to a race, to a country and so on, is it not? The identification of oneself with the greater, with India, with England, and so on, is the craving for continuance. When you call yourself a Hindu, or a Muslim, or a Christian, is it not an indication that the term, the name, is of greater significance than yourself? The name, the label, covers the poverty of your inner being; you are petty, shallow, and through identification you hope to escape from your own emptiness. So the name, the country, the idea, become all-important, and for that you are willing to die and to kill. This craving for identification is exploited. Nationalism, the economic frontier, inevitably leads to war; nationalism is of recent growth, a poison that is destroying man, setting man against man.

Through nationalism, the unity of man is not possible; the nationalist can never comprehend the brotherhood of man. Nationalism is the new religion, and it can only breed hatred and disaster.

Organized religion and nationalism have set man against man, and through them there is no hope for man. They have been the cause of untold misery and degradation. Ignorance does not lead to enlightenment; ignorance must cease so that there can be enlightenment. Organized belief, which is organized religion, and organized identification, which is nationalism, must come to an end so that man may live peacefully with his fellowman. Through belief and through patriotism there can never be happiness for man.

Must you not go beyond and above the things made by the hand or by the mind to find truth? Right thinking, which comes with self-knowledge, alone can deliver you from the conflict and sorrow of existence.

Question: You have talked of exploitation as being evil. Do you not also exploit?

KRISHNAMURTI: Critical capacity is necessary for self-knowledge, and credulity only leads to obstinacy and to illusion.

What do you mean by exploitation? Does it not mean the use of another for your own profit, either materially or psychologically? Material exploitation is minimized when the essential needs are intelligently understood and limited. To have much is a bothersome thing, as those who have much know. The limiting of needs can come about only when needs are not used for psychological gratification; when the essentials of existence—food, clothes, and shelter are not made the means of self-aggrandizement. When things, made by the hand or by the mind, are given greater significance than their sensate value, then exploitation begins. When needs are used to gratify acquisitiveness, greed, then exploitation begins. Needs have their own limited significance—to feed one, to clothe one, to shelter one—but when needs become psychological necessities, then exploitation begins. A happy man does not depend for his happiness upon things, either made by the hand or by the mind; he has the treasure of the greatest significance. A man who has not that treasure makes sensate values predominant and thereby causes strife and misery.

The problem of psychological exploitation is more subtle and more profound. Psychologically we depend on things, on relationship, on ideas, or belief. Things, relationship, and ideas become all-important when they are used as a means of covering up the inward poverty, the inward emptiness. Being inwardly poor, insufficient, fearful, uncertain, we seek security, certainty, riches in those things made by the hand or by the mind. This search is the beginning of exploitation. We are aware of the results of seeking psychological security in things: war and degradation, class and national division, man against man, confusion and misery, the modern civilization the world over. Then you are the things and without them you are lost. In relationship, too, what happens if security is sought? Dependence breeds possessiveness, fear, jealousy, anger, and so on. The object of dependence becomes all-important, and so name, family, position become significant, with the result of conflicting division and misery. This dependence is the outcome of inward emptiness, which you try to cover up through gratifying relationship. When you are inwardly poor, things made by the mind—knowledge, idea, belief—become overwhelmingly important, which gives rise to imitation, to the worship of authority, to the acceptance of systems, to thoughtlessness.

The outward exploitation of man by man is comparatively easy to recognize and to understand and to minimize, but the psychological exploitation of man by man is far more difficult to recognize and to transcend. Its ways are subtle and hidden. It causes far greater conflict and misery than the outer exploitation of man by man. This psychological exploitation is far more important to understand and so put an end to than the material exploitation of man, which is also necessary. For however well-regulated or organized the material welfare of man is, the inner conflict and confusion always overcome the outer. This self-expansive process through things, through relationship, and through knowledge is the beginning of exploitation. Only understanding and love put an end to such exploitation and not legislation.

Question: What is the difference between surrendering to the will of God in suffering and what you are saying about the acceptance of what is?

KRISHNAMURTI: Are you surrendering to the will of God? Or are you surrendering yourself to what you consider God? What you know is not the real. If you surrender to a higher will, then the higher is the projection of your own thought. There is gratification and comfort in such surrendering, but conflict and sorrow come to an end only through awareness and understanding. To understand *what is* there must be awareness, a passive intelligence and not the surrender to a formulation, however satisfying. To understand *what is,* effort is a hindrance, for effort, as I pointed out, exists only when there is distraction. To understand *what is* there must be no distraction, no effort. To understand what you are saying, I must not be distracted; I must give my whole attention. It is extremely arduous to be aware of *what is,* for our very thinking has become a distraction. We consider *what is* with prejudice, with a bias in its favor or against it, with condemnation or identification. *What is* is the actual, the real, and to desire to change it is to run away from *what is*. Only in understanding *what is* is there fundamental transformation. To understand *what is,* the conflict of the opposite must cease, for the opposite is the negative continuation of *what is,* the becoming which creates the opposite. The becoming is the denial of *what is.* To understand arrogance, the distraction of its opposite must cease, the effort of becoming, positively or negatively, must come to an end. If the feeling that is termed as *arrogance* is not named, then that feeling withers away. The response, pleasant or unpleasant, to a challenge withers away if it is not named, but as I pointed out love is utterly different. If love is the opposite of hate then it withers away.

This desire to accept *what is* is again a wrong approach. There is acceptance only when there is the desire to become; a fact does not demand acceptance; when there is a compulsion to evade *what is,* then there is an urge to accept it. To understand *what is* needs passive awareness. A mind that is caught in the net of time is translating *what is* in terms of the past and the future and so is incapable of understanding *what is.* A mind that is seeking escapes, distractions, however worthy and subtle, cannot understand *what is.* Without understanding *what is,* life is a constant conflict and pain; without being aware of the significance of *what is,* the real is not. Without the real there is no joy, no happiness.

December 14, 1947

Tenth Talk in Madras

Right thinking is essential to dissolve the many problems with which we are confronted each day. It is important to find out how to think rightly, how to understand the problems rightly rather than what should be the thought and attitude regarding the problem. We are accustomed to be told what to think about the problem and not how to think about it. How to think is essential, not what to think. To seek a mere solution to a problem brings about wrong thinking, and right thinking comes about in understanding the problem, *what is.* Right action can take place only with right thinking and right thinking comes with self-knowledge.

What is thinking? I wonder if we have ever asked ourselves that question. What is the process of thinking? It would be good if we could talk this over together, but as that is not possible with such a large audience, nevertheless I hope you will partake silently in what is being said. This is a discourse in which both you and I are taking part; if you allow yourself to become the mere listeners, then real communication between us ceases. Communion between us can exist only when our hearts are open to each other. Do not let us close our hearts with verbal misunderstandings and prejudices.

What is thinking, the process of thinking? As we know it, it is a response of memory, is it not? Memory is the accumulation or residue of experience. So thinking, which is the response of memory, is always conditioned. You have an experience and you respond to it or interpret it according to your background, memories, the residue of previous experiences. This response of memory is called thinking. Such thinking only strengthens conditioning, which only produces more conflict and sorrow. The constant response of the residue of experience is called thinking. Life is a series of challenges and responses but the response is conditioned and this response of memory is called thinking. But the challenge is ever new and the response is of the past.

Believing is not thinking, believing is only conditioned response, which is binding, causing conflict and sorrow. According to your belief, background, conditioning, you experience; this experiencing leads only to further conditioned thinking. The so-called thinking, the response to challenge which is ever new, is limited, within the frame of reference, memory, and so brings further conflict, further confusion, and further sorrow. This so-called thinking is not really thinking but what, then, is thinking? The response of memory to challenge is not thinking. Have you ever asked yourself what you mean by thinking? What is thinking? As it is a new question put to you, a new challenge, what is your response to it? Since you have not thought about it, what is your immediate response? You are silent, are you not? Please follow this with a little care. A new problem is presented to you; and since you have not "thought" about it—that is, since there is as yet no response of the frame of reference, memory—there is a natural, unforced hesitancy, a quietness, a stillness of observation. Is that not so? You are silently watching, you are not interpreting the new problem according to the frame of reference, memory, but your mind is very alert, one-pointed, without effort, and as the question is vital, your mind is not asleep, alert but passive. The mind is alertly passive, awaiting the true answer to the problem. Now this alert yet passive state is true thinking; right thinking comes with the ending of the response of memory. Since it is confronted with a new problem, your mind is still, quiet but not dull, asleep, alertly aware but passive. It is not active for it is not even seeking an answer, for it does not know it. This state of alert, passive awareness is thinking, is it not? It is the highest form of thinking, there is neither positive nor negative response of memory.

Now is it not possible to meet our every human problem with this ever new, alert, passive awareness? When we do, then the problem yields its full significance and thereby comes to an end. But when we try to solve the problem by thinking about it, which is to follow the response of the memory, modified or unchanged, then we further complicate the problem by interpreting it according to our conditioning, and so bring about further conflict and sorrow. You can experiment with this for yourself. Take any problem that you have, any vital and intimate problem; put aside your conditioned responses and look at the problem anew. This passive, alert awareness is the highest form of thinking; this awareness dissolves our problems with their conflicts and pain.

Question: I dream a great deal. Have dreams any significance?

KRISHNAMURTI: When are we awake? When there is a crisis, when there is an intense problem, either of pleasure or of pain; the problem is an awakening, but our instinctive desire is to escape from it through so many different ways, and thereby we put ourselves to sleep once again. When there is a problem, what is your response to it? You try to solve it according to the frame of reference, according to some principle, to some teachings which only put you to sleep again. So when there is a pleasurable challenge you pursue it, craving more of it, which only dulls the mind and heart, putting you to sleep again; when the challenge causes pain you avoid it, which only helps to dull the mind and heart. Challenge demands earnest attention, clear perception, and understanding, which may necessitate further action; but we refuse, or so identify with the problem that sleep is induced. This is generally what happens to us and only very rarely are we awake. In those rare moments there is no dream; in those moments of full wakefulness there is neither the dream nor the dreamer, experience nor the gatherer of experience. What is the significance of dreams? During the so-called wakeful state, during the day, the conscious mind is actively engaged in earning a livelihood, occupied with some complicated technical job, learning, wrangling, avoiding, enjoying, or with prayer and worship. It is constantly and superficially active, but when it goes to bed the surface mind becomes fairly quiet. But consciousness is not just the superficial layer. Consciousness has many layers: layers of hidden motives, pursuits, fears, and so on. These hidden layers project themselves into the now peaceful, superficial layer, the conscious mind, which upon waking is aware that there was a dream. The conscious mind is so occupied with its daily activities that it is incapable of receiving during the day the intimations, the hints, of the hidden layers. Only when the superficial layer, the conscious mind, becomes quiet, then the deeper layers can project themselves. These projections, with their symbols, become dreams. There are dreams without consequence and dreams with significance. The dreams that are the outcome of bodily weariness, of indulgence, of ailments, and so on, we are not here considering.

Dreams are the intimations of the deeper layers of consciousness. The conscious mind receives these intimations through symbols, through pictures, which need translation, interpretation. I do not know if you have noticed that as the dream proceeds there is also at the same time an interpretation of what is taking place. Dreams demand interpretation, that is, if you are at all aware, you want to know their significance. There is the luxury of going to a psychoanalyst, the dream interpreter who will unravel it for you after many months, for a great deal of money. But most of us have neither the money nor are we near one. They will become the new priests if we are not wise; we will exploit them and they will exploit us, which is a most unfortunate factor in human relationship. You have had a dream of some significance; you want to understand it; you are anxious about it. You try to interpret it, and your interpretation of it will be according to your prejudices, fears, and so on. According to your likes and dislikes, you translate your dream and so miss its full significance. The interpreter is too anxious, too agitated, and so he cannot fully understand his dream. Only when the interpreter is alert and yet passively aware, choicelessly watchful, then only does the dream yield its full meaning. So the dream is not so important as the dreamer, the interpreter. He is of greater significance. In understanding himself, he is then open to all the hidden layers of consciousness and so frees himself from conflict and sorrow.

As long as the interpreter exists, he must always dream and be anxious about his interpretations. Is it necessary to dream? Dreams come to an end only when the conscious mind is alert and passively aware during the waking hours, so that the hidden layers can give their intimation without being misinterpreted; it is possible only when the conscious mind is not entangled in the conflict of problems, when it is still and not made still; it is possible only when there is integration of all the layers of consciousness so that the superficial layer is the profound. If you will experiment you will see that though the superficial layer is occupied with outward activities, yet because it is choicelessly aware, the intimations, the projections, as they arise, of the hidden layers, are being understood. Thus there is a freedom, an integration of the different and separate parts of consciousness. Only when there is an understanding of the different parts of consciousness, and thereby a complete integration of the parts, then only the dreamer ceases to dream. For dreams are a disturbance, and when these disturbances stop, then only can consciousness penetrate deeply, beyond itself. When there is no disturbance, then on waking there is a renewal; there is always an ending, so there is always the ecstasy of renewal.

As the fields are allowed to lie fallow after they are tilled, sown, and harvested, so must the conscious mind allow itself to be passively aware. As the field renews itself when allowed to lie fallow, so does the mind renew itself. This creative renewal must take place from moment to moment. When you have a problem you struggle with it, not completely understanding it, and so carry it over to the next day. There is never an ending, but continuity is strengthened. Only in ending is there a renewal, and in continuity there is sorrow. To live the four seasons in a moment is to be blessed with the ecstasy of renewal. It is not the renewal of desire with its endless conflicts and pains, but a rebirth of the ever new, of the ever fresh.

Question: We see the significance of what you say, but there are many important problems which demand immediate attention, such as the struggle between capital and labor.

KRISHNAMURTI: Now, either we deal with problems with the reformist mind, seeking an immediate solution, which only breeds further problems and further reforms, or approach the problem as the end of a total process, which demands right thinking. So how are you approaching the problem—as a reformer, in its widest sense, or as a seeker after truth? It is very important to be clear what your approach is. If you are concerned with mere immediate reform, solution, then it will inevitably lead to more conflict, more confusion, more sorrow. This attitude, that of the politician, that of the man committed to a system, causes disaster and misery. Or are you considering the problems of daily existence—starvation, economic frontiers, the struggle of capital and labor, and so on— from the point of view of a man who is seeking the whole meaning of existence?

The individual or the group craving for power and position leads to every kind of corruption and disaster, socially and psychologically. Whether power, violence, is used in the name of the state or in the name of religion, it cannot possibly bring about order and peace in the world; on the contrary, it will breed multiple miseries. Power, exercised by a government of the right or of the left, in the name of the people or of a system, will not give man even his physical security. Without understanding the true meaning of existence, to merely organize society according to any particular pattern is to cultivate conflict, confusion, misery. To merely encourage revolution, to carry out a particular system of thought, is to be utterly indifferent to man's struggle and misery.

Must we not consider the total process of man and not take one issue and try to solve it separately? This process is more psychological than mere material struggle; the hidden conflicts and confusion always shadow the outer existence, and without comprehending inner issues, to merely regulate outward events is the work of the thoughtless; and the reformer and the politician are involved in this superficial activity. Such activity breeds more conflict, more confusion, more misery, which is exactly what is taking place at the present time. Without understanding man's relationship to man, there can be no happiness for him in any system nor in any immediate reform. Right relationship between man and man cannot be brought about by mere legislation, nor by mere social controls. Right relationship can exist only when you understand yourself; for what you are the world is; your problem is the world's problem. You cannot bring order and peace in the world without first bringing, through self-knowledge, order and peace within yourself. You must begin with yourself and not with a society which you have created. Your relationship with another is society, and according to your thoughts and actions, you bring about misery or happiness.

Question: Are we not shaped by circumstances? Are we not the creatures of our senses?

KRISHNAMURTI: The implications in this question are profound and we must consider them thoughtfully. We are shaped by circumstances, but there is surely greater significance to life than mere sensate values. The discovery of what is beyond the sensory values lies through self-knowledge. Without self-knowledge, all knowledge leads to misery and to illusion. Without self-knowledge, there is no foundation for right thinking and right action; without self-knowledge life is a contradiction and despair.

There is the idea that matter is in movement in itself, and the other formulation is that God or idea moves upon matter. The one is supposed to be materialistic and the other so-called religious. The materialistic formulation implies the control of environ-ment as a means of shaping, controlling the individual, and so he is not important in himself. So circumstances, environmental influence, outward and scientific knowledge become all-important. It is essentially based on sensate value. The religious formulation admits of an absolute value, that the individual is sacred, an end in himself, not a mere tool in the hands of the state, and so on. The materialist, the extreme leftist says that there is no absolute value, that man is merely the product of the senses and of environmental influence, and he changes his values according to sensory demands. So the control of environment, of matter, of the individual, becomes all-important, shaping him according to a system, compelling him to shape himself according to a pattern of thought, so that he functions effectively in a mechanized society. To understand, do not take sides nor be on

the defensive; understanding comes with freedom and not with a biased intelligence.

To the so-called religious, the individual is all-important, for he is created in the image of the idea; in him the absolute value exists, which is translated in multiple ways; he is a spiritual entity, fashioning his own end, and so utilizing the environment for that purpose, and hence environment is not all-important. We need not enlarge and explain further the religious point of view.

Both these formulations are theories, beliefs; both have their sacred books, both have their propagandistic organizations, both have their high priests, their central authority, their binding dogma and discipline, their future hope and the way to realize it, and so forth. Both meet in moments of grave crisis, national or economic disaster. To the religious, the individual is sacred only so long as there is no danger to his state or to his system; when there is, the individual is sacrificed to war, to be regimented and controlled by the state and so on.

So the materialist and the religious are both approaching the problem with a prejudiced mind, a mind conditioned by a belief, by a dogma. But to find truth, we must be free from belief and dogma. Obviously, one of the facts is that man is the result of environmental influences; man is the result of his sensory cravings; his relationship with another, based on sensate value, creates society of which you and I are the product. When you call yourself a Hindu, a Christian, or a Muslim, you are the product of your environment. You are conditioned to believe—and you do—in God or in no-God. You go to the temple or to the church according to your conditioning. Environmental influences, economic and social, have shaped your mind. But to find out if you are only the result of environment, merely the product of matter in movement in itself, or if you are something more, you must go deeper and deeper into the creator of sensate values and go above and beyond thought itself to find truth. Thought is still the result of the senses. You have to experiment with yourself; there must be self-awareness, which is self-knowledge, to discover how deeply your thoughts and feelings are sensory and what is beyond thought. If you accept that which is gratifying, God, then you are akin to the materialist who denies. For denial and acceptance are both hindrances to him who is seeking truth. You are living and experiencing according to your conditioning. But those who are living according to their conditioning, or according to their gratifying or arbitrary decision, will not discover the truth.

If you want to find the truth, you must begin obviously with the senses; in understanding the sensory values, you enter into the question of consciousness; if you pursue further, not verbally but actually, you will discover *what is*. If you approach a problem from the point of its opposite, then the significance of the problem is not understood. For the opposite is the outcome of its own opposite. Belief or nonbelief cannot be understood if they are treated as opposites; then there are merely responses to a conditioning. When the religious is in opposition to the materialistic, this very belief breeds conflict; the materialist, by his very denial, fosters belief. When the left is treated as an opposite to the right, then the left is the continuation of the right.

In the understanding of *what is,* ever profoundly, there comes a tranquillity that is not self-induced. When the mind is utterly still, not only in its superficial layers, but in the entire consciousness, when all desire is still, there comes into being that which is real. Acceptance is the very denial of truth.

December 21, 1947

Eleventh Talk in Madras

From our daily contact with our neighbors and with the incidents of our existence, we must observe the increasing confusion and misery, socially and religiously. How are we to understand this mounting conflict and disaster and bring order and happiness out of it? Most of us are concerned, vaguely or intensely, with this problem of conflict and sorrow. Those who are taken up with systems as a means of producing order and peace are not concerned with man's happiness, but with their particular system, with their particular solution. So we are not considering any system or organization of society, but how to bring about order and peace out of this conflict and confusion.

To go far you must begin near; you must begin with that which is close, that which is near, close to yourself. You are the center of all this conflict and sorrow, of this confused puzzle and cruelty. In trying to understand this confusing puzzle, we seem to miss this basic factor, you, the individual. You are the center in the whole structure of society. So what is the relationship between this confusion and misery and yourself? This confusion and misery does not come into being by itself; you and I have created them; they are the outcome of any system, capitalistic, communistic, or fascist. You and I have brought about this conflict and antagonism in our relationship with each other. What you are the world is. What you are within you project without, which is society. Your problem is the world's problem. This is a basic fact, is it not? Yet we seem to overlook this fact and give importance to systems, to ideas, as a means of bringing about revolution in values. We seem to forget that you in your relationship with another build the structure of society, either bringing about order and peace, or conflict and confusion.

So, we must begin near; we must begin with our everyday existence, with our daily thoughts, feelings, and actions. To bring about a radical transformation in your life, you must consider the means of right livelihood, your relationship with the near or with the distant, and your ideas and beliefs. Your livelihood is now the outcome of envy and not based on the requirement of daily needs. The means of livelihood has now become the way of acquiring power, position, prestige, and so on, which breed conflict and antagonism; this progressive becoming, from the clerk to the manager, from the priest to the bishop, has created a society in which competition and ruthlessness are inevitable. If you are only concerned with daily needs and not with the acquisition of power, then you will find the right means of earning a livelihood. Envy is the most destructive factor in our social relationship, which ultimately leads to power politics. The clerk seeking to become the manager, and the manager the director, is one of the causes of misery and destruction. He who is seeking power and position is directly responsible for war and confusion.

Our relationship is a process of self-isolation; each one is building a wall of self-enclosure, which excludes love, only breeding ill will and misery. In this so-called relationship, jealousy, dominance, passion are inevitable, for each one is seeking security, and so relationship is conflict, from which one tries to escape through various ways, gross or subtle. There can be love only when this self-isolating process of gratification ceases. Are not beliefs and formulations distorting our thought process? Giving wrong values to things made by the hand or by the mind is stupidity; this stupidity is the guiding factor in our daily life. It is this stupidity, as belief in a religious or political system, that sets man against man. Stupidity breeds envy and ill will, conflict and misery.

Such is our daily existence; to bring order out of this confusion is the beginning of virtue. The outward confusion is the projection of our inward state, of our inward conflict and misery. To bring order out of this inward confusion is virtue. Virtue can only come into being through self-knowledge. You can bring about peace and happiness only through self-knowledge and not through any system, religious or political. To know yourself is very arduous, but it is easy to follow and discipline yourself after a system, to give yourself over to a party of the right or of the left. To follow authority puts an end to thought and to self-knowledge. To be aware of your daily thoughts, feelings, and actions is strenuous, and so you escape into social activities and reforms, into addictions of every kind. The thoughtless are consumed with the reformation of society, of confusion and misery, which are the results of their inward daily thoughts and activities.

Self-knowledge is not the knowledge of some supreme or higher self, which is still within the field of the mind, but the knowledge and the understanding of your thoughts, feelings, and actions from moment to moment. From this self-knowledge and understanding there comes right thinking and right action. Right action can be understood when there is self-awareness, but right action is difficult to understand when it is considered theoretically. No system, religious or secular, can bring happiness, peace, and order out of this conflict and confusion and misery, for you have created it, you and I have created it through our envy, ill will, and stupidity. In self-knowledge alone is there hope for man and not in any system or leader. For self-knowledge brings about order and peace; it brings freedom which is virtue. In this liberation alone can the real come into being.

Question: Can an ignorant man, with many responsibilities, understand and so carry out your teachings without the aid of another, without resorting to teachers and books?

KRISHNAMURTI: Can understanding be given by another? Can love be taught? Can a guru, a teacher, or a book lead you to love? Can they teach you how to be merciful, to be generous, and the way of understanding? Can you follow another and be free? Can you accept authority and yet be free? Surely there is creativeness only when there is freedom, inward freedom, when there is no fear, no imitation. Who is the ignorant man? An ignorant man is he who does not know himself; the learned man is ignorant if he does not know himself. The merely learned man, by giving wrong value to knowledge, is caught in the net of his own stupidity. Understanding comes only through self-knowledge, the knowledge of your total process, and not one part of it, the psychological or the physical, for they are interactive. Self-knowledge is arduous, for it demands constant awareness, which is not introspection. Introspection is a process of self-improvement, with its conflicts and condemnations, its morbidity and confusion. But awareness is wholly different from introspection. Awareness is a process of your everyday thought, feeling, and action with their condemnation, justification, or identification. To understand, there cannot be condemnation or identification, so when there is alert passivity, understanding comes. So self-knowledge is the beginning of wisdom.

The questioner wants to know if an ignorant man, with many responsibilities, can understand and carry out the teachings without the aid of a teacher or a book. If he accepts authority of any kind there can be no understanding. Authority is ever blinding, whether it is outer or inner. Responsibility implies relationship, does it not? Relationship is a process of self-knowledge, revealing the ways of the self, the ways of the thinker. There is no existence in isolation; to be is to be related. A man who seeks to avoid the world is still related; he is running away from conflict and not understanding it. In relationship, which is activity between you and another, the ways of the self are revealed. Surely, to know yourself, what you think and feel and do, you don't have to go to a guru or to a book, do you? To think out, to feel out every thought and feeling is arduous; to see their implication and meaning demands earnest and swift pliability. None can assist you in this pursuit. You and I can talk over a problem, go into it significantly with the thoroughness of a consecrated mind, with that penetrating interest. You go to another, to a teacher, only when the deep interest to understand is gone, when interest itself is the search, devotion itself. Therein lies the misfortune. When you are interested, when you are aware of the significance of relationship, then that very awareness unfolds the ways of your thoughts and actions.

So the problem is not whether you should go to teachers and books, but to be aware, to be aware simply of what you are thinking, feeling, and doing when you talk to your friends, to your wives, and children. Be aware and discover self-knowledge. If you are aware, you will perceive that conflict and pain increase, for then you begin to see the significance of your thoughts, feelings, and actions. To escape from conflict and pain you turn to teachers and books; in them there is no understanding of your conflict and pain. The teachers and books introduce other problems and other miseries. There is no creative joy in following, in copying an example; creativeness comes into being only where there is freedom. Only when the activities of the self, of the thinker, are quiet and still, then only is there the ecstasy of the real. Only in that state, when the mind is not burdened by its own self-created fears and hopes, conflicts and sorrow, is there creative joy. This joy cannot be taught by another, or given to you by another. It comes into being only when the problems are understood and so dissolved. To be aware from moment to moment is arduous, demanding swift pliability. Our minds are made dull through fear, through copying and tradition, through the worship of authority, and the pursuit of a system; it is difficult to break away from those things that make us dull and stupid. To break away necessitates action and invites perhaps more conflict; and unwilling to face it, we turn to teachers and books who pacify us, gratifying us and thus increasing our dullness and stupidity.

Question: What is that awareness of which you speak? Is it the awareness of the supreme, universal consciousness?

KRISHNAMURTI: Awareness is a simple act—to be aware of the tree, of the flower, of that passing bird, of the relationship between one and another, of the thoughts, feelings, and actions. You must begin near to go far. You cannot be aware of something that you do not know. You verbally assert that there is a universal consciousness, but you do not know it; either you have been told about it or you have read about it. So it is still within the field of the mind, of memory. You are trying to be aware of that which is distant, far away, and not be aware of that which is near. It is more convenient and comforting to be aware of a formulation, of a speculating hope, than to be aware of your thoughts, feelings, and actions from moment to moment. To be aware of your daily thoughts, feelings, and actions is discomforting, painful, and so you would rather think of something in the distance, gratifying. To be aware of that which is close, to be aware of relationship, its self-enclosing process, its

cruelty, its thoughtlessness, is very disturbing; so, being conscious of the immediate pain which direct awareness brings, we would rather speculate about universal consciousness, whatever that may mean, which is an escape from the actual, from *what is*. That of which I am speaking is the awareness of *what is*. The understanding of *what is* leads to great heights. In being aware of *what is* there is no possibility of self-deception.

Understanding comes with the awareness of *what is*. There can be no understanding if there is condemnation of or identification with *what is*. If you condemn a child or so identify yourself with him, then you cease to understand him. So being aware of a thought or a feeling as it arises, without condemning it or identifying with it, you will find that it unfolds ever more widely and deeply, and thereby discover the whole content of *what is*. To understand the process of *what is* there must be choiceless awareness, a freedom from condemnation, justification, and identification. When you are vitally interested in fully understanding something, you give your mind and heart, withholding nothing. But unfortunately you are conditioned, educated, disciplined through religious and social environment to condemn or to identify, and not to understand. To condemn is stupid and easy, but to understand is arduous, requiring pliability and intelligence. Condemnation, as identification, is a form of self-protection. Condemnation or identification is a barrier to understanding. To understand the confusion, the misery in which one is, and so of the world, you must observe its total process; to be aware and pursue all its implications requires patience, to follow swiftly and to be still.

There is understanding only when there is stillness, when there is silent observation, passive awareness. Then only the problem yields its full significance. The awareness of which I speak is of *what is* from moment to moment; of the activities of thought and its subtle deceptions, fears, and hope. Choiceless awareness wholly dissolves our conflicts and miseries.

Question: I am very interested in your teachings; I would like to spread them and which is the best way?

KRISHNAMURTI: Truth cannot be repeated; when repeated it becomes a lie. This repetition is not truth, and so propaganda is a lie. Truth is to be experienced directly. Repetition is a mere copy. That which you repeat may be a truth to him who has experienced it, but when it is repeated it becomes a lie. In this terrible net of lies, called propaganda, thought is caught.

You have read or heard a formulation, an idea which appeals to you, gives you gratification, and you want to tell it to your friends, you do propaganda for it. Have words greater meaning than nervous and verbal significance? Surely not. So what you are spreading, an unfortunate term, is really words, and do words dissolve our aches and sorrows, our problems? For instance, say you believe in reincarnation and you do propaganda for your belief. What are you spreading? You are spreading your conviction, your conclusions, clothed in words; and through words, through explanations, you think you have solved a complex human problem. You are caught in the lie that the word is the thing. Surely the word *God* is not God, but you are caught in the illusion that the word is God. So you spread the word. The word becomes all-important, the label, and not *what is*. You want to catch others in the net of words in which you are caught; this is propaganda. Words, explanations, set man against man. Then you will create a new system based on Krishnamurti's words which you, the propagandist, will spread for other propagandists. And what have you achieved

by this? Whom have you helped? It is the height of folly to spread someone else's experiences, words, and thoughts.

You experience what you believe, and so it is a conditioned experience, and so not a significant, vital experience. There can be vital, true experience only when the process of thinking ceases. This significant experience you cannot spread, as information, to cover up the inward and so the outward confusion. If you give your mind and heart to a direct problem, such as nationalism or caste, it is comparatively simple to understand. Nationalism is a poison which is destroying man. This poison of race and caste is spreading more and more throughout the world. It is setting man against man; it has become a cunning instrument in the hands of the exploiter, and you want to be exploited, for nationalism feeds your craving for self-expansion. You cannot be a nationalist and yet talk of peace, for they are a contradiction. This, surely, you can understand by putting aside your nationalistic spirit, your caste, and so on; then only can you talk about the poison of nationalism, and only then can you spread your understanding.

Your understanding will be shown by your thoughts and actions and not by the rituals you perform or by the organizations to which you belong. There is hope only in the transformation of yourself and not in a system, either of the right or of the left. Belief separates man and sets man against man, and there can be communion only when there is love. It is by the thoughts and acts of your life that communion can be established, and not by mere words. To him who is seeking truth, the truth of words, the truth of relationship, the truth of idea, become all-significant. Truth is not some vague abstraction, but it is to be discovered in the very thoughts, feelings, and actions of our daily existence. Words become very important when the word is the thing.

So if you want to spread these teachings, live them and by your life you will communicate.

Question: Is marriage necessary for women?

KRISHNAMURTI: In marriage, sexual relationship, companionship, communion, love are implied. Without love, marriage becomes, for man or for woman, a source of gratification, of conflict, of fear and pain. Love comes into being only when the self is absent. Without love, relationship is sorrow, however physically exciting it might be; such relationship breeds contention and frustration, habit and routine. Without love there can be no chastity, and sex becomes an all-consuming problem. Without love, the ideal of chastity is an escape from the conflict of desire, and without understanding craving, the ideal leads to illusion and pain. The licentious and the ideal both deny love. The pursuit of the ideal and indulgence give importance to craving, to the 'me', and when the 'me' is emphasized, love is not.

There are other problems involved in this question. One of them is fulfillment. The woman or the man seeks fulfillment in the child. When the woman is deprived of this, she is starved, as she is starved when there is no love. Men seek fulfillment, when deprived of love, either in things or in children or in activity, which are all distractions. So things and action and children become all-important, leading to further confusion and further misery. Man also seeks to escape through fulfilling himself in activity, in distractions and addictions of every kind, from amusement to worship. So man and woman seek to fulfill herself through things or property, through family or name, through ideas or beliefs, and so they become all-important, thus giving to them false or wrong impor-

tance, which causes inward and so outward conflict and misery.

Now is there fulfillment? The craving to become can only lead to frustration, to conflict; in this becoming there is always fear and the conflict of its opposite. The craving for fulfillment, for continuity, is only when there is frustration. Being empty, there is a craving for fulfillment. Without understanding *what is,* which is emptiness, frustration, we pursue fulfillment, the covering up of *what is.* Only in understanding *what is,* which is the emptiness, the shallowness, the pettiness, can there be radical transformation. This transformation is true revolution. But to merely pursue fulfillment is moral and social chaos. A man who is happy, creative, is not seeking fulfillment through property, through marriage, or through ideation; he is not escaping through passion nor is he seeking fulfillment. We cease to be creative, happy, when we are imitative or merely functioning according to the responses of memory. The response of memory is generally considered thinking; such thinking is merely the response of the frame of reference. These responses are not right thinking. Right thinking comes into being only when there is no response to memory. In this passively alert awareness there is creative being. In this state, the life of becoming, with its fulfillment and conflict, fades away. This state is love. Because our hearts are dry, we fill them with the things of the mind, which give rise to multiple problems.

Love is not a thing to be learned; it comes into being when you, the problem, cease. Have you not found yourself to be happy without a conscious or unconscious cause? Then you are in communion with all nature and man. But unfortunately you are so occupied with your own thoughts and problems, envies and fears, that you are incommunicado; this isolating process prevents you from knowing your wife or your husband

and child; you are sheltering behind a wall of your own making, and without breaking down these walls there can be no communion, no love. Without love, to become chaste, to become a celibate is unchaste. Where there is love there is chastity, there is incorruptibility.

Question: I have been listening to what you have been saying, and I feel to carry out your teachings I must renounce the world I live in.

KRISHNAMURTI: You cannot live in isolation; to exist is to be related. You can live in isolation only in an asylum. You can live happily with the world only when you are not of the world, involved in its worldliness. The world is made up of things, of relationship, and of ideas and the values you have given to them. These valuations cause conflict, and from this misery you desire to escape, which is called renunciation. You may give up your house but you will be attached to your wife; you may renounce your wife but you will cling to idea, to belief. Wrong valuation breeds conflict, confusion and misery. Only right valuation or understanding of property, of name, of belief puts an end to sorrow.

To understand yourself is to understand the giver of values. Without understanding yourself, there is no renunciation of the world; without self-knowledge there can be only escape, called renunciation, which gives birth to endless problems and miseries. It is like a stupid man renouncing stupidity but he is still stupid; his very attempt to become clever is still stupid. If he becomes aware of what is stupidity, which is himself, then surely he will understand greatly. In understanding *what is,* is the beginning of wisdom; the awareness of *what is* opens the door to reality. But escape leads to illusion and not to the discovery of that which is the real. To give right value to property, to relationship,

to ideas is arduous. To escape through renunciation is comparatively easy, and to build a wall of self-enclosing isolation does not lead to happiness. Property has a meaning only according to your valuation. If you are inwardly insufficient, empty, then property becomes enormously important, from which arises the problem of attachment and renunciation. All psychological valuation is the outcome of the craving for self-expansion; this self-expansion process is to cover up this inward poverty, and so the activities of the self are in their very nature an escape, causing conflict, confusion, and sorrow. Happiness lies in understanding the full meaning of *what is* and not in running away into isolation.

Question: Life hurls at us one problem after another. Will the state of awareness of which you speak enable one to understand and dissolve, once and for all, the whole question of problems at one stroke, or have they to be dissolved one after another?

I feel certain deep urges which need to be disciplined. What is the best way of disciplining?

KRISHNAMURTI: If the creator of problems is not understood, then problems are inevitable; if he is deeply and fully comprehended, then problems will cease, or as they arise are understood immediately and dissolved. To merely deal with the symptoms without understanding the cause does not bring about a cure, so to be concerned only with problems without understanding the creator of them is to be in constant conflict. The thinker is the creator of problems, and he resists or disciplines his thoughts in order to meet what he has created. Discipline exists only as a measure of resistance; otherwise thought is not disciplined. If through discipline, habits and self-enclosures are brought about, then fear and anxiety are warded off and achievement and success are gained. Discipline, which is resistance, comes into being when there is no understanding. In understanding a problem, the problem ceases to be, and not in resisting it. If you understand the cause of arrogance and its effect, then you do not have to discipline against it. The disciplining against arrogance is the pride of becoming. So to understand *what is* is strenuous; to understand *what is*, which is arrogance, there must be no distraction, the distraction of the conflict of its opposite, humility. To understand, there must be complete concentration on *what is,* concentration which is not exclusive. The discipline against temptation is the building up of resistance, and resistance is violence, which is death. This self-enclosing process of discipline prevents understanding and communion. A man disciplined in righteousness has no love, for he is enclosing himself within the walls of his becoming. Awareness of the process and of the meaning of discipline brings about intelligence, and that which is intelligent is never resisting, but pliable and swift. That which is pliable is enduring.

Now let us consider the other question, whether problems are to be solved one after another as they arise, or whether it is possible to uproot the cause of all problems. If the maker of problems can be fully understood, then the conflict and sorrow of problems will cease. The creator of problems is the thinker, is it not? Problems do not exist apart from the thinker. Is the thinker separate from his problems? Is the thinker separate from his thoughts? If he is separate, then problems will continue indefinitely; if he is not, then there is a possibility of putting an end to all psychological problems. Does not the thinker separate himself from his thoughts, from his problems, in order to resist or protect himself from all change, while transforming his thoughts or grappling with his problems? Is this not a cunning

trick, an illusion on the part of the thinker to safeguard himself? But if the thinker is the thought, is the problem, inseparable, then he, the maker of problems, can begin to dissolve himself and not be concerned with the change of thought, with the solution of the problem.

Now, if you are aware, you will observe that the thinker has separated from his thought, and on this your philosophies, your sacred books, and beliefs are based. There are only thoughts and not the thinker of thoughts; put aside the qualities of the thinker, his thoughts, where is the thinker? The thinker is not. Set aside the qualities of the self, memory and his attributes, and so on, where is the self? But if you assert that the self is not the thinker but some other entity beyond and above him, he is still the thinker, only you have pushed the thinker further away, but he is still within the field of thought. Now why does the thinker separate himself from his thoughts, his problems? He perceives that thoughts are transient, modified according to environmental influences, that he can shape his thoughts according to the pattern of craving. Since he is seeking permanency, he himself becomes the permanent entity, giving himself continuity. How does the thinker come into being? Obviously through craving. Craving is the outcome of perception, contact, sensation, desire, identification, the 'me' and the 'mine'. The thinker is the product of desire, and having produced the 'I', the 'me', then the 'I', the thinker, separates himself from his thoughts, feelings, and actions. He remains in the illusion of permanency, brooding over his thoughts and problems. So as long as the thinker is separate from his thoughts, ever-increasing problems will continue.

When the thinker is the thought, then what happens? Then the thinker himself is undergoing a transformation, a radical, fundamental transformation. This, as I have said, is right meditation. The passive, yet alert, awareness of the ways of the thinker brings self-knowledge. With self-knowledge there is the beginning of meditation. Meditation is the ending of thought, in which the continuance of the thinker ceases. The thinker in disciplining his thought from which he has separated himself, gives continuity to himself through property, family, through knowledge and belief. Problems will continue as long as the thinker separates himself from his thoughts. When there is an awareness of the total process, then only is there self-knowledge; self-knowledge is the beginning of wisdom. Time, as memory, ceases only through self-knowledge.

December 28, 1947

Radio Talks, India, 1947–48

❋

A New Approach to Life

We realize the confusion and the sorrow which exist in us and about us. Politically and socially, this confusion is not a passing crisis like so many that have been, but a crisis of extraordinary significance. There have been wars, economic depressions, and social convulsions at different periods. But this crisis cannot be compared with these recurring disasters; this crisis is not of any particular country nor the result of any particular system, religious or secular; but it is a crisis in the very worth and significance of man himself. So, we cannot think in terms of patchwork reforms nor seek out substitution of one system for another. To understand it, there must be a revolution in thinking and in feeling. This confusion and sorrow is not the result of mere external events, however catastrophic they may have been; but it is the outcome of confusion and misery in each of us. So, without understanding the individual problem, which is the world problem, there cannot be peace and order within and so without. Since you and I have brought about this degradation and misery, it is utterly futile to look to a system for a transformation of the present condition. Since you and I are responsible for the present chaos, you and I have to bring about in ourselves the transformation of values.

This transformation of values cannot take place by any legislation nor through any outer compelling agencies. If we look to them, we shall find similar misery and confusion repeated. We have been reduced to this state of conflict and confusion by giving predominance to sensory values, and sensate values always breed dullness of mind and heart. Sensory values make our existence mechanical and uncreative.

Food, clothing, and shelter are not an end in themselves. But they become so when the psychological significance of man is not understood. Regeneration can take place only when you, as an individual, become aware of those conditions that limit thought and feeling. This limitation is self-imposed by the mind which is ever seeking its own security through property, through family, and through idea or belief. This psychological search for security necessitates the cultivation of things, made by the hand or by the mind. And so, things, family or name, and belief become all-important, because happiness is sought through them. Since happiness cannot be found in them, thought creates a higher form of belief, a higher form of security. So long as the mind is seeking self-protective security, there can be no understanding of relationship between man and man; then relationship is mere gratification and not a process of self-knowledge.

It is important to understand the significance of right relationship. There can be no existence in isolation. To be is to be related. And without relationship there is no existence. Relationship is challenge and response. The relationship of one with another is society; society is not independent of you; the mass is not a separate entity by itself, but it is the product of you and your relationship with another. Relationship is the awareness of interaction between you and another. Now, what is this relationship based on? You say it is based on interdependence, mutual assistance, and so on; but apart from the emotional screen which we throw up against each other, what is it actually founded on? On mutual gratification, is it not? If I do not please you, you get rid of me in different ways; and if I please you, you accept me as your wife, your neighbor, or as your friend, or your guru. This is the actual fact, is it not? Relationship is sought when there is mutual gratification, satisfaction; and when you do not find it or it is not given to you, you change your relationship, you seek a divorce; or putting up with *what is,* you try to find gratification elsewhere, or you change your guru, your teacher, or join another organization. You move from one relationship to another until you find what you seek, which is gratification, security, comfort, and so on. When you seek gratification in relationship, there is ever bound to be conflict. When in relationship security is sought, which is ever evasive, there is the struggle to possess, to dominate, and the pain of jealousy, of uncertainty. Self-assertive demands, possessiveness, the desire for psychological security and comfort deny love. You may talk about love as responsibility, as duty and so on, but actually there is no love, which can be seen in the structure of modern society. The manner you treat your husbands and wives, your children, your neighbors, and your friends is an indication of the lack of love in relationship.

What then is the significance of relationship? If you observe yourself in relationship, do you not find that it is a process of self-revelation? Does not your contact with another reveal, if you are aware, your own state of being? Relationship is a process of self-revelation, of self-knowledge; since it reveals unpleasant and disquieting thoughts and actions, there is a flight from such relationship into a comforting and soothing one. Relationship becomes of very little significance when it is based on mutual gratification; but it becomes very significant when it is self-revealing. Love has no relationship. It is only when the other becomes more important than love, there begins relationship of pleasure and pain. When you give yourself over utterly and wholly—when you love—then there is no relationship as mutual gratification or as a process of self-revelation. There is no gratification in love. Such love is a marvelous thing. In it there is no friction, but a state of complete integration, of ecstatic being. There are such moments, such rare, happy, and joyous moments when there is love, complete communion. Love recedes when the object of love becomes more important; then a conflict of possession, of fear, of jealousy begins, and so love recedes; and the further it recedes, the greater the problem of relationship becomes, losing its worth, its meaning. Love cannot be brought into being through discipline, through any means, through any intellectual urgency. It is a state of being which comes when the activities of the self have ceased. These activities must not be disciplined away, suppressed, or shunned, but understood. There must be an awareness and so an understanding of the activities of the self in all its different layers.

Without self-knowledge there can be no right thinking. Right thinking can come into being only when each one is aware of his every thought, feeling, and activities. Through this awareness in which there can be no condemnation, justification, or identification, every thought can be completed and understood. Thus the mind begins to free itself through its choiceless awareness from its self-created impediments and bondages. Only in this freedom can reality come into being.

Our problem then is not adherence to any particular system of thought—political or religious—but for the individual to awaken to his own conflict, confusion, and sorrow. When he becomes conscious of his strife and pain, the inevitable response is to escape from them through beliefs, through social activities, through amusements, or through identifying himself with political action either of the right or of the left. But the confusion and the sorrow are not solved through escapes which only intensify strife and pain. The escapes which religious organizations offer as a means of resolving this confusion are obviously unworthy of a thoughtful man; for, the God they offer is the God of security, and not the understanding of confusion and pain in which man lives. Idolatry, the worship of things made by the hand or by the mind, only sets man against man; it offers not the dissolution of sorrow of man, but an easy escape, a distraction which dulls the mind and the heart. Likewise are the political systems; in them man finds easy escapes from his present existence. For in them the present is sacrificed for the future. But the present is the only door through which understanding can come into being. The future is ever uncertain, and only the present can ever be transformed by fully and deeply understanding *what is*. So, organized religions and political systems cannot resolve this confusion and sorrow of man.

Man himself, you yourself, have to face this confusion by putting aside all systems and all beliefs and trying to understand what is actually taking place within yourself. For, what you are the world is; and the world cannot be regenerated without first transforming yourself. So, the emphasis must be laid not on the mere transformation of the world, but on the individual himself, on you; for you are the world and the world is not, without you. For this transformation, the leader—spiritual or secular—becomes a hindrance, a degenerating factor in civilization. This regeneration can take place only when—setting aside all the impediments such as nationalism, organized religions, organized beliefs, and those barriers that set man against man, like caste, race, systems, and so on—you understand yourself by being aware of your daily thoughts, feelings, and actions.

Only when thought is free from the sensory values made by the hand or by the mind, can there be the realization of truth. There is no path to truth. You must sail on the uncharted sea to find it. Reality cannot be conveyed to another, for that which is conveyed is already known, and what is known is not the real. Happiness does not lie in the multiplication of blueprints or systems nor in those values which modern civilization offers, but it lies in that freedom which virtue brings; virtue is not an end in itself but it is essential, for in that freedom only, can reality come into being. The mere pursuit and the multiplication of sensate values can lead only to further confusion and misery, to further wars and disasters.

There can be peace and order in the world only when you as an individual—through self-knowledge and so through right thinking, which is not of any book nor given by any teacher—set aside those values that bring strife and confusion. The purpose of man is not this constant strife and misery, but the realization of that love and happiness which comes into being with reality.

Talk broadcast and published by kind courtesy of All-India Radio, Madras, October 16, 1947

The Way of Living

The human world in which we live is made up of individuals, and without the individual society would have no existence. The world's problems are only problems of relationship between man and man. Hence the individual problem is the world problem. The world is only the individual in his relations with others based on what he thinks of himself.

Man is the product of a total world process and is not a separative force; his being is not founded in antagonism. What affects the individual affects the world deeply; there is no separation; the regeneration of the individual is immediately and totally reflected in the transformation of the world.

Without the regeneration of the individual, there can be no fundamental revolution. Without a basic revolution of values, a true and lasting order is not possible. It is our concern to bring about this revolution. It is a revolution in feeling and thinking and thereby in acting. These three are not separate but are a unitary process. They are interrelated and mutually dependent.

Only when we have brought about order and peace in our own lives, when we are out of this confusion, can there be the comprehension of the real, which alone can bring happiness to mankind. Without this comprehension whatever we do will lead only to further disaster and sorrow.

You, the individual, are far more important than any system, religious or social. The systems are preventing man from solving his problems. Systems have become much more

urgent than the suffering of man. Patterns of action destroy human freedom and lead man into confusion and misery. Only in the understanding of *what is,* of the present, the actual, is there a possibility of transforming it. The world can be changed only in the present, not in the future, only here, not elsewhere.

If we look to systems which are patterns of action, we necessarily create leaders and gurus, who take us away from the central problem of our own suffering. Suffering cannot be overcome through any belief or through any pattern of action. No leader, political or religious, can bring about order in ourselves. Each one of us has to understand the confusion and sorrow that is in us, which we project into the world. This projection is society with its violence and degradation.

We suffer at different levels of our consciousness, physical and psychological. This suffering takes different forms within each one of us, but we must distrust the dissimilar and concentrate on the similar.

There is economic chaos brought about by the overemphasis on sensate values. We try to solve it by further increase of sensate values, through expansion of production of things. We look for greater satisfaction to the machine and thereby give importance to things, to property, name, and caste. If we look round or into ourselves, we see that property, name, and caste have become extraordinarily important, and as they have assumed such predominant value, naturally they bring conflict between man and man. We use things made by the hand or by the machine as a means of escape from our psychological conflict and distress.

So mere rearrangement of things according to any pattern of action, whether of the extreme left or of the right, will have little significance if there is no comprehension of the psychological confusion and misery in which each one of us lives.

So the emphasis should be laid on the conflict within the individual. It is of no value to attempt all the time to bring order into the outward existence; for the inner, the psychological will always overcome the outer, however well and cunningly organized and legislated.

This psychological conflict in ourselves is of the greatest importance. It manifests itself in our relationship to things, to people, and to ideas. It is this false relationship which causes suffering. And to bring about true relationship is the task of each one of us who is trying to solve this appalling chaos and agony in the world.

There cannot be any isolation from the world, for to be is to be related. Without understanding relationship, true action is not, for what we call action is merely movement within the framework of ideology. Such movement is bound to create further sorrow and suffering. Relationship is communion and this communion is prevented when the isolating process is strong. In relationship each one of us is merely seeking security on different levels of our existence. The search for gratification through things, through people, and through ideas brings about isolation, a self-enclosing wall, which prevents relationship. Though we think we are related, what we are actually doing is to look over the wall of isolation, but always remaining within the walls and thereby bringing greater suffering to ourselves and to others. Relationship in isolation inevitably leads to cruelty and fear.

But relationship need not be a process of isolation. It can be a process of self-revelation, which is the understanding of ourselves. Such understanding is a total process. This self-knowledge which comes through relationship cannot be found in books, in the guru, or in any leader. If you look to them, you are merely avoiding immediate action. So it is very important to understand the function of relationship to things, to people, and to ideas. Suffering comes into being when this relationship, instead of being a self-revealing action, becomes a self-enclosing movement.

So when there is suffering, we should not try to seek a solution for suffering. We should rather look into relationship, which is the primary cause of sorrow. Sorrow is the effect of false intention in relationship. Whenever we seek in relationship gratification, escape, or security, we approach another with a motive, and in such approach there is violence. And because of violence in relationship, there is violence in the world.

The ideal of nonviolence is the avoidance of the understanding of violence. The idealist who is seeking to be nonviolent avoids thereby the fundamental transformation of violence. Nonviolence is merely an idea, but what is actual is violence. Violence can be understood and transformed when the fictitious ideal is taken away. The idea of the opposite becomes an obstacle to *what is*. The opposite of violence is itself violence, never love, which is its own eternity. The idealist who is pursuing the opposite can never know this love. He is always merely concerned with becoming nonviolent, which is always the expression of the self, whether it is positive or negative, whether asserting or denying. We must abandon the ideal to solve the process of suffering. Knowledge, which is mere memory, must be put away because the present cannot be understood through the past, but the past can be understood in the present. The problem of violence cannot be solved through thinking because the roots of thinking and of violence are the same. Only when there is cessation of the thought process will violence come to an end. It ceases when awareness, free from condemnation or justification, embraces violence in compassionate understanding. This cessation of thought is 'being' and 'being' is ever creative. Then only is there reality, the bliss of which must be discovered to be known.

Violence throughout the world is not to be overcome through the patterns of action either of the left or of the right. Violence is a symptom of inner emptiness, which neither violence nor nonviolence can fill, for the very struggle to fill this emptiness leads to more violence. To be free from violence we must understand this emptiness. This will happen when we are alone, but not isolated. Aloneness is freedom from belief in any form, from all hindrances that crowd our life. In this freedom alone, reality comes into being. Reality is the fullness of understanding and love.

This love is not born out of suppression of hatred and violence. He only will know it who has seen the face of violence and has not turned away from it, has not covered it up with an ideal, which is again violence both in intention and in result. Love is not the goal, the distant end of a weary path; it is hidden in the acceptance of the actual and therefore of the real. In love of life there is truth, not in the ideal, which is violence to truth. Truth alone can set us free and in freedom alone can there be love of man.

This freedom is not independence, which is mere isolation. This freedom knows no man-made frontiers. It is the freedom of the mind born from compassionate understanding. This freedom is always individual, never political or economic. It is always an inner discovery. Nobody can grant it nor is it a result of struggle. It comes of its own, silently and swiftly, when the mind looks at its own limitations in humble understanding.

It is this freedom alone that can renew the world. Only those in whom it is born are truly nonviolent because they are nonviolent to truth. They are the forerunners of the greatest revolution—the revolution to the real.

Talk broadcast and published by kind courtesy of All-India Radio, Bombay, February 2, 1948

The Way of Peace

Wherever we may live, each one of us is aware that there is in the world an ever-mounting confusion. This loss of orientation, this degeneration of values is not restricted to any particular class or nation. Wherever we live, at whatever level of society we move, we are aware in our relationship to the outer world and to the inner world of ideas, that there is conflict and misery that seem to have no end.

Many solutions have been offered for this confusion—solutions economic and political, social and religious. And yet no system can bring about peace. Systems with the ideologies and their patterns for action are merely concerned with outward changes and adjustments. They are unable to bring about a radical transformation, for they strive towards a result, a goal, which is the outcome of superficial knowledge, calculation, and frustration. Their knowledge is not integrated. The experts who offer well-thought-out formulas are obsessed with preconceived achievements, and are incapable of understanding the psychological complexities of the human mind and heart.

The systems, being entirely concerned with results and not with the means, can only offer patterns of action and variations of ideas. As long as peace is conceived in terms of opposing ideologies, there cannot be peace. As long as peace is a matter of which side wins, the victor is invariably faced with disaster because in order to conquer he has to let loose powers which enslave him. The way of peace is to understand the fallacy of the idea that peace is the result of strife, the outcome of a physical or mental conflict between military or ideological antagonists. Peace is not the result of a struggle; peace is that which remains when all conflict is dissolved in the flame of understanding; peace is not the opposite of conflict nor the synthesis of opposites.

Systems, philosophical and economic, are turned out in large numbers by the specialists, and these various systems compete with each other for power. After all, experts and specialists can only offer their opinion; they cannot offer the true solution, for the true solution is completely outside all systems. A system may be technically sound and yet inapplicable except by compulsion, and there cannot be peace through compulsion. There can be no peace without the removal of the causes of chaos. And the roots of sorrow must be seen by each one before they wither away. Yet we do rely on specialists because each one of us does not want to think out for himself the problems of peace, but prefers to rely on the experts, the politicians, the economic planners. But surely peace is not of the realm of ideas. You can see for yourself that peace is not the product of a thought process. Our thinking is conditioned and therefore limited. Limited thinking is invariably erroneous and always a source of conflict. To rely on systems, however technically perfect, is to avoid the responsibility of being directly concerned with peace.

The war, this evergrowing tragedy, is after all merely the spectacular and bloody expression of our daily life. War is not an accidental result of an irresponsible society. This misery, this violence, this appalling chaos in the world is the result of our daily actions in relationship to things, to people, and to ideas. As long as this relationship is not fully and deeply understood, there can be no peace in the world. Peace and happiness do not come into being by themselves, or by chance. To be happy and peaceful one has to pay the price. This price may appear enormous, but in reality it is not so very great; the only price to pay is the clear intention to have peace in ourselves and so live in peace with our neighbors. This intention is essential. The price of peace is the freedom from the causes

that bring in their wake strife and violence, antagonism and envy. Peace is a way of life, not the result of strategy on the part of the individual or of a group. It is a way of life in which violence is not suppressed by the ideal of nonviolence, but in which violence in its effects and causes is deeply understood and therefore transcended.

To understand violence there must be clear awareness of violence to its various expressions. The causes of violence are complex and various. Nationalism, class antagonism, acquisitiveness, the lust for power, and the innumerable beliefs from which our minds suffer all bring about violence. Acquisitiveness, which is the basis of our present civilization, has divided man against man. In our desire to possess, to dominate peoples' thoughts, feelings, and work, we have divided ourselves into classes, class governments, class struggles, class wars, and also into Hindus and Muslims, Americans and Russians, workers and peasants. The power over things made by the hand is the least disastrous; it is the mental, the psychological slavery of man to man that is so brutalizing and disintegrating. The real causes of war are hidden in our unwillingness to keep inwardly, psychologically, free. As long as we are not ready to abandon our beliefs, dogmas, ideologies, and systems of thought, patterns of behavior, and the various compulsions— which are merely chains provided by society in order to control without understanding— the problem of violence will continue. These chains will bring about inevitable chaos and misery to all the schemes for social or political, economic or religious transformation.

And yet we can live extremely simply and wisely, and therefore peacefully, if our minds and hearts are not burdened by possessiveness, whether of things made by the hand or by the mind. What we need in the way of food, clothing, and shelter will come to us easily and sanely when our lives will be free from violence. This freedom from violence is love. The expert, economic or religious, political or social, is leading us to disaster. Each one must concern himself with the creation of a new society or a new culture, free from the causes which are destroying and disintegrating the world in which we live. So it is for you, the individual, to realize that it is by your own transformation, by freely paying the price for peace, by your gladly abandoning nationalism and class security, ideologies and organized religions, that you can bring peace to the world. Your own transformation is of the utmost importance because you yourself are the cause of the confusion in the world in which you live, and the way of your life will immediately transform the world about you, or continue further the chaos and sorrow.

What you are is of the highest importance and not the assertions of the experts. It is your everyday conduct that is decisive in bringing about peace to the world; it is not mass movements impelled by physical and psychological compulsions that can bring about peace and happiness to man. Unless you cease to yield to pressure—physical or mental, religious or political—you will continue to be the creator and the victim of this appalling misery. Therefore you the individual are the world problem. You are the only problem because all the other problems are created by your unwillingness to tackle yourself first and to understand yourself deeply and fully.

The problems of the world are your own problems merely magnified and multiplied. They are not in any way strange to you— they are the same problems of food and shelter, of affection and freedom, of peace and happiness. You are a part and an expression of the world, and the world is reflected in you fully and completely. You cannot separate yourself from the world because the world affects you and you affect the world, whether you like it or not. All attempts to estrange yourself from the world will inevitably lead to decay, to the withering of the mind and the heart. You have made the world and you have to transform it. It is by your conduct, by your way of living, by fundamentally regenerating yourself that you can create a new world free from want and strife, from exploitation and war. This fundamental regeneration, this complete transformation will come if you are aware of your thoughts, feelings, and actions. Be aware of how you behave in your daily life, how you are conditioned by the past and the surroundings, how you act from memory, from greed, from imitativeness and submissiveness. Do not condemn your life. Be compassionate to yourself, but do not justify yourself. Without condemnation and justification, see yourself as you are, watch yourself thinking, feeling, and acting until you begin to understand yourself. This flame of understanding brings about disentanglement, which makes for true simplicity. It is this simplicity of mind and heart that will bring about the transformation of the individual and will immediately transform the world in which you live.

You will become aware of violence in your daily life. If you condemn it, you will create the opposite—the ideal of nonviolence which only perpetuates violence by involving you in an endless conflict with violence. To remain in a state of conflict is itself violence. To cultivate an ideal of nonviolence while all the time living in violence is hypocrisy—a betrayal of the truth of the actual—and so the greatest form of violence. An ideal is always something that is not; it is an imaginary fiction, this opposite. The actual is the only thing that exists. Being fictitious, the ideal is noneffective and therefore sustains violence in some form or the other. But in the full and pliable awareness of violence with its various implications, there is freedom from it and not merely substitution by another form of violence.

Love alone can transform the world. No system, either of the left or the right, however cunningly or convincingly devised, can bring peace and happiness to the world. Love is not an ideal, but it comes into being when there is respect and mercy, which all of us can feel and do feel. We must show this respect and mercy to all. It is the way of our being and it comes with the richness of understanding. Where there is greed and envy, where there is belief and dogma, there cannot be love. Where there is nationalism or attachment to sensate values, there cannot be love. And yet it is love alone that resolves all our human difficulties. Without love life is crude, cruel, and empty. But to see the truth of love, each one must be free from those self-enclosing processes that are destroying the individual and disintegrating the world. Peace and happiness come when the mind and heart are not burdened by those ways of life that are constantly isolating.

Love and truth are not to be found in any book, church, or temple. They come into being with self-knowledge. Self-knowing is an arduous but not a difficult process; it becomes difficult only when we are trying to achieve a result. But to be just aware from moment to moment of the ways of one's thoughts, feelings, and actions without condemnation and justification brings a freedom, a liberation in which alone there can be the bliss of truth. It is this truth that will bring peace to the world. It is this truth that will make each one of us a blessing in our relationship, a source of happiness.

This war, which seems so catastrophically imminent, cannot be prevented by any spasmodic effort of diplomacy or by the game of conferences. Pacts and treaties will not stop the war. What can put an end to those recurring wars is goodwill. Ideologies in their very nature cause conflict, antagonism, and confusion, and so goodwill is destroyed.

Ideologies become all-important when the individual and his inward happiness are denied. Then you and I become merely pawns in the game of powerseekers, and where there is hunger after power, whether it be individual or collective, there must be bloodshed and sorrow.

The way of peace is simple. It is the way of truth and love. It starts with the individual himself. Where the individual accepts his responsibility for war and violence, there peace finds a foothold. To go far one must begin near and the first actions are within. The sources of peace are not outside of us and the heart of man is in his own keeping. To have peace, we must be peaceful. To put an end to violence each one must voluntarily free himself from the causes of violence. Diligently one must put himself to the task of self-transformation. Our minds and hearts must be simple, creatively empty, and watchful. Then only can love come into being. Love alone can bring peace to the world, and then only the world will know the bliss of the real.

Talk broadcast and published by kind courtesy of All-India Radio, Bombay, April 3, 1948

Bombay, India, 1948

--- ✳ ---

First Talk in Bombay

When there is communion on the same level and at the same time, there is understanding. Listening is an art, whether to a problem or to each other. To commune there must be no prejudice, no fear, no resistance. Deep and full attention is the beginning of understanding. Understanding is instantaneous, ever in the present; it is not the outcome of growth, not of time. When the heart is dry, the mind fills it with words, but this is not understanding. The realization of truth is ever in the now, and not in the morrow. To receive truth the heart must be open, vulnerable. None can give you truth; it must come to you. To receive it, to directly perceive it there must be no defense, no safeguards, no walls of resistance.

Understanding comes with the awareness of *what is*. To be aware of *what is*, of the obvious, of the actual, without interpreting, without translating, is the beginning of wisdom. The truth of *what is* is passed over when the mind is burdened with prejudice, with belief, is distorted with effort. To understand exactly, the actual puts an end to conflict. To be aware of exactly what one is, from moment to moment, brings freedom from conflict and confusion. It is the beginning of wisdom. To understand the actual, *what is* frees thought from the process of time. Time is a destructive process; it creates confusion. The psychological process of becoming breeds time, and time is not the solvent of problems. There can be understanding of *what is* only when there is no condemnation of, nor identification with, *what is*. To be aware of the actual is already the beginning of intelligence, but to be unaware and to struggle only breeds habit.

What is is never static; it is ever in movement, ever undergoing modification; and to follow it, a very alert and passive mind is necessary. It must be free from conclusions, from answers, from belief, and from knowledge to follow the swift movement of *what is*. To know *what is*, the actual, is to transcend it.

There is confusion and sorrow; there is individual and collective suffering. This misery is everywhere. How are we to grapple with it? How are we to understand it? What is your response to this misery? From your response, you will be able to directly understand your relationship to this mounting confusion. Those who derive benefit from this misery, worldly or psychological, have their peculiar response and action. They want things to continue as they are. Then there are those whose response in the midst of this misery is to protect what they have, seeking security at different levels. There are others whose response is towards legislation, towards reform, towards outward order; or to try to solve this problem according to a system either of the left or of the right; or seek out a leader, a guru, political or religious, to lead them out of this increasing suffering. All these are various methods of escape from the problem itself. Then escapes become far more important than the problem itself; the ideology, the guru, the bank account, the psychological security become far more important than sorrow itself; then the leader, the authority, is far more significant than misery itself; then organization, rituals, assume dominating importance. These become all-important, and not the misery of men. When ideologies and their authorities—either of the right or of the left, religious or secular—assume power, humanity, you, are sacrificed.

What is the cause of this mounting confusion and sorrow, inwardly and outwardly? You have to discover the cause and not merely repeat the authorities of the right or of the left. You must know the truth of it and not repeat the assertions of others, however wise and learned. In discovering for yourself the truth of the cause of sorrow, there is freedom from sorrow; truth liberates and mere repetition is ignorance. It is important to understand this—that truth liberates and you must discover it. When sensate values predominate, there is confusion; there is sorrow when the values of the mind dominate eternal values; there is confusion when the fabrications of the mind fill the heart. When things made by the hand or by the mind assume supreme importance, then there is conflict, confusion, and sorrow. When the value of things dominates, then belief and ideology possess significant influence. From this confusion we try to escape, and the very search for the real becomes a flight from *what is*. He who seeks, struggles to find truth, can never find it; but in understanding *what is,* truth comes into being. To understand, there must be still, silent observation and alert, passive awareness.

Destruction is keeping pace with existence. Frustration follows action; the wave of confusion is ever covering our life; death is ever our companion. Some have freed themselves from confusion and sorrow, but confusion and sorrow continue. Each one must free himself from this confusion and sorrow, and then only can there be happiness and peace in the world. This freedom is not to be found tomorrow, but in the now. Time does not bring understanding; understanding is ever in the present. You must free yourself from misery now and not wait for tomorrow. To wait for tomorrow is to be caught in the wave of death and confusion. If you postpone, you are caught in the wave of strife and misery. You must perceive the truth now, for truth is the liberator and not your effort, not your craving for freedom, for happiness. Truth must be perceived now and not be postponed; in postponing you give birth to confusion. Truth alone can bring about creative revolution, the revolution of renewal. Change is a modified continuation; the revolution of the left is the continuation of the right. But this creative revolution is not a modified change, but the abandonment of change altogether. While thought is changing, moving from the known to the known, there cannot be renewal. This revolution can only take place in the individual. Individuality comes into being in relationship. This relationship creates society; society is not a separate entity, existing by itself. It is the outward projection of the inner relationship between man and man. The mere change of the outer has little significance without a fundamental transformation in the psychological activities.

Without self-knowledge, there is no foundation for right thinking and action. No system can transplant self-knowledge, the knowledge of the ways of the mind and heart. Systems can and do modify and change the outer activity of man, but man always transforms the system according to his inner demands. Until I in my relationship with you understand and thereby bring about fundamental transformation, I am the cause of conflict and confusion, destruction and misery, exploitation and ruthlessness. This understanding does not lie in the future, but always in the present. If you look for it in the future, tomorrow, then you are caught in the wave of confusion and death. When there is absorbing interest there is immediate understanding and action. If there is no psychological transformation now, it will not come tomorrow, in the future. Change, modified continuity, will take place with tomorrow, but it is not fundamental transformation. This transformation can take place only now and not in duration, in time. So how can you who are the result of the past, your thought founded on the past, on yesterday, on time, step out of time? Time ceases when there is complete understanding. This timeless being is not an illusion, a self-induced hallucination. When a problem is completely understood it leaves no residue, memory; memory is time. The self, the continuation of memory, breeds time, the ever-accumulating past. The freedom from the self takes place only when each problem, as it arises, is completely and deeply understood.

Question: I am born with a certain temperament, a certain psychological and physical pattern, whatever may be its reason. This pattern becomes the major single factor in my life. It dominates me absolutely. My freedom within the pattern is very limited, the majority of my reactions and impulses being rigidly predetermined. Can I break away from the tyranny of genetic factors?

KRISHNAMURTI: Each one of us is the result of his father and mother who in turn were the product of their parents. Their beliefs, their hopes and fears, their craving for security, their gods and their temples, their knowledge and their superstition, their envy and ambition is the structure of society, the environment in which each one is held. He is a part of the environment; he is the result of the past in conjunction with the present. He is held in a psychological and environmental influence. The son is the father, modified. Existence is the product of the past through the present to the future. It is the outcome of time. You are the result of yesterday, modified by today, giving birth to tomorrow. Now, the questioner asks, can he step out of time? Can he break away from the pattern of the past?

When *what is* is interpreted then thought slips into the unreal, into theory, into speculation and credulity. To understand *what is* is arduous. What is it that conditions you? What is it that limits thought? What is it that creates the pattern in which thought is caught? Is it not thought itself? If thought ceases, the pattern is broken. Thought is the outcome of yesterday, of the past; it responds to every challenge, which is ever new, according to the pattern of yesterday. Can thought free itself from the burden of yesterday? Only when thinking, as we know it, ceases. This cessation of thought is not an escape from thought.

You seem puzzled; you are waiting for an answer from me for this question. But the answer is in the question itself. In understanding *what is*, the problem itself, the solution is found. The very problem holds its own solution. If you look to the answer, then the problem is not understood; but in studying the problem itself, without the anxious search for the answer, the problem ceases. If you look for an answer you will find it; but it will be according to your convenience, to your gratification.

So the problem is this: thought is conditioned, fixed in a pattern. Thought responds to challenge, which is ever new, according to the past, thus modifying the new. Thought, which is the product of yesterday, can only respond in terms of yesterday, of time. When you ask, "How can I break away from the tyranny of conditioning?" you are asking a wrong question. Thought can never be free. Thought only knows continuity, not freedom. Freedom is when thought is not. There is freedom only when the process of continuity ceases. Thought gives continuity. So thought must be aware of its own conditioning and not try to become something. The becoming gives continuity to thought and thus there is no freedom from conditioning. Thought must cease for freedom to be. When thought is active, positively or negatively, then it is conditioning, giving birth to modified continuity.

Can thinking cease? What is thinking? The so-called thinking is the response of memory. Memory is the residue of experience. When there is a challenge, thought, which is the result of yesterday, responds. Challenge, which is ever new, is met with the old, and so the new is not completely understood. This incompleteness of an experience leaves a mark which we call memory. Have you not noticed that when you understand an experience completely that there is no memory of it? It is only an incomplete act that leaves a mark. The response of memory is called thinking. Can there be a state in which memory is not functioning? When time ceases, there is such a state which alone transforms, which alone is creative.

January 18, 1948

Second Talk in Bombay

The understanding of *what is* is arduous; for, *what is* is never static, it is in constant movement. A mind that wishes to understand it must be swift and pliable. All problems are always new and the mind must be fresh to grasp their full meaning. Every crisis is new and the mind must be unburdened by the past to understand it fully.

There is an urgency of inward revolution which alone can bring about a radical transformation in the outer circumstances of life, in society. Action without this constant inward revolution becomes repetitive, static. This action is society. This action of relationship between man and man is society. So society without this creative, psychological revolution is ever becoming crystallized and constantly has to be broken. Outward revolution has no significance without the inner, psychological transformation of the individual. In the social structure there is ever the seed of decay, and only the individual can ever be in constant and creative revolution. Society is always static and only in the individual is there hope. Can there be any relationship between the creative, revolutionary individual and the ever static society? Social revolution through any means is always static, as there is no inward revolution of the individual. Mere change in the outward structure of man has little significance without psychological revolution of the individual. If relationship is not the outcome of inward revolution, then that relationship which is the social structure makes the individual static, repetitive. Each one is aware of the disintegrating factor in relationship, and so in the social structure of the present civilization.

It does not need specialists to tell us an obvious fact that society is disintegrating, crumbling. So there must be new builders to create a new social order; the new structure must be built on a new foundation. The new architects are not the politicians of the left or of the right, nor are they any party specialists. The new architects must be you and me, the individual. To look to authority, to leaders is to sustain disintegration. Through self-knowledge, you and I must rediscover lasting values; they must be newly discovered by each one.

So, you and I must become creative because the problem is urgent. You and I must be aware of the causes of the collapse of society, and build a new structure whose foundation is based on our creative understanding. This creative understanding is negative thinking, and negative thinking is the highest form of meditation. To understand what is creative thinking, we must approach the problem negatively. A positive approach to a problem is imitative and therefore disintegrating. For, understanding comes not through any positive system, or positive formula, or conclusion, but through negative understanding.

One of the fundamental reasons for the disintegration of society is that you, as an individual, have been imitative outwardly and inwardly—outwardly the mere cultivation of technique, and inwardly copying, which comes from fear and the desire to be secure. Our education and our religious life is based on imitation, to fit into a formula, to be Hindus or Christians, Muslims or Buddhists. This prevents creative existence. Where there is imitation, there is the disintegrating factor of a leader. Where there is worship of authority, there must be disintegration also, which prevents creative understanding. In the happy moments of creativeness there is no repetition, no copying. Where there is regimentation and the worship of authority, there must be disintegration and collapse of true values. The substitution of one authority for another is still to be in conflict, and so there cannot be creative understanding.

Where there is becoming there must be copying and authority. Becoming creative admits the process of time. In becoming, there must be the authority, the example, the ideal, the tomorrow. In being, there is the cessation of time, and so it is a state of immediate transformation.

Question: What is your solution to the problem of starvation?

KRISHNAMURTI: The answer to any human problem lies in the problem itself. The answer is never outside the problem. If we can understand the problem itself with all its significance, then the answer comes. But, if you have a ready-made answer or a formula for the problem, then you will never understand the problem. For, the answer, the conclusion, the formula intervenes between the problem and its understanding, which distorts the understanding of the problem.

Will any solution offered by any system, either of the left or of the right, put an end to starvation? When I am asked whether I have a solution to this question, in this question is implied whether I have a system which will put an end to starvation. Now, can any system bring about the ending of starvation? Why have systems become important? They have become important because we think they will solve the problem. Through a pattern of action we hope to solve this question. By outward compulsion it is hoped that man can be fed. Systems become important because each one thinks that through legislation, through compulsion, through some outward action, we can feed man.

Why have food, clothing, and shelter become so predominantly important in man's life? They are necessary. But, why have they become such an all-consuming problem? Why have things made by the hand or by the mind become so extraordinarily significant in our lives? If we can answer this question, that is, if we can find the truth of this, then they will assume their true value. Then, they will not become the dominant influence in our lives. When systems become important, the feeding, clothing, and sheltering of man become of secondary importance; then we will kill man to maintain the system, and the problem of starvation will continue. If we do not look to a system, but understand what are the significant implications in the problem itself, then we will find the right means which will bring about the right end.

Why have you and I given such an extraordinary significance to property, whether made by the hand or by the mind? We give importance to sensate values because we use them as a psychological means for self-expansion. Property has very little meaning in itself; but property becomes extraordinarily significant in giving you power, position, prestige, and so on. Since it gives you power and authority, you cling to it, and on this you build a system which destroys compassion and generosity and thereby the feeding of man. So long as you and I use property, name, belief—which are food, clothes, and shelter on a different level—as a means of self-expansion, there must be starvation, conflict between man and man. As long as the state or a group of people are using food, clothing, and shelter as a means of gaining power, starvation will continue. So, a system does not offer a solution to the problem of starvation; a system is ever in the hands of a few, and so the system becomes important.

Only when you and I are aware that we are using property—things made by the hand or by the mind—as a means of self-expansion, and see the falseness of such an action, then only can there be happiness in our relationship with man. After all, take away your name, your title, your possessions, what are you? You are nothing. To cover up this fear of being nothing, property, name, family, ideas become all-important. This psychological emptiness of man must be understood and not covered up; and to understand it, there must be the freedom from the desire for self-expansion through property, family, idea. So, this question of starvation is more a psychological problem than mere legislation and enforcement. If you see the truth of this, then you put an end to the process of self-expansion through essential needs and therefore help to bring about a new social order. If you do not give predominance to sensate values, then this problem can be solved simply. Then, the scientists and others can give us all food, clothes, and shelter; but, as they themselves are caught in the self-expansive process, they are not a help to man. So, the solution of the problem lies in your understanding of this self-expansive process, and its disintegrating action in your relationship to essential needs. If you truly understand this, there will be an inner revolution which will create a new social structure.

In understanding *what is*, truth comes into being. It is the perception of truth that is liberating and not the clever systems or ideation. Ideas breed further ideas and opposition and in no way bring happiness to man. Only when ideation ceases is there being, and this being is the immediate transformation which truth alone gives.

Question: You say we can remain aware even in sleep. Please explain.

KRISHNAMURTI: Consciousness is of many layers. It is not merely a superficial layer. Consciousness is made up of hidden intentions, unrevealed motives, unsolved problems, tradition, memory, the impingement of the past on the present, the continuation of the past through the present to the future: all this and more is consciousness. This is not a theory, but we are studying *what is*. This is actually what is consciousness. The many layers of memories, the many unsolved problems which we call memory, the racial instincts, the past in conjunction with the present which is time giving birth to the future—all this is consciousness.

Now, most of us are functioning within the superficial layers of consciousness. As I see that some of you are not interested in what is being said, please listen to it merely as information. But, if you will go into it deeper, you will see that what I have said is a fact. As I have said, I have not studied any religious or psychological books. I am not using any jargon of the psychologists. Being aware of oneself, one discovers all these and greater things. In one's self is the whole of wisdom. Self-knowledge is the beginning of meditation, and without self-knowledge there is no right thinking. Without self-knowledge, there is no basis for thought. We are exploring consciousness and you can explore it directly as I am talking; be aware and experience, not merely verbally.

As I was saying, most of us function in the superficial layers of consciousness; so we remain shallow and our action brings further confusion and misery. There is liberation from sorrow only when the whole of consciousness is fully and deeply understood—which is not a matter of time. Since we function within the superficial layers of consciousness, naturally action creates problems. Such action can never solve our problems. These superficial layers are always the breeding ground of problems. Most of our daily activities are the responses of these superficially cultivated layers. Now, when you have a problem, you try to solve it superficially, worrying over it, struggling with it as a dog with a bone; and yet, you do not find the right solution for it. Then, what happens? You go to bed with it, and when you wake up, you have either seen a new way of looking at it, or you have solved it. In this there is nothing extraordinary or mysterious. These superficial layers of consciousness have thought about this problem during the day, trying to translate it according to its immediate demands and prejudices. During the so-called sleep, the superficial consciousness is somewhat quiet, relaxed, temporarily inactive. Then, into that superficial layer, the hidden projects its intimation which becomes the solution. So, when you wake up and

when the superficial layer becomes active, the problem is reexamined and understood. This process is not reserved for the occultists nor the dream experts. It is in everyday life an obvious fact which can be observed by you, for yourself. The superficial layers can be quieted during the day, and the problem understood directly, if you are open to the intimation of the hidden layers of consciousness.

The next point involved in this question is the intimation of the hidden layers of consciousness. Most people live a superficial existence unaware of the vast hidden sources, treasures of extraordinary importance, of great delight and joy. Because we are unaware during the waking hours of these movements, they appear as dreams when we are asleep. Because the superficial layers of consciousness are active during the waking hours, and do not receive the intimations of the hidden, such intimations become dreams. These dreams need interpretation and the expert interpreter comes in and becomes important. There need be no interpretation if there is constant and direct contact with the hidden layers of consciousness. This can happen only when the mind has a space interval between thought and thought and between action and action.

Then, the other point involved in this question is that of subjective experience, such as conversation with another, remembering words, remembering scenes and various activities. I do not know if it has happened to you that, upon waking, you remember having had a long talk with somebody, remembering words or a word of extraordinary significance and potency, having had a discussion with a friend, with a guru, with a Master and so on. Now, what are all these subjective activities or experiences? Is not all this within the field of consciousness, and therefore a projection of itself which is translated upon waking as a conversation, a direction received from a Master, and so on. But the discussion and the Master are still within the field of consciousness, and so a projection of its own content as a Master, a word, a scene, giving them significance.

So, the remembrance of an event within the field of consciousness is still an intimation or projection of thought, and therefore a product of thought, and therefore not the real. Reality comes into being when thought ceases, when thought is not creating.

The next point involved in this question is whether during sleep it is possible objectively to meet a person. What is the person? The person is obviously identified thought. The objective person whom you met in sleep is only his thought which he projected and which is identified with him by you. This identified thought you meet objectively. You are also the identified thought which is constantly projecting itself. Thought, which is like a wave, is identified, given a name; and that you meet objectively, which assumes the form of a person.

But, all these explanations have no meaning whatsoever without self-knowledge. You may repeat what I said. But repetition is a lie; it is mere propaganda and is not true. These things must be experienced. The division between the superficial layers of consciousness and the deeper layers is very narrow. Since most of us are occupied with the waking consciousness, with its worries, with the earning of a livelihood, the tension of relationship, the anxiety of belief—all these prevent the exploration of yourself at deeper levels. You cannot dig consciously into the deeper layers of consciousness; for, any action on the part of the superficial mind becomes a hindrance to the uncovering of the deeper layers. But, when the conscious mind is still, the hidden projects itself swiftly. When in those silent moments the hidden gives its intimation, there is a new joy, a new understanding. This joy and this under-

standing we translate into immediate action; or, we want the joy to be repeated. This craving for repetition prevents further intimation and further joy.

What is important is to understand that there cannot be right thinking and so right action without self-knowledge. This knowledge is not limited to the superficial layers of consciousness, but is the complete understanding of the whole process of consciousness. This understanding is not a matter of time. If there is intention to understand, then there is perception, and the urgency of that intention depends on honesty. The passive and yet alert awareness unfolds the deeper depths of consciousness. The discovery and experiencing of *what is* brings creative joy. In understanding *what is* without your interpretation, truth comes into being, and it is this truth which liberates and gives joy.

Question: You say that full awareness of the problem liberates us from it. Awareness depends on interest. What creates interest? What makes one man interested and another indifferent?

KRISHNAMURTI: To understand a problem, no previous conclusion or answer must intervene between yourself and the problem. Because our minds are filled with conclusions and remembrances of responses, we are never directly in relationship with the problem. We either quote religious books or the assertion of leaders or gurus, which prevents the complete understanding of the problem. We are never directly in relationship with the problem. There is a screen between us and the problem—the screen of quotation, of conclusion, a favorable answer—which prevents the full significance of the problem from being understood. So, to be aware of a problem directly is extremely arduous. Now, let us experiment with this. If you have a problem, what is your response to it? Your instinctive response is to look for an answer. This search for a solution indicates the avoidance of the problem, and not the comprehension of the problem. When you are aware that you are seeking an answer rather than the understanding of the problem, the search for an answer is put aside, and you are directly confronted with the problem. When you are thus directly confronted with the problem, you will begin to be aware of the full significance of the problem, and the problem will yield its full content and will cease to be. To fully understand a problem is to be aware of the escapes. These escapes take different forms—the desire for a solution, the acceptance of authority, memory as conclusion, and so on—and if you are not aware of them, emphasis is laid on the escapes and not on the problem itself.

Now, every problem is a new problem, a new challenge. Life is a process of challenge and response. This challenge is ever new; but the response is ever conditioned and limited, and the challenge is always translated in terms of the old, and so there is never understanding of the problem or of the challenge completely. We meet the challenge anew at moments of great crisis.

Interest in a problem is either stimulated or the very urgency of the problem itself demands it. If it comes into being through influence, it soon fades away. Nothing real can be discerned through influence, through stimulation. To be influenced is to lose the pliability of action. A man who is influenced soon loses the integrity of his own experience and understanding. Where there is earnestness, there is interest, and that earnestness does not depend on moods. Earnestness is not a thing to be cultivated. Where there is sorrow and not an avoidance of it, there is earnestness. If you are not interested in the understanding of sorrow, mere stimulation or influence cannot bring about a sustained ex-

ertion. Stimulation and influence soon weary the mind, leaving it dull and wasted.

What makes us indifferent? Why is there no vital, significant interest in our action? Is it not because our minds are distracted? The cinema, the guru, the temple, and drinking help us to avoid the intensity and the purposive direction of our lives. They are distractions, and distractions inevitably dull the mind. The guru and drinking, though momentarily stimulating, destroy the swift pliability of the mind. Because you desire gratification and not understanding, you pursue distractions which inevitably weary the mind. Most of us are not open to sorrow. We avoid it. Being discontented, we try to run away from discontent. Thus, thought itself becomes a distraction.

What is important is to find out why each one of us is indifferent or superficial. Why is one caught in this net of suffering? The answer lies in discerning for oneself the causes that make one dull and insensitive to suffering, to the open skies, to the passing birds, to the tears of our relationship. To be sensitive is to be vulnerable, and it is only in that state of sensitivity that understanding can come.

January 25, 1948

Third Talk in Bombay

Question: What are the real causes of Mahatma Gandhi's untimely death?

KRISHNAMURTI: You must approach the question either as a personal loss or as one of the events in the world crisis. If it is a personal loss, then the significance has to be understood. There is in most people the tendency to identify oneself with something greater, whether it is a person, the nation, or an idea. This craving for identification with a person or with an idea is an indication of one's own poverty of being. The identification with a person brings a sense of personal loss when anything happens to that person. Similarly, when there is an identification with a nation or a group, and when that nation is conquered or becomes a conqueror, there is depression or elation. This desire to identify exists; for, in oneself, one is empty, shallow, without substance; and by identifying oneself with a country, with a leader, with a group, one becomes something, one is something. This identification leads to extremes of thoughtlessness and ruthlessness. If you identify yourself with a person, with a group of people, then you are responsible for any calamity that may happen to that person or to that group. Through this identification, exploitation comes into being.

What are the causes that have brought about this assassination? Each one is responsible for what is happening in the world at the present time. The various incidents that are taking place at the present time are not unrelated incidents but related. The real cause of this murder lies in you. The real cause is you. Because you are communalistic, you encourage the spirit of violence, of division, of caste, of ideology. Obviously, you are responsible and it is foolish merely to blame the murderer. You have all contributed to the murder.

It is inevitable when a so-called nation is made up of separate groups, each seeking power, position, and authority; then, it is bound to produce not one man's death but thousands. Similarly, organized religion with its dogma and belief will inevitably produce conflict and confusion. When belief becomes stronger than affection, then there is antagonism between man and man—belief in ideology, in patriotism, and so on. In how many different ways each one tries to isolate oneself from another. This isolation is the real cause of strife and misery.

This assassination is an indication of the present trend in the world's affairs. Wrong means for a right end is justified; ruthlessness as a means to world peace is morally encouraged; war is justified because it will bring about peace. Justification of evil has become a necessity, which makes for an unprecedented crisis in man's relation to man. The sacrifice of the present is another indication of man's ruthlessness to man. This liquidation of the present human life for a future utopia is another indication of the utter ruthlessness that comes when there is identification with an ideology. The sacrifice of the present to the future is a sacrifice to darkness because the future is uncertain and cannot be predicted. "To save man, man must be killed" is the greatest form of illusion. For a future security, your present security is denied. Surely, only in the present and not in the future lies understanding. Comprehension is in the now and not in the tomorrow.

The justification of evil and the sacrifice of the present for the unpredictable future are the two tendencies that are making the world crisis of an extraordinary character. Does this not prevent love between man and man? Without love there is no solution for any problem. Without love there can be no transformation of the present chaos. The worship of the intellect cannot bring about a solution to our miseries; but, only affection, love, can bring happiness to man. When the intellect becomes supreme, the heart is empty. You will fill it with the things of the intellect and so allow cunning and ruthlessness, deceit and antagonism to prevail.

Since you are responsible for the world crisis and for the various incidents in this crisis, you have to radically transform yourself. For this transformation you must be aware of your ways of thinking, feeling, and acting. Through this awareness, earnestness and serious intention come into being. Mere outward transformation will not bring about happiness to you. Only when there is an inward revolution, a psychological transformation, only then can there be peace and happiness in you and so in the world.

Question: Can we realize the truth of what you are speaking immediately, without any previous preparation?

KRISHNAMURTI: To put the problem differently, can you understand directly or comprehend a problem immediately? In understanding *what is,* truth comes into being. It is truth that gives freedom, and not the mere analysis of the problem, nor the mere search after the cause of the problem.

Life is, is it not, a series of challenges and responses. If your response to a challenge is conditioned, then that challenge, not being understood, leaves its mark, its residue, which further strengthens the conditioning. So, there is constant residual memory, accumulation, scars, which prevent the understanding of the new. The question is whether one can understand a problem so completely that it leaves no residual memory. For it is the memory that prevents the understanding of truth. For truth to come into being, mind must be free from the scars of yesterday. Since every problem is new, only a fresh, unscarred mind can understand it. A problem which you have had yesterday, for example, has undergone a change today; and when you meet it, your mind must equally have undergone a transformation so as to meet it anew. So, to understand the truth of a problem, you must come to it afresh, without the scars of yesterday. To be free from yesterday's memory, each experience must be completely understood. It is the incomplete experience that leaves memories, and through the screen of these memories the new cannot be understood.

A problem can be understood immediately, and the truth of it seen directly, when the mind is not interposing between the problem and yourself the various screens of escapes, such as the desire for a comforting answer, a gratifying conclusion, a repetitive intention. Understanding comes when the mind is not burdened with the past, when the mind is still. This stillness is not the product of compulsion, of discipline, of a practice; but it comes into being when you are directly in relationship to the problem itself.

To perceive truth does not need preparation. Preparation implies time, and time is not the means to the understanding of truth. Time is continuity, and truth is timeless. Understanding is noncontinuous; it is from moment to moment. Understanding is not cumulative. It is this open quality that is necessary for immediate understanding, unclouded by theories, fears, and conclusions. Only then is there communion. When the mind and heart are open, then only can truth come into being.

Question: Does Gandhiji continue to exist today?

KRISHNAMURTI: You want to know the truth of continuity. This indirect question regarding Gandhiji's continuity is an inquiry about your own continuity. Most of you probably believe in reincarnation and continuity. So, your belief is preventing you from finding the truth of this question. We will experiment to find the truth of this matter directly, now and not tomorrow. To invite the truth concerning continuity, you must put away your beliefs. Even though you may have proofs of continuity, they are still in the field of thought; the mind can fabricate and deceive itself. So, to find the truth of this challenge, you must come to it afresh, with a mind that is unburdened. For truth to come into being, all these impediments of the mind, the creations of the mind, must be set aside. When the mind is clouded with anxiety, hope, with the longing for continuity, it is incapable of understanding. To understand, you have to be aware of the various hindrances, now, that prevent the mind from receiving truth.

Now, what is continuity? Either there is continuity for the spiritual entity or for memory. Either you are a spiritual entity or merely a bundle of memory. This memory gives itself continuity through experience. If you are a spiritual entity, that entity is timeless and so it has no continuity; it is not in the net of the past, the present, and the future. For, that which is real, spiritual, cannot be thought of, formulated, caught in the net of time. It cannot evolve, it cannot progress or grow. It cannot become. Since you are thinking in terms of becoming, continuing, you are not a spiritual entity. If you are a spiritual entity, then death and life are one. Then there is immortality. If you are a spiritual entity, then you will not be concerned with death, nor with becoming, and the complications of acquisitiveness and envy. But, since you are concerned with these things, you may not quibble with the assertion that you are a spiritual entity, which implies a state of being in which time is not. Since you crave for continuity, you are concerned with death, so you are not a spiritual entity.

So, we can put aside the belief that you are a spiritual entity and concern ourselves with the desire for continuity. What is that continuity? Obviously, it is memory identified with property, name, relationship, and idea. If you had no memory of yesterday, then things would have very little significance. You are seeking continuity and establishing it through property, through family, through idea. This continuity is the 'me', the 'I'. You want to know if this 'me' continues. Now, what is this 'me'? Is it not the name, the qualities, your bank account if you have one, your position, your character, your idiosyncracies, and so on? All this is memory, is it not? I am stating what actually is and not dealing with theories and speculations. We must know the truth of this, and it is truth that liberates and not theories and explanations concerning continuity.

What causes continuity? Obviously, identified memory. How did this memory come into being? There is perception, contact, sensation, desire, and identification; from these arise the idea of me and mine. You perceive a car and then contact it; you have the sensation and then the desire to possess it. So, the 'me' is the residue of memory. However much this memory may divide itself into the higher and lower self, this division is still within the field of memory, and therefore it is not true. Memory is incomplete understanding. Have you not noticed that when you understand something completely, wholly, the memory of it has faded away?

Love is not memory. It is not a state of being. It is not a continuity. There is a continuity when there is sensation and memory, which is not love. So, continuity is memory. Through identification, the various separate and broken memories are given a continuity.

Through continuity, is there renewal? The 'me' continues from memory to memory, the 'me' which has divided itself into the high and the low. This whole process of identification is the 'me' with its continuity through memory. Now, will this continuity bring a renewal? Will continuity bring the understanding of truth? Certainly not. That which continues has no renewal. That which was of yesterday, though modified today, cannot have freshness, newness. Memory can only renew itself and this renewal through memory is not the renewal of a new birth. So, continuity of memory is not a renewal. There is renewal only when there is an ending. There is a new birth only when there is death to yesterday, to the identified memory. You will continue, obviously, as long as there is identified memory, but in this continuity, there is no renewal.

Memory is the product of time, and through time, the timeless cannot be. There must be death, an ending, for the real to be—death to acquisition, to memory. There is continuity when thought is identified, and that continuity can never be open to the real. Only when there is death from moment to moment, an ending of psychological memory, then only is there renewal, a rebirth. Through the process of time, through identified memory, reality can never be. Only when thought, which is the product of time, ceases—then only is there the real.

February 1, 1948

Fourth Talk in Bombay

Ideas cannot bring about transformation in the world. Ideas only create further ideas in opposition or in acceptance, which inevitably create separate groups and bring about conflict and misery. Ideas cannot fundamentally change man. They do affect his superficial life, modifying his actions and his outward relationships. But, ideas do not radically transform his being. He either opposes them or accepts them and therefore isolates himself—which only creates further antagonism and strife. Only the state of being can bring about fundamental transformation. This state of being is not an idea or a mere formulation, but it comes when thought as ideas ceases.

The mind cannot solve our human problems. The mind can invent theories, systems, ideas; it can bring about different patterns of action; it can organize existence; it can invent and formulate. It cannot solve the human problem because the mind itself is the problem, and not the problem which it projects outside itself. The mind itself has become the problem, and its fabrications fur-

ther complicate life, bringing conflict and misery. The substitution of one idea for another, or the change of ideas, does not transform the thinker. So, the thinker himself has become the problem. Thought can be modified, changed; but the thinker remains apart. The thinker is the thought. They are not separate, they are a joint phenomenon and not separate processes. The thinker, by manipulating, modifying, changing thought according to circumstances, safeguards himself by this action. The picture remains; only the frame is changed. But, the picture is the problem and not the frame. Thought is not the problem, but the thinker. This action of modification, change, of his thought, is a clever deception on the part of the thinker, leading him to illusion and endless misunderstanding and conflict. So, only when the thinker ceases is there being, and it is only the state of being that can bring about radical transformation.

It is important to understand this—that ideas cannot transform man; modification of thought cannot bring about radical revolution. There is radical revolution only when the thinker comes to an end. When do you have creative moments, a sense of joy and beauty? Only when the thinker is absent, when the thought process comes to an end. Then, in the interval between two thoughts, is creative joy. Being alone can bring about transformation.

How to bring about an end to the thinker is our next question. But, that very question is erroneous. For, it is still the thinker that is putting this question, thereby giving himself continuity. Only when the thinker is aware of his activities—then only the thinker comes to an end. With great beauty or in moments of great sorrow, the thinker is temporarily driven away, and within that period there is that extraordinary sense of infinite happiness and bliss. It is this creative moment that brings about enduring revolution. It is this state of being, in which the thinker is not, that gives renewal. In this silence when the thinker is absent, does reality come into being.

Question: Can one love truth without loving man? Can one love man without loving truth? What comes first?

KRISHNAMURTI: Love comes first. To love truth, you must know truth. To know truth is to deny truth. What is known is not truth. What is known is already encased in time and ceases to be truth. Truth is an eternal movement, and so cannot be measured in words or in time. It cannot be held in the fist. You cannot love something which you do not know. But truth is not to be found in books, in images, in temples. It is to be found in action, in living.

The very search for the unknown is love itself, and you cannot search for the unknowable away from relationship. You cannot search for reality, or for what you will, in isolation. It comes into being only in relationship, only when there is right relationship between man and man. So, the love of man is the search for reality. In relationship only, I am beginning to know myself.

Relationship is the mirror in which I am discovering myself, not my higher self, but the whole total process of myself. The higher and the lower selves are still within the field of the mind. Without understanding the mind, the thinker, it is not possible to go beyond thought and be open to the real. So, the understanding of myself in relationship is the beginning of life. I do not know how to love you—you in whose relationship I come into being. How can I search for the real and therefore love the real? I cannot exist without you. I cannot be in isolation. In our relationship, between you and me, I am beginning to

know myself; and the understanding of myself is the beginning of wisdom.

The search for the real is love in relationship. To love you, I must know you; I must be receptive to all your moods, changes, and not merely enclose myself in my ambitions, pursuits, and desires. Without you, I cannot be. If I do not understand this relationship, how can there be love? Without love, there is no search.

To say that one must love truth, one must know truth. Do you know truth? Do you know what reality is? Do you know what God is? To know is to encase it in memory. What is known is within the field of time, and so it is no longer truth. How can a dry heart know truth? It cannot.

Truth is not something distant. It is near, only we do not know how to search it out. To be open to it, you must understand relationship, not only with man, but with nature, with ideas. To understand, there must be open communion; there cannot be an isolating process, a withholding. To understand, there must be love, and without love there can be no understanding.

So it is not man or truth that comes first, but love. It comes into being only in understanding relationship. Truth cannot be invited. It must come to you. To search for truth is to deny truth. It comes into being when you are open, when you are completely without any barrier, when the mind is no longer creating. It comes into being when the mind is still. This stillness is not the product of compulsion, repetition, or concentration. To induce stillness is to seek a reward, and truth is not a reward. Where there is search for reward and the avoidance of pain, truth is not.

Question: You cannot build a new world in the way you are doing it now. It is obvious that the method of training laboriously a few chosen disciples will not make any difference to humanity. No doubt you will leave a mark like Krishna, Buddha, Christ, Mohammed and Gandhiji. But, they have not changed the world; nor will you, unless you discover an entirely new way of approaching the problem.

KRISHNAMURTI: A few do free themselves from confusion, conflict, and sorrow, but the vast majority are held in the net of time and sorrow. Is it possible for each one to break through this net and be free? If they are not free, then the wave of destruction and chaos will always overcome the living. The questioner says that the past teachers have not set the vast majority of mankind free. Since they are not free, the wave of destruction and the wave of life are always together. The questioner wants to know if there is an entirely new way of approaching this problem.

The wave of misery is stronger than the wave of happiness; and if each one does not awaken, then the wave of destruction will be more powerful, and so man is doomed to strife and pain. The problem is, is it not possible for each one to step out of this net of strife and pain, out of this net of time? Can you, who are here, free yourselves immediately from sorrow? If you can, you will be able to help another to transform himself immediately. If you think that you will become free from sorrow, then you will never be free, for the becoming is part of this destructive wave. Either you understand now or never. The now is ever in the present and the present has no time. The present is also the tomorrow. The postponement of the now until tomorrow is not the present; it is the invitation to the wave of destruction.

As long as you think in terms of becoming or being something tomorrow, then it sets up the process of conflict and pain. Confusion exists because you are thinking in terms of becoming. Can this becoming come to an end? It is only then that there can be a radical transformation. Becoming is a process of time and being is free of time. Where there is the psychological process of time, there must also be the wave of destruction and misery. In being, only, can there be transformation and not in becoming. In ending, only, there is renewal and not in continuity. So, can each one of us stop thinking in the process of becoming? I say you can do it. You can do it only when there is profound interest, when the thought process ceases entirely.

It is the thinker that is ever striving to become. He is the creator of time. It is only when the thinker ceases that there is being. Only when you give your mind and heart entirely to understanding, then only truth comes into being—which alone liberates you from sorrow. Then only is there a radical transformation. You can step on to the shore from the river at any point. The river of becoming is destruction and sorrow. The river of becoming ceases when you understand the time process. But, to understand, you must give your heart and mind.

Question: When I listen to you, all seems clear and new. At home the old, dull restlessness asserts itself. What is wrong with me?

KRISHNAMURTI: Existence is challenge and response. The challenge is always new and the response ever old. You met me yesterday, but since yesterday I have been modified; you have the picture of me of yesterday; so the 'me' is absorbed into the old. You do not meet me anew. You have only the picture of me of yesterday. So, your response to challenge is ever conditioned. While you are listening to me, you forget temporarily all your anxieties, your strife, and pain. You are listening quietly, trying to understand. But, when you go away from here, you are back into the old pattern of life or action. The new is always being absorbed into the old—the old habits, customs, memories, and ideas.

So, the problem is how to free thought from the old, from yesterday, so as to live continuously in the new. Why is it that we do not meet the new afresh every minute? Why is it that the old absorbs the new and modifies it? Is it not because the thinker is always the old? Is not your thought founded on the past? When it meets the new, the past is meeting the present, the now. The experience of yesterday, the memory which is dead, is meeting the new, which is alive. So, how is the mind to free itself, as the thinker? How is the psychological accumulation to come to an end? Without freedom from the residue of experience, there can be no meeting of the new. To free the thought process, which is of yesterday, is arduous. For, beliefs, tradition, and education are a process of imitation, building up the store of memory. This memory is constantly responding. This response we call thinking. So, thought can never meet the new. Thought is the outcome of incomplete experience. It is only when experience is completed without leaving a mark—then, only, thought as a response to memory ceases.

Love is not memory. Love is not a process of thought. It is a state of being. Love is eternally new. To bring about a revolution in thought and feeling, every thought and feeling should be thought out from moment to moment. Every response must be fully understood, not casually looked at and thrown aside. There is freedom from accumulating memory when every thought and feeling is thought out and felt out completely to the end. In this ending, there is renewal. There is an interval between this ending and the arising of another thought. In this space of silence, creativeness comes into being. If you will experiment with your thought and feeling, you will discover the practicality of this in your daily life. You will discover for your-

self this creative interval, which is not of any theory or of any religion. It is a direct experience. If you cling to that experience, it ceases to be the new, the eternal. This creativeness is happiness.

A happy man is not concerned whether he is rich or poor, to what caste he belongs or to what country. He has no leaders, no temples, and no gods of promise or fear, so he lives in peace and does not cause enmity. You are not creative in the sense explained by me already, so you are antisocial at the different levels of your consciousness. So, you breed strife, confusion, and antagonism. To be practical and effective in your relationships, you must be happy. There can be no happiness if there is no ending. There can be no happiness in continuity, in becoming. In ending there is a rebirth, a newness, a joy, an ecstasy. In becoming there is decay, strife, and pain.

Question: You never mention God. Has He no place in your teaching?

KRISHNAMURTI: You talk a great deal about God, don't you? Your books are full of it, you build churches and temples, you perform ceremonies. This pursuit of God indicates the shallowness of your search. Though you repeat the word *God*, your acts are not godly, are they? Though you worship God, your ways are ungodly. Though you mention God, you exploit others; and the richer you get, the more temples you build. So, you are only familiar with the word *God*. But, the word is not God, the word is not the thing.

To find the real, all the verbal utterances of the mind must cease. The image of reality must cease for reality to be. For reality to be, the image and the temple must cease. For the being of the unknown, the mind must put aside its content, the known. To pursue God you must know God. To know what you are pursuing is not to know God. The response which urges you to pursue is born of memory, so what you seek is already created. That which is created is not eternal, it is a product of the mind.

If there were no books, if there were no gurus, no rituals, and other forms of escape, all that you would know is sorrow and an occasional glimmer of happiness. Then, you would want to know what is the cause of sorrow. Then, you would not escape through fanciful illusions. You may invent Gods and other things, but if you really wish to find out the whole process of suffering, then you will not escape, then you will have no addictions, then you will be faced with *what is.* Then only will you find out what reality is.

A man in sorrow cannot find reality. He must be free from sorrow to find it. That which is the unknown cannot be thought about. What you think about is already the known. You can think only of the known. Thought moves from the known to the known, from the secure to the secure. But, what is known is not the real.

So when you think about God, you think about what is known and the known is in the net of time. The real can only come into being when the mind ceases to create, when the mind is still. This stillness is not a product of compulsion, discipline, or self-hypnosis. There is silence only when all problems have ceased, like the pool that becomes quiet when the breezes stop. So, the mind becomes quiet when the agitator, the thinker ceases. For the thinker to come to an end, all thoughts which he manufactures must be thought out. It is vain to erect a barrier against thought. Every thought must be felt out and understood. When the mind is still, the reality, the indescribable, comes into being. You cannot invite it. To invite it is to know it, and what is known is not the real. The mind must be simple, unburdened of ideation and belief. For reality to come into being, do not seek it, but understand the

causes that agitate the mind and heart. When the creator of problems ceases, then there is tranquillity. In that tranquillity, the blessing of the real comes.

February 8, 1948

Fifth Talk in Bombay

There is so much sorrow and so little happiness in our life. When there is happiness, the problems of power, position, and achievement disappear. When there is happiness, the struggle to become ceases, and the divisions between man and man come to an end. All conflicts come to an end when there is happiness. Happiness comes only with the highest form of intelligence. Intelligence is the understanding of sorrow; it is not the outcome of sorrow. We know sorrow is always with us, a constant companion, ever increasing, without end. We know sorrow in different forms, physical and psychological.

We know remedies to overcome physical pain; but, psychological pains are more complex, and to seek remedies for these is to avoid the understanding of them, which alone can put an end to pain. The psychological suffering is more complex, demanding greater attention, deeper penetration, and wider experiencing. But, sorrow, whatever it be, at whatever level, is still painful and agonizing.

Does suffering come to an end through effort, through thought process? Physical pain can be overcome by a thought process. But the psychological suffering—anxiety, frustration, the innumerable aches—can they be transcended by effort, by thought? So, what is suffering? What is effort? What is thought? If you can understand this problem directly, then you will destroy this ache, this burning loneliness and pain.

What is suffering? Is it not the desire to become, with its varying actions and frustrations that lead to conflict and disintegration? This desire to become, negatively or positively, is sorrow.

Will effort, the action of the will, put an end to sorrow? When there is frustration we try to overcome it, we try to battle against it. This positive action in varying degrees and in multiple forms, positively or negatively, is called effort. Effort exists or comes into being when there is the anxiety to change *what is*. Change is modified continuity. I am this and I want to become that, the opposite of what I am, but it is still the continuation of what I am in a different form. So, the gaining of the opposite, in which is always effort, is the modified continuity of *what is*. To become nongreedy is the modified continuity of greed, only under a different name—it is still greed. In the pursuit of the opposite is implied becoming and the becoming is the cause of sorrow.

Can the thought process bring an end to sorrow? What is thinking? Thinking is a response of memory. If there were no memory, there would be no thinking. Memory is the residue of experience which is not completely, fully understood. Only the incomplete experiences leave their mark, which we call memory. So, suffering is not solved through memory. In dealing with sorrow, three things are involved—thought, memory, and effort. As pointed out already, thought cannot resolve sorrow. What can bring about that happiness is not the result of effort. Happiness is not a result. It comes into being spontaneously, uninvited. If you seek happiness by getting rid of sorrow, you will not understand sorrow. When you try to resolve sorrow through the thought process, you create the problem of sorrow at a different level. When you use effort to overcome sorrow, you create duality, the opposite; and the opposite is always within the field of its own cause.

What can put an end to sorrow? Sorrow can be understood only when you become aware of the process of thought, of memory, of effort. When you are aware, you are neither condemning nor justifying; condemnation, justification, or identification create a barrier to understanding. When this justification and condemnation disappear, then you are aware, you perceive; there comes an alert passivity. In that awareness, sorrow comes to an end.

Question: You say that love is chaste. Does it mean it is celibate?

KRISHNAMURTI: To understand any problem there must be no offensive or defensive response. There must be inquiry without bias, without being tethered to tradition or belief. When the mind is tethered, it is tied to an attitude, it cannot be free to discover what is true. If you are anchored to a haven of belief or to a prejudice, you will never find the truth of any problem. So let us inquire together without being anchored to any conclusion—which is in itself an arduous task. Prejudice distorts.

In this question is involved the complex problem of sex. Religion, gurus, and tradition have condemned sex, as it is said that it prevents man from realizing the highest, and that to realize the highest, celibacy is necessary. Tradition and authority must not stand in the way of finding truth; they become a hindrance to a man who is seeking truth. In extremes there is no stability. The opposite is fictitious and truth is not found in it. To understand, there must be no fear nor the pursuit of pleasure and indulgence.

Why has sex become such an intense, burning problem to most of us? Why is man caught in sensate pleasure? If we do not understand this, mere self-discipline or superficial legislation will not solve this problem. It has become a burning issue because it is stimulated by every possible means in modern society. Newspapers, cinema, and magazines stimulate eroticism. Advertisements, to attract your attention, use the picture of a woman. Outward and inward stimulation is encouraged, is sedulously cultivated. The present society is essentially the outcome of sensate value. Things, power, position, name, and class have become of vital significance. Sensory values have become predominantly significant in your lives. Your emotions and thoughts are imitative and so have ceased to be creative. Your organized religion is mere copy—following authority, tradition, and fear, merely following the example, the ideal. Religion has become routine, religion has become the vain repetition of rituals, practicing of disciplines, the imposition of beliefs which merely breed habit and imitation. When the mind and heart are caught in copying, they wither. The heart and the mind must be swift and pliable, capable of deep penetration and understanding. But, when they are made into a record-playing machine, they cease to be. So, inwardly, there is no creative response, but dullness and emptiness. Your lives are hollow, empty, a routine of earning money, playing cards, going to the cinema, and the reading of books. Such a mind and heart function without depth and compassion. How can such a mind be creative? Since your life is without compassion, without joy, you have only one pleasure left, which is sex; therefore, it becomes an ever increasing problem. Your ideals, your disciplines, will not free you from this problem. You may suppress it, you may hold it down; but suppression is not creative understanding and happiness. There is a constant state of fear without love. Happiness can only come in the state of self-forgetfulness, and sex is used as a means of brief self-forgetfulness.

In understanding this problem fully you will find the answer. To all the major problems of life there is no categorical answer of yes or no. But in understanding the problem clearly, you will find an answer. The answer to this question is that the problem will exist so long as there is no creative understanding, so long as you are not free from copying, from the various forms of psychological habits. It is only in bringing about a radical transformation in your lives, a revolution of values, this question of sex will have a different meaning. Then, life itself undergoes a rigorous and deep transformation.

Those who are trying to be celibate in order to achieve God are unchaste for they are seeking a result or gain and so substituting the end, the result, for sex—which is fear. Their hearts are without love, and there can be no purity, and a pure heart alone can find reality. A disciplined heart, a suppressed heart, cannot know what love is. It cannot know love if it is caught in habit, in sensation—religious or physical, psychological or sensate. The idealist is an imitator and therefore he cannot know love. He cannot be generous, give himself over completely without the thought of himself. Only when the mind and heart are unburdened of fear, of the routine of sensational habits, when there is generosity and compassion, there is love. Such love is chaste.

Question: You say that this present crisis is without precedent. In what way is it exceptional?

KRISHNAMURTI: You are familiar with crises of varying types, at different periods throughout history—social, national, political. Crises come and go. Economic recessions and social depressions get modified and continue in different forms. The present crisis is different because it is in the field of ideation. Now, you are all justifying evil as a means to a righteous end. Evil was recognized to be evil, murder as murder; but now, murder is used as a means to a righteous end, and so evil is justified. This justification of evil cannot bring about peace in the world. War is not a means of peace. The sacrifice of the present for the future is considered worthy. The future must ever be uncertain, and to sacrifice the present for the unpredictable, and to justify it, is another form of negation of life.

In this is implied the employment of wrong means to achieve a right end, which can never be, for the end is in the means. Means and end are not separate; they are a joint phenomenon, and to separate them is to bring about bloodshed, destruction, and misery.

We have exploited man and his necessities. But now, we are exploiting his ideas, and the exploitation of ideas is more devastating and destructive.

Another indication of this exceptional crisis is that man is forgotten and systems have become all-important. Man is no longer of any significance, but systems are. For a system, millions are destroyed, and the destruction is justified because the system promises a beneficial result. Systems are patterns of action, and actions without understanding the purpose of man cannot be justified, however noble or ignoble they are. Systems cannot solve man's problems. Systems are the outcome of experts and of incomplete knowledge. The specialists give importance to their inventions. But, only the integration of the individual can solve the present crisis.

One of the reasons for this crisis is the importance that man is giving to sensate values—property and name, caste and country. Values of things, whether made by the hand or by the mind, have become the predominant influence in your lives, and so there is the quick recurrence of wars.

This crisis is exceptional. So, an exceptional action is necessary. As I have said, thought process will not make a man free from this crisis; only the state of being, which is timeless action, must come. This state of being comes with individual transformation. When you transform yourself, you will discover that there is an action which is not productive of a further wave of destruction and misery. So, your regeneration must be timeless. For, if you look to tomorrow, you are inviting confusion and sorrow.

Question: Are there no perfect gurus who have nothing for the greedy seeker of eternal security, but who guide, visibly or invisibly, their loving hearts?

KRISHNAMURTI: This question is put over and over again in different forms—whether a guru is necessary or not. Does a loving heart need a guide? A loving heart needs no guide, for love is its own eternity. A loving heart is generous, merciful, it respects; then, it knows that which is without a beginning, without an end. But, most of you have no such heart. Your hearts are dry and empty, filled with the things made by the mind. Being empty, you go to another to have it filled. You go to another to find eternal security which you call God. You go to another to find that permanent gratification which you call peace. Because your hearts are dry, you seek a guru who, you hope, will fill it with the gratification which you call love.

Can anyone free your heart, whether the guru is visible or invisible? Gurus can give patterns of action, they may tell you what to think, but not how to think. They may give you disciplines and words to repeat; but these are things made by the mind and so the heart is ever empty. Your practice, your meditation, your imitations, only make your heart dull and weary, terrorizing your family and yourself. Will you know love through compulsion?

Without love, you cannot find reality. Without being tender, considerate, how can you know the real? Through a technique, love is not captured.

Disciplines and practices, rituals and mere knowledge make for a dull and insensitive mind. A restless mind becomes only a dull mind when it is held within the narrow groove of a discipline. Without sensitivity, this swift movement of truth cannot be discovered.

The pursuit of gurus wastes the pliability of the mind and heart. This constant search for gratification, which you call the search for God, wearies the mind, using it wastefully. For, that which is used constantly wears itself out. Since you seek gratification, you will find a guru who is gratifying. But, this is not understanding. This does not bring about happiness and there is no love. The search for gratification, calling it by a noble name, only destroys.

Love is ever new. Without its perfume, its beauty and goodness, to search for a guru is a waste of time and action. Where there is love, there is no need for a guru; on the contrary, the guru becomes a hindrance. For, love is virtue. Virtue is not a practice. Virtue brings freedom. It is only when there is freedom that the eternal comes into being.

So, our problem is how to awaken the dull and the empty heart to the beauty and richness of love. You must be aware your mind is dull, that your thought process has no significance, and that your heart is empty, filled by things made by the mind. Just be aware, passively aware without condemnation, without justification. Be open to discover *what is*. In this passive yet alert awareness, there comes a transformation. In this stillness, in this tranquillity, the indescribable comes into being.

February 15, 1948

Sixth Talk in Bombay

The problem of existence is not at one level, but at different levels of action, and they are all interrelated. The psychological problem is related to the physical; and if we try to solve the problem of food, clothing, and shelter on its own level, we shall find that we shall not come to a true solution. No problem can be solved on its own level. Departmental thinking can in no way solve the problem of existence. We have to think of our existence as a whole, as a total process, and not an unrelated action at different levels. Our life is a movement of contradictions. We talk of peace and our actions are for war; we think of freedom and our life is regimented; we seek creativeness and our mind is the result of imitation and habit; we are poor and seek riches; being violent, we pursue the ideal of nonviolence; we desire to be happy, and we do everything to bring about unhappiness.

Now, to choose one of the contradictions is to avoid action; choice at all times is a process of avoidance of action. Choice will not bring about integration, but only right thinking will. There can be no right thinking when there is contradiction. When we know how to think rightly, contradiction will cease. We will have to find out what is true thinking and not be caught in choice—choice between good and evil, peace and war, poverty and riches, regimentation and freedom.

As contradiction is the very nature of the self, which is the seat of desire, merely to choose one of the desires does not lead to understanding. Choice between the essential and the nonessential is still the outcome of desire. Choice is desire, and desire in its very nature is contradictory. So, choice only strengthens the self, only the self-enclosing process of the 'you' and the 'me'. The understanding of desire is the beginning of self-knowledge. Without self-knowledge there is no true thinking. If you do not know the total process of yourself—not only through the responses of your daily activities but by being aware of the different psychological levels—then you live in a state of contradiction. To choose one of the contradictions only strengthens the enclosing process; and so, such action breeds further contradiction. So, choice between the opposites does not lead to happiness, does not bring peace. Only right thinking can bring about happiness. Happiness is not an end in itself. It is a byproduct of something far greater than the result of choice.

Right thought and right thinking are two different states. Right thought is merely a conformity to a pattern, to a system. Right thought is static; it involves the constant friction of choice. Right thinking or true thinking is to be discovered. It cannot be learned. It cannot be practiced. Right thinking is a movement of self-knowledge from moment to moment. This movement of self-knowledge exists in the awareness of relationship.

Mind can be disciplined to conform to a pattern of right thought; but disciplining, which is the movement of a pattern, can never result in right thinking. Right thought always has a result in view and so it can never go beyond itself; whereas, right thinking comes into being through the awareness of the activities of the self, which must be experienced and discovered from moment to moment. So, right thinking has no goal, no end in view. Desire is never static and so the self is never still. It is ever struggling to gain and to avoid. The self is not only the higher, but the lower self. This division is arbitrary, and so not real; this division is a form of escape; this division—which so many indulge in—is still within the field of consciousness, and so still within the thought process.

Right thinking can only come into being when there is awareness of every thought and feeling, the awareness not only of a particular group of thoughts and feelings, but of all thoughts and all feelings. The unfolding of these thoughts and feelings is put an end to by condemnation, and condemnation is choice. Condemnation is a form of inaction for understanding demands action, not choice. Though you think that choice brings about action, if you examine closely you will find that choice invariably leads to inaction, to isolation. Choice can never bring about understanding, as condemnation only builds resistance, preventing understanding; choice is another form of self-protective response. This inaction, which outwardly seems so active, has led man to destruction and misery. This inaction, projected outwardly as the social structure, brings about disintegration.

There can only be creative action through right thinking. Right thinking is a constant discovery of the full significance of every thought and feeling. To be passively yet alertly aware of every movement of thought and feeling, of the motives, of the intentions that are hidden, brings about right thinking. It is only right thinking, which is the outcome of self-knowledge, that can solve the many problems that confront each one of us.

Question: Is not the longing expressed in prayer a way to God?

KRISHNAMURTI: In this question there are several things involved, not only prayer, but concentration and meditation. What do we mean by prayer? In prayer is there not involved petition, supplication? The state of open receptivity, the state of sensitivity without the self-enclosing process of demand, is surely not prayer, but one of the highest forms of meditation. Most prayers are petitions or the search for guidance. This petition for guidance indicates, does it not, that being confused, being in pain, you seek clarity and joy through what you call God. You and I have created the confusion, the misery, this utter want of love; and so, you pray for a higher entity to clear up this confusion and conflict. But, since you have created this force of destruction and violence, you have to clear it up, and not someone else. When you pray for something, it generally comes into being. But you have to pay the price for it. The price is not understanding; the price is another form of conflict and misery. What you demand, you receive, and this gift is the outcome of your own self. How can God answer your particular demands? Can the immeasurable, the unutterable be concerned with your petty little worries, miseries, confusions, and your national calamities which you have created for yourself? So, what is it that answers? Surely, your own hidden layers of consciousness. It may bring a momentary clarity, gratification, but such answers are not of the highest. At the moment of prayer, you are faintly silent, in a mild state of receptivity, and so the active mind being comparatively still, the hidden projects itself and you have an answer. It is your own layers of consciousness that respond and not that which you call God. Reality must come to you, you cannot go to it. If you invite it to help you to solve your problems, to give you the direction for conduct, then it ceases to be the real. The small voice that is heard in prayer, when the mind is superficially quiet, is the intimation of your own being. This voice surely is not the voice of God. How can a mind that is confused, craving, ignorant, petitioning, understand reality? Reality can come into being only when the mind is absolutely still, not asking, not seeking; when desire ceases, only then reality comes into being.

Concentration is a process of exclusion. Concentration is brought about through effort, compulsion, and direction. So, concentration is a process of exclusion. This concentration takes different forms. You know the concentration that is demanded in earning your livelihood. But, concentration that is demanded in so-called meditation is what we are concerned with here. As the mind wanders when you try to meditate, you try to fix your mind on a picture or an image or on a phrase. But since your mind insists on wandering off, you try to force it back on the object of your interest. This constant battle with your thoughts is generally called meditation. You try to concentrate on something in which you are not interested, and so there is multiplicity of thought and vagrancy. So, you spend your energy in warding off. If you can concentrate on your particular desire or object, you think you have at last succeeded in your meditation. But, surely, this is not meditation. Meditation is not an exclusive process, a process of building up resistance. So, concentration as exclusion is not meditation. Concentration becomes a form of escape. To sit in front of a picture of your Master, your guru, of an image, or to do rituals is also an escape. For, without self-knowledge, there is no right thinking; and without true thinking, what you do has no meaning, however noble your intentions are. These escapes only dull the mind and weary the heart.

It is comparatively easy to concentrate. A general planning war, planning the butchery of man, is very concentrated. A businessman trying to pull off a deal is concentrated. A man who is interested in anything is naturally, spontaneously concentrated on it. But concentration is not meditation. The concentration on what you want, what you desire, is not meditation. Meditation is understanding. Meditation of the heart is understanding. How can there be understanding if there is exclusion? How can there be understanding when there is petition? Understanding comes when there is freedom. You are liberated from that which you understand. Understanding is the way, the foundation of meditation. Prayer and concentration lead to obstinacy, to fixation, to illusion. Understanding brings about freedom, clarity, and joy. Understanding comes when the right significance of all things is gathered. To be ignorant is to give wrong values. Stupidity is the lack of comprehending right values.

How is one to establish the right value of property, of relationship, of ideas? For the true to come into being, you must understand the thinker, must you not? If you do not know the thinker, which is yourself, what you choose has no meaning. If you do not know yourself, your action of choice has no foundation whatsoever. So, self-knowledge is the beginning of meditation, not the knowledge that you pick up from books, from authorities, from gurus, but that knowledge which comes into being through passive awareness, experience, and discovery. Without self-knowledge, there is no meditation. If you do not understand the ways of your thoughts, your feelings, and your desires, the patterns of action which are ideas, then there is no foundation for thought. The thinker who merely asks, prays, or excludes without understanding himself must end in confusion and illusion. So, the beginning of understanding is self-knowledge, being aware of every movement of thought and feeling, to be aware of all the layers of consciousness.

To know the deep activities, the concealed motives and responses, the conscious mind must be still to receive the projections of the hidden layers. The conscious mind is occupied with the daily activities connected with earning a living, of exploiting others, of anger and greed, of running away from problems. This conscious mind must understand its own activities and bring about tranquillity to itself. It cannot bring about tranquillity by mere regimentation, by compulsion, by discipline. It can bring about tranquillity by becoming aware of its own activities, by observing silently its actions towards its immediate relations and others. Thus, a conscious mind becomes fully aware of its own

activities, thus bringing about tranquillity to the superficial layers; then only is it in a position to receive the intimations of the hidden layers of consciousness. Only when all these projections have been understood, and the whole consciousness is unburdened of the past, then only can it receive the eternal. As the pool is quiet when the breeze has stopped, so the mind is quiet when the thinker, the creator of the problem, ceases. Then, only, that which is immeasurable comes into being.

Question: Why is your teaching so purely psychological? There is no cosmology, no theology, no ethics, no aesthetics, no sociology, no political science, and not even hygiene. Why do you concentrate on the mind only and its workings?

KRISHNAMURTI: If the thinker can understand himself, then he will have solved all his problems. Then only is there creation. Then only is there reality. For then, what he does will not be antisocial. Virtue is not an end in itself. Virtue brings freedom and there can be freedom only when the thinker ceases.

It is important to know the process of the mind, the bundle of memories it creates, the 'me' and the 'mine'. Because the thinker is confused, his actions are confused. Because he is confused, he seeks order and peace. Because he is ignorant, he seeks knowledge. Because he is in contradiction, he seeks out authority for conduct, which is ethics. Because he is confused and driven by desires, he is antisocial. Because he does not understand himself, he cannot understand reality. So, if the thinker, the mind, can understand itself, then the whole problem is solved; then there will be no antisocial actions; then it will not exploit another or things as a means of self-expansion, thus causing conflict between man and man; then there will be no caste, no nationality, no division of belief;

then there will be love. So, the importance is not in cosmology, nor in theology, nor in hygiene, though hygiene is necessary and theology and cosmology are unnecessary; but what is important is to understand the ways of the mind, the self.

Is the thinker different from his thoughts? If thought ceases, is there a thinker? When the qualities of the thinker are removed, where is the thinker? Is there the 'me' without its qualities? So, thoughts themselves are the thinker. There are only the thoughts and not the thinker. The thinker has separated himself from his thoughts in order to safeguard himself and to give himself permanency. He can always modify his thoughts according to circumstances, and yet he remains. When he begins to modify himself, to transform himself, the thinker ceases. Because he is afraid to cease, he is occupied with the modification of thought. The thinker is not, if the thought is not. And the mere modification of thought does not do away with the thinker. So, it is one of the cunning actions of the mind to separate the thinker from his thoughts, and to be very concerned with them. So, the self gives itself permanency; but it is not permanent, whether the higher or the lower self; for it is still in the field of memory, within the net of time.

Why I am laying so much emphasis and urgency on psychological transformation is because the mind, the self, is the cause of our strife and misery, of our confusion and antagonism. Without understanding this, merely to reform, merely to trim the superficial actions has very little meaning. We have pruned our thoughts for generations, and have brought about such confusing madness and misery. Now, we have to go to the very root of the problem of existence, of consciousness, which is the 'me' and the 'mine'. Without understanding the thinker and his activities, mere superficial social reforms have very little significance, at least for the man

who is earnest. So, it is important for each one to find out for oneself on what to lay emphasis, whether on the superficial, the outward, or on the fundamental. If you are persuaded by me to lay emphasis on the inward nature of man, then you will merely be imitative, and you will equally be persuaded by another to lay emphasis on the outer. So, you must think out this problem very earnestly and not wait for somebody to tell you on what to lay emphasis. What fundamental value is there in trimming the environmental influences and conditions? When man is inwardly sick, diseased, and confused, power politics and organized religions, ideologies and systems cannot heal this burning disease. Help comes only when the cause of disease is eradicated, the disease in yourself. An earnest man is concerned with the understanding and with the eradication of the disease. There will be outward order and peace when there is inward order and peace, for the inward always overcomes the outward. A happy and peaceful man is not in conflict with his neighbor. It is only the ignorant man that is in conflict, and his actions are antisocial. A man who understands himself is at peace, and so his actions are peaceful.

Question: You have said that all being is in love only, and that what we call progress is merely a process of disintegration. Chaos is always with us, and there is no progress or regress in chaos.

KRISHNAMURTI: There is technological progress, but otherwise we are rapidly disintegrating. This technological progress is worshipped. But, is there progress of our mind and heart? The transforming energy comes through love and where there is charity. All technological progress without love leads to destruction and disintegration. From the cartwheel to the jet plane is progress. But, do you, your psychological being, evolve at all?

What is the thing that evolves, and towards what? Ignorance can never evolve to wisdom. Greed can never become that which is not greed. Greed will always be greed though it progresses. Ignorance through time can never become wisdom. Ignorance must cease for wisdom, greed must cease for the being of nongreed. When you indulge in the talk of evolving or progressing, you mean becoming. You are this and you will become that; you are a clerk and you will become the manager; you are the ordinary priest and you will become the bishop; you are evil and you will eventually become good. This becoming you call evolving. This evolving, becoming, is merely a continuity of *what is* in a modified form, and so becoming can never bring about transformation. In becoming, in continuity, there is never rebirth. Only in ending is there being. Where there is love, there is no compulsion. When you love, the 'me' and the 'mine' ceases. It is the 'me' and the 'mine' that is ever in search of continuity, it is ever seeking growth. That which grows knows decay and that which continues knows death.

Question: We know that thought destroys feeling. How to feel without thinking?

KRISHNAMURTI: We know that rationalization, calculation, bargaining, destroy love. Love is dangerous. For, love might lead you to all unpremeditated action. You control it by rationalizing, and thereby bring it to the market place. Where there is thought process, which is naming or terming, love is destroyed. You have a feeling of pain or pleasure. By terming it, by giving it a name—that is, by thinking about it—you have modified it and therefore reduced it. When you feel generous and open, your mind comes in and begins to rationalize your generosity; then you become

charitable through organizations and avoid direct action. As love is dangerous, you begin to think about, and so minimize, it and slowly destroy it.

Is it possible to love without thinking? What do you mean by thinking? Thinking is a response to memories of pain or pleasure. There is no thinking without the residue which incomplete experience leaves. Love is different from emotion and feeling. Love cannot be brought into the field of thought; whereas feeling and emotion can be brought. Love is a flame without smoke, ever fresh, creative, joyous. Such love is dangerous to society, to relationship. So, thought steps in, modifies, guides it, legalizes it, puts it out of danger; then one can live with it. Do you not know that when you love someone, you love the whole of mankind? Do you not know how dangerous it is to love man? Then, there is no barrier, no nationality; then, there is no craving for power and position, and things assume their values. Such a man is a danger to society.

For the being of love, the process of memory must come to an end. Memory comes into being only when experience is not fully, completely understood. Memory is only the residue of experience; it is the result of a challenge which is not fully comprehended. Life is a process of challenge and response. Challenge is always new but the response is ever old. This response, which is conditioning, which is the result of the past, must be understood and not disciplined or condemned away. It means living each day anew, fully and completely. This complete living is possible only when there is love, when your heart is full, not with the words nor with the things made by the mind. Only where there is love, memory ceases; then every movement is a rebirth.

February 22, 1948

Seventh Talk in Bombay

This evening I will answer questions only. If you can listen with right awareness, without prejudice, we shall understand more deeply and extensively. So, if I may suggest, it would be good if you listen without the effort made to listen; and though you may have defenses of prejudice, it would be well if you would understand. Put the armor of prejudice aside, and let us think together of the various problems we shall deal with this evening.

Question: Are ideals the only thing between ourselves and madness? You are breaking a dam which keeps chaos out of our homes and fields. Why are you so foolhardy? The immature or unsteady minds will be thrown off their feet by your sweeping generalizations.

KRISHNAMURTI: This question is put with regard to what I have said concerning ideals, examples, and the opposites. So, I will have to restate what I have said about ideals.

I have said that ideals in any form are an escape from the understanding of *what is*. Ideals, however noble and however fine, have no reality; they are fictitious. It is more important to understand *what is* than to pursue or to follow an ideal or an example or a pattern of action. You have innumerable ideals—peace, nonviolence, nongreed, etc.—within which your minds are enclosed; they are not really factual, they are nonexistent. Since they are nonexistent, of what value are they? Do they help you to understand your conflict, your violence, your greed? Are they not a hindrance to such understanding? Will this screen of ideals help you to understand arrogance and corruption? Can a violent man be nonviolent through the ideal of nonviolence? Must you not put aside the screen of ideals and examine violence? Will the ideal help to bring about understanding? Is

evil understood through the ideal of good? Or is evil transformed—not through the ideal, not through the pursuit of its opposite—but in facing it without resistance and understanding it. Does not the ideal in any form prevent the understanding of *what is*?

Surely, you have each one tried the pursuit of the opposites and are caught in the conflict bred by the opposite. You are familiar with the constant struggle of the opposites, of the thesis and of the antithesis, and hoping to arrive at a synthesis—capitalism in conflict with the left—hoping to arrive at a synthesis, that synthesis again creating its own opposite, and again producing a synthesis, and so on and on. We are familiar with this state.

Now, is this struggle necessary? Is not this struggle unreal? Is not the opposite itself unreal? What is the real, the actual? The opposite is fictitious, not real. The actual is greed. The ideal of nongreed is nonexistent; it is the creation of the mind giving it an opportunity to escape from *what is*.

If you have no ideals, will you collapse, will you fall apart? Are your ideals acting as a dam against evil and unkind action? Is your ideal of nonviolence preventing you from being nonviolent? Obviously, it is not. So, ideals are nonexistent except in theory, and therefore valueless. An idealist is really a man who is escaping, avoiding direct action with regard to *what is*. By removing the ideals, will the weak-minded be thrown off their feet? The weak-minded are thrown off their feet anyhow by the politicians, by the gurus, by the priests, by the innumerable ceremonies and exploitations. But, the man who is strong anyhow disregards the ideals and pursues what he wants. So, neither the weak nor the strong pay any attention to ideals. The ideal is a convenient easy cover for false and thoughtless action. The ideal of the opposite is a hindrance to the direct understanding of *what is*. You can understand *what is* only when you are not escaping from it through the fantasy of an ideal. The ideal prevents you from looking at it, examining it, and dealing with it directly. As you do not want to deal with it directly, you invent the ideal and so *what is* can be postponed.

So, our problem is how to transcend, to go beyond that which is—not how to go beyond the opposites which the mind has created. Obviously, *what is* can be understood completely, wholly, when you are aware of the whole psychological significance of *what is*. You understand *what is* only when all escapes have ceased. To acknowledge *what is*, whether it is greed or it is a lie, requires an honesty of awareness. To be aware that one is greedy is already the beginning of freedom from greed. Seeing the truth in the false and truth as truth is the beginning of understanding. It is the perception of truth that liberates, and not the pursuit of the opposite or of the ideal.

Question: Will sexual urge disappear when we refuse to name it?

KRISHNAMURTI: This question needs considerable explanation. The process of naming or terming is quite a complex problem, and to understand it, we must go into the whole problem of consciousness.

What do we mean by consciousness? Consciousness is surely the state of experiencing which is the response to challenge. The beginning of consciousness is challenge, response, and experiencing. The experience is named or termed or given a label, as pleasant or unpleasant, and it is recorded and put away in the mind. So, consciousness is a process of experiencing, naming, and recording. Without these three processes, which are really a unitary process, there is no consciousness. This process is going on all the time at different levels. This song is repeated

in different moods, with different themes; but it is always, at whatever level, the same process of experiencing, naming, and recording. This is the theme, this is the record that is being played.

Now, what would happen if we put an end to naming? Why do you give a name to an experience, calling it pleasant or unpleasant, meritorious or unworthy, good or bad, and so on? We give it a name either to communicate or to fix it in memory, which gives it a continuity. To have no continuity, the mind is not, condemnation is not. You must give continuity to an experience; otherwise, self-consciousness ceases. Therefore, you give a name to an experience. The giving of a name to a feeling, to an experience, is instantaneous. The mind which is the record keeper, which is memory, labels a feeling in order to give itself stability and continuity. But, supposing you did not term the feeling—which is quite arduous because the naming of the feeling is instantaneous—what would happen to a feeling? If you did not, the record keeper, the mind, could not grapple with the feeling. He cannot give it substance, strength; so the feeling withers away.

You can experiment with it in your daily life and discover for yourself what happens to a feeling when you do not term it. You will discover an odd thing happening. You will find that the feeling withers away. The naming of a feeling, of an experience, gives permanency to the thinker, the record keeper. We know what happens when we give a name to a feeling, to an experience. We give a continuity to that experience, upon which the mind feeds and so becomes vital. When you give a name to a feeling, you put it within the framework of reference, so the very nature of terming an experience is to give continuity to consciousness, to the 'me' and 'mine'. We are so swiftly and unconsciously doing it all the time. This record is being played at different levels with different themes, with different words, all the time, whether waking or sleeping. By not terming a feeling, the feeling withers away.

Now, you have learned a trick. You will say to yourself, "I know how to deal with unpleasant feelings, how to put an end to them quickly; I will not name them." But, will you do the same with the so-called pleasant feelings? You want to continue the so-called pleasant feelings, pleasant emotions, that give you substance, and these you want to maintain. So, you will begin to choose those that are pleasant and term them; and those which you call unpleasant, let them wither away by not naming them. By this process you are inevitably sustaining the conflict of the opposites; whereas, if you do not term a sensation, a feeling, whether pleasant or unpleasant, it comes to an end. So, the thinker, the record keeper, the creator of the opposites withers away.

But, is love a sensation, an emotion which can be termed and so given a continuity; or by not naming it, will it wither away? When you love some person and when you think of him, what happens? You are only dealing with the sensations caused by that person. You are concerned with emotions, sensations of that person; the more you give emphasis to them, the less there is of love.

Now, the questioner asks whether the sexual urge will disappear when it is not termed. It will disappear, obviously. But, if you do not understand the whole process of consciousness, which has been explained carefully, the mere putting an end to an urge, whether pleasant or unpleasant, does not bring about the eternal quality of love. Without love, merely to put an end to an urge has no meaning. You will become dry as an idealist. Where there is love, there is chastity. The man who is passionate, who craves after the ideal of chastity, will never know love. He is caught in the conflict of opposites; and as the ideal is nonexistent, he

lives in illusion. Such a man is empty of heart, and he fills it with the things made by the mind, which are ideals. Once you open the door to the understanding of your whole being, you will discover great riches. But to discover, there must be freedom to experiment. Freedom comes through virtue, not becoming virtuous, but being virtuous.

Question: Why can't you influence the leaders of a party, or members of a government, and work through them?

KRISHNAMURTI: For the simple reason that leaders are the factors of degeneration in society and governments are the expression of violence. How can anyone who attempts to understand the truth work through instruments opposed to reality?

Why do we want leaders, political or religious? Because we want to be directed, we must be told what to think and what to do. Our education and our social system are based on compulsion and imitation. When there is confusion, you look to another to lead you out of it. Can any leader, political or religious, liberate you from your own misery? For, in leadership is implied power, position, prestige. The leader becomes the exploiter of the follower, and the follower exploits the leader. The leader feels lost, frustrated without a follower; and the follower feels confused and uncertain without direction. So, it is a mutual process of exploitation when there is a desire for power, position, and a craving for guidance. When the leader becomes the authority to whom everything is referred, politically or religiously, then you are merely the record player, and so you become thoughtless and uncreative. So, what is important is to understand your own sorrow and confusion and your disastrous existence. To understand it, need you have a leader? Surely not. What you need is attention to look closely and clearly with eyes that are not biased. You have to be aware of your own thoughts and feelings, which is self-knowledge and which no leader can give you. The leader becomes important only when he helps you to run away from yourself. Then, the leader can be worshipped, put in a cage and whispered about. Thus, the leader becomes a degenerating factor in society. A society that is creative has no leader because every individual in it is a light unto himself.

Question: By what mechanism do we change the world when we change ourselves?

KRISHNAMURTI: The individual problem is the world's problem. The individual with his inner conflicts, with his psychological struggles and frustrations, with his anxieties and hopes, creates the world of relationship about him. What he is, the world is. The individual and the world are not separate processes. They are inseparable, they are one process. The world is you, and the world is not apart from you. This is not a mystical statement but an actuality. What you are, that you project outwardly, which becomes the world. However cunningly and diligently the outer is systematized, regulated, and constructed, the inner will inevitably overcome the outer. So, there must be the transformation of the inner, not in opposition to the outer, not in antagonism to the many, to the collective.

As you are a total process, you must begin with yourself. By transforming yourself you will inevitably affect the complex state of relationship, that is, the world in which you live. You cannot transform the world, the world has no referent. The individual has a referent, which is you, so you must begin with yourself, not for individualistic perfection which leads to isolation, to segregation. Nothing can exist in isolation. This isolation which takes the form of self-improvement is

destructive to understanding, for it is a process of self-enclosure.

So by transforming yourself you bring about a revolution in the immediate world of your relationship. So, the mechanism of transformation is brought about swiftly by your action of understanding. As long as you are acquisitive, envious, and nationalistic, you will inevitably create the structure of a society in which these things are encouraged and maintained. These are ultimately the causes of war. As long as you are seeking power, position of authority, you will inevitably bring about conflict between man and man. The way of peace is your responsibility, as you are responsible for the way of war. As belief and ideology, organized religion and nationalism separate man from man, creating antagonism between man and man, you who are the creator of this antagonism, and so of destruction, must transform yourself. So, regeneration must begin with yourself, yourself who is a total process of man. This regeneration is not opposed to another individual or to the collective world. The other and the collective is a total process as yourself, and to have antagonism for another is to be antagonistic to yourself. So, you have to be aware of every thought, every feeling, and every action.

So, in understanding yourself completely, you will find love. It is only love that transforms. Without love, there can be no peace and happiness in you and so in the world.

Question: What is true and what is false in the theory of reincarnation?

KRISHNAMURTI: It is important in understanding this question that we should have an inquiring mind and an open mind. Inquiry implies the search for truth. Truth is not according to any system at all. It is not in the net of belief or dogma. This inquiry is impeded when there is prejudice and dishonesty of thought. Mere quotation of an authority, however ancient or learned, will not yield the freedom of truth. Inquiry must be free from prejudice and belief; if you are tethered to them, you can wander only within the radius of your own bondage, but within it, truth can never be.

What is the thing that reincarnates? What is the continuous quality that comes into rebirth? There are only two states that have a possibility of continuing: one, the spiritual entity called the soul or the other, the 'me' and the 'mine'. The spiritual entity must be something that is not created by the 'me' and the 'mine'. It cannot be the outcome of a thought process. It must be, if it is the spiritual entity, something beyond ignorance and illusion. If it is something other than me, it must be timeless, and that which is timeless cannot evolve, grow, become. It is deathless. If it is deathless, it is beyond me, beyond my consideration and not within the field of my consciousness. So, you cannot think about it; you cannot inquire if it can or cannot reincarnate. Since it is timeless and deathless, and as you are concerned about death and time, you cannot inquire into it. To speculate upon the nature of the spiritual entity is an escape, and speculation about the unknown is an escape and a definite hindrance to the understanding of truth.

You are really not concerned about the continuance of the spiritual entity but with the continuance of yourself, the 'me'—the 'me' and the 'mine' with its achievements and failures, with its frustrations and bank accounts, with its characteristics and idiosyncracies. You want to know if the 'me' of your property, the 'me' of your family, the 'me' of your beliefs, if the 'you', which is a physiological as well as a psychological process, has a continuance when the physical existence ceases.

What do you mean by continuity? We have examined more or less what we mean by 'me' and 'mine', the name, the characteristics, the achievements at all different levels of consciousness. What do you mean by continuity and what is it that gives continuity? What is it that clings to continuity, continuity in the form of permanency? If you are assured of permanency, then you would not cling to continuity. You seek permanency or security in possessions and in things, in family or in belief. When the body dies, the permanency of things and the permanency of family are gone, but the permanency of idea may continue. It is the idea that we want to continue. The thought, the idea of 'me'—will it continue? This continuous becoming from experience to experience—will this formulation of 'me' continue? Thought identified as the 'me' continues, has substance. Like the electronic waves, thought has existence. This thought, when identified by you, *is* you; and so, thought as you continues.

Now, what happens to that which continues? What happens to that which is in constant becoming, moving from experience to experience? That which continues has no renewal. That which moves from experience to experience, which is becoming, is constantly reconditioning itself, and so it has no renewal. The 'me' identified with thought has continuance, but that which continues is in constant decay, for it is moving from experience to experience, accumulating, and so acting within the net of time. There is only renewal when there is constant experiencing without the accumulation of experience, which is without yesterday. That which ends has a beginning, but that which is continuous can have no regeneration, nor transformation. Only in death is there renewal, the death to the moment, to the day. Only in ending is there love. Love is new from moment to moment. Love is not continuous. It is not repetition. That is the greatness and beauty of love.

Some of you will probably say that I have not answered about what is true and what is false in the theory of reincarnation. If you will ponder over what I have said, you will see that I have pointed out what is true and what is false. To the deep problems of life, there is no categorical yes and no. It is only the thoughtless that seek the yes and the no to a problem. In inquiring into this problem, we have found the truth of continuity. Life and death are one, and he who knows it dies every minute. Immortality is not the continuance of identified thought. The mortal cannot seek the immortal. Immortality comes into being when the thought process as the 'me' and the 'mine' ceases.

February 29, 1948

Eighth Talk in Bombay

Life is, from birth to death, a constant strife and pain, a constant battle with oneself and so with one's neighbor. Is this battle necessary or is there a different approach? Life, existence, is a constant process of becoming, from *what is* to something else. Becoming is always a strife. Becoming is always repetitive. Becoming is cultivation of memory. This cultivation of memory is called righteousness, and righteousness is a process of self-enclosure. We know the battle of being poor and of becoming rich, of being petty, small, and of becoming profound. Becoming is the cultivation of memory, and without memory there is no becoming. This struggle is considered righteous, and so righteousness is a form of self-enclosure, self-isolation. To this struggle we have given significance. We have accepted it as a worthwhile, a noble part of our existence, this battle of suffering.

Is life meant to be a process of struggle, sorrow, and pain? Surely, there must be a different way of living. This new way of living can be understood only when we understand the full significance of becoming. In becoming, there is always repetition and the creation of habit. In becoming, there is the cultivation of memory which lays emphasis on the self. The self, in its very nature, is travail and is contradictory.

Virtue is never a becoming. Virtue is being in which there is no strife. You cannot become virtuous, you are or are not virtuous. You can always become righteous, but never become virtuous. Virtue becomes freedom and a righteous man is never free. If you attempt to be virtuous, you merely become righteous. In understanding the process of becoming, in which there is strife and pain, there is being which is virtue. In the freedom of virtue, truth comes into being. Truth can never come to the righteous man, for he is enclosed in his becoming. If you try to become merciful, generous, then the emphasis is laid on becoming, on the self, the 'me'. The 'me' can never be merciful. It can enclose itself in righteousness, but it can never be merciful. A righteous man can never be a virtuous man.

If you are aware of the way of virtue, you will see that there is no building up of resistance. Mercy, generosity, self-confidence, freedom from envy, do not come into being through the cultivation of virtue. When virtue is cultivated, it becomes a resistance. But, if you are aware of the process of becoming, which is to understand the ways of the self, then there comes being.

How is one who is caught in the struggle of becoming to step out of it? All that can be done is to be alert and passively aware of this process of becoming. Becoming is to set up resistance, and resistance is the cultivation of memory, which is righteousness. Be aware without choice, without condemnation, and you will find that the wall of resistance drops away. Then only, in freedom, can truth come into being. Being is virtuous; being brings order and freedom. The man of will, which is the man of resistance, by his self-enclosing action is never free, and so truth can never come into being. It is only by the recognition of *what is* without choice and condemnation and following its movement swiftly and easily, that freedom from *what is* comes into being. It is in the understanding of *what is* that truth is revealed.

Question: Are not religious symbols an explanation of a reality too deep to be false? The simple name of God moves us as nothing else. Why should we shun it?

KRISHNAMURTI: Symbols surely exist as a means of communication. Do we need symbols to communicate with reality? Reality cannot communicate itself to us when our mind is crowded with the means of communication which are symbols—either the cross, the crescent, or the Hindu symbols.

Why is it not possible to experience directly that which is without the intermediary of symbols? Are not symbols, to a man who is seeking a direct experience, a distraction? What happens when you have symbols? Each group of people has its own symbols, and these symbols become more important than the search for reality. The symbol is not the real. The word is not the thing. The word is not God. But the word has become important. Why? Is it not because we are not seeking that which is above and beyond the creations of man? So, symbols have become important and we are willing to destroy each other for them.

The word *God* gives us a certain stimulation. But we think that stimulation, nervous as well as verbal, has some relation with the real. But, has a sensation, which is a thought process, any relation to reality? Has thought, which is the outcome of memory, response to a conditioning, any relationship to reality? So, has a symbol, which is the creation of the mind, any relationship to reality? Is not a symbol a fanciful distraction from reality? For the real to be, the symbol has to be discarded. But, we crowd our minds with symbols because we have not got the other. If you love you don't want the symbol of love. If you have the symbol, the picture, the ideal, then you do not love.

Why is it not possible to appreciate things directly? You love a tree or a person not because of what it represents, not because it is a manifestation of life or reality, not because it is an outward expression of an inward state—which are easy explanations. When one is able to love life, not because it is the manifestation of something, then in that very love of life one will find what is real. If you treat life as a manifestation of something, then you abominate life, then you want to run away from life; or you make of life a bore and a routine which make you escape from the actual.

A mind that is caught in symbols is not a simple mind. Only a simple mind, unpolluted, and a clear heart, uncorrupted, can find the real. A mind and a heart caught in words and phrases, in patterns of action, are never free for the real to be. It is only when the mind strips itself of all its accumulations that the real can come into being.

Question: What do you advise us to do when war breaks out?

KRISHNAMURTI: Instead of seeking advice, may I suggest that we examine the problem together? To follow the advice of another in moments of crisis leads to our own destruction. Whereas, if we were able to understand the whole implication of war, then we would be able to act truly for ourselves. We would not act according to our conditioning, and that conditioning is strengthened through propaganda and by various other means to impress upon us the necessity of going to war. As we are now conditioned by the so-called love of the country, by economic frontiers, by ideologies—religious or political—we will inevitably jump to arms. To such people, there is no problem; their action is definite and clear-cut; it is called duty and responsibility and they become the cannon fodder.

You have a problem only when you begin to question the causes of war, which are not merely economic, as some would like to make out, but much more psychological. War is only a bloody and a spectacular projection of your daily life. War comes into being only when you, in your relationship with another, breed conflict which is the result of your inward strife and misery. This is projected outwardly as antisocial action, and causes disaster and misery. Through greed, acquisitiveness, and envy you are killing, destroying, and maiming thousands. So, when you begin to inquire into the causes of war, you are beginning to understand your relationship with another, you are questioning your whole way of living. According to this inquiry, intelligent or superficial, you will respond when war comes. A man who is nonviolent, who is not the idealist who is striving to become nonviolent, to him war is a great disaster and not productive of peace. So, he will not enter it naturally; he may be shot or he may be imprisoned. He will naturally disregard the consequences.

The idealist, as I have previously explained, is incapable of being free from violence. As your life is based on conflict and violence, if you do not understand that way of life now, how can you act tomorrow with understanding when there is a calamity? How can you, who have been conditioned by nationalism, by class security, by envy, be free of your conditioning at the moment of war? You have to free yourself from these causes of disaster before war comes into being.

War breeds its irresponsibility, and many like this freedom from responsibility. The government will feed you and your family and so on. War gives you an escape from the boring routine of your daily life. It is an ugly business, killing; but at least it is exciting. Also war acts as a release to criminal instincts. We are criminals in our daily life, in the world of business, in our relationships; but it is all very carefully hidden, covered over with a righteous blanket and legalized. War gives a release from this hypocrisy, and at last we can be openly violent. So, it depends upon your conditioning how you will act when you are called to arms. But, those of us who are earnest, if we can understand how we are violent in our daily life and understand it by actually facing it, if we can be aware of violence in our speech, in our thoughts, in our feelings, and in our actions, we will see that when war comes, we shall be able to act truly. It is only by being aware of *what is* and not trying to transform it, trying to make it into something else, that understanding comes. A man who is pursuing an ideal will act falsely because his response will be based on frustration. If you are aware of your daily thoughts and actions without choice and condemnation or justification, then you will be free from those causes that bring about war.

Question: Can a man who abhors violence take part in the government of a country?

KRISHNAMURTI: Government, if it is not completely authoritarian, is supposed to represent you. You elect those who are like you. So, government in a so-called democracy is what you are. What are you? You are a mass of conditioned responses of violence, greed, acquisitiveness, desire for power, and so on. So, the government is what you are. How can a man who has really no violence in his being belong to a structure which is violent?

Can a man who is seeking reality or to whom reality has come have anything to do with a government, with a country, with an ideology, with party politics, with systems of power? How can a man who has given himself over to another, whatever it is, to a party, to an ideology, to a guru, find the real? He cannot.

You ask this question about government because you like to rely on outside authority, on the alteration of environmental influences, for the transformation of yourself. You hope that leaders, governments, ideologies, systems which are patterns of action will somehow transform, bring about order and peace in your lives. Surely, this is the basis of your question. Can another—be it a government, a guru, or an ideology—give you peace and order? Can another give you love and happiness? Certainly not. Peace can only come into being when confusion, which you bring about, is completely understood. But without understanding the causes of our misery, you look to some outward agency to bring you peace and happiness. The outward is always overcome by the inner, and as long as the psychological conflict in various forms exists, however well built and orderly the outer structure, the inward conflict and confusion will always overcome it.

So, without isolating yourself, the transformation must begin not in opposition to the outer, but to bring—not only to yourself and so to the outer—peace and happiness.

Question: You don't seem to think that we have won our independence. According to you, what would be the state of real freedom?

KRISHNAMURTI: Freedom becomes an isolation when it is nationalistic, when it is exclusive, and when it is class-ridden. Isolation inevitably leads to conflict, for nothing can exist in isolation. To be is to be related.

To isolate yourself in a national frontier invites confusion, starvation, and so on. Independence as a process of isolation ever leads to conflict and war. Independence with most of us implies isolation. When you have isolated yourself as a national entity, have you gained freedom? Have you gained freedom from exploitation, from class struggle, from starvation, from priests, from leaders? Obviously you have not. You have driven out the white exploiter and the brown has taken his place. Both are ruthless.

You do not want to be free. You fool yourself with words. Freedom implies intelligence—intelligence not to exploit, but to be merciful and generous and not to accept authority as a form of security. Virtue is necessary for freedom. But, righteousness is an isolating process. Isolation and righteousness always go together. Virtue and freedom are co-existent.

A group of people calling themselves a nation will build self-enclosing walls of isolation and so can never be free. It becomes the cause of strife, suspicion, antagonism, ultimately leading to war. Freedom must begin with the individual, which is a total process, a total process of man. If he isolates himself in economic frontiers or in righteousness, he is the cause of disaster and misery. If he liberates himself from greed and violence, then he will have direct action upon the world of his relationship. This regeneration of the individual is not in the future, but now. If you postpone, you are inviting the wave of darkness and confusion. You will understand only when you give your full attention, when you give your mind and heart to that which needs immediate comprehension.

Question: My mind is restless and distressed. Without getting it under control, I can do nothing about myself. How am I to control thought?

KRISHNAMURTI: First we must understand thought and the thinker. What do we mean by thought, by thinking? Is the thinker different from his thoughts? Is the meditator different from his meditation? Are the qualities different from the self? Before thought can be controlled, whatever that may mean, we must understand the thinker and his thoughts. Does the thinker exist when he ceases to think? When there are no thoughts, is there the thinker? If there is no thought, there is no thinker. But, why is there the division between the thinker and his thoughts? Is this division real or is it fictitious?—this fiction which the mind has created for its own security. We must be very clear if the thinker is separate from his thought and why he has separated himself. Are you not aware that your thoughts are separate from yourself? From this arises the idea that there are the controller and the controlled, the observer and the observed.

Most of you think that the thinker is separate, the higher self dominating the lower self, and so on. Why is there this separation? Is not this separation still in the field of the mind? When you say that the thinker is the atma, the watcher, and the thoughts are separate, surely it is still within the field of the thought process. Does not this division exist because the thinker gives himself permanency through the division? He can always modify his thoughts, put a new frame round him; but he remains apart and thereby gives himself permanency. The thinker without thought is not. He may separate himself. If he ceases to think, he is not. This separation of the thinker from his thought gives permanency to him. The thinker perceives that thoughts are transient, and so he cunningly makes himself permanent by calling himself the atma, the soul, the spiritual entity. But, if you observe closely, putting aside all the acquisitive knowledge of what others have said, however great, you will

perceive that the observer is the observed, that there is only thought. There is no thinker apart from the thought. However wisely, deeply, and extensively he may separate himself, build a wall between himself and his thought, he is still within the field of thought. So, the thinker is the thought.

When you ask how thought can be controlled, you put a wrong question. When the thinker begins to control his thoughts, he is merely controlling them in order to give himself continuity, or because he finds his thoughts painful. When you become fully aware of the fact that the thinker is the thought, then you are no longer thinking in terms of dominating or modifying, controlling or channeling your thoughts. Then thought becomes more important than the thinker; then the understanding of the thought process is the beginning of meditation, which is self-knowledge. Without self-knowledge, there is no meditation, and meditation of the heart is understanding.

So, we are concerned with the thought process itself. We are free from the idea of discipline and from the idea of control of thought, which is a great revolution. There is a freedom only when you see the falseness that a thinker is separate from his thought. When you see the truth of the false, then there is freedom from the false.

Thought is the result of sensation and the mind is the recorder, the accumulating factor. Consciousness is experiencing, naming, and recording—which I have explained previously. This recording is memory. Challenge is always new and response is the old, so memory, which is the record of the past, meets the new. This meeting of the new by the old is called experience. Memory has no life in itself. It revivifies itself by meeting the new. The new is giving life to the old, which is to strengthen the old. In translating the new according to its own conditioning, memory comes to life. Memory has life only as it meets the new. This revivification is called thinking. Thinking can never be new, for thinking is the response of memory, which is vitalized by the new. Thinking can never be creative, for it is always the response of memory.

A controlled mind is not a free mind. As thoughts wander all over the place, how is it possible to bring order out of this confusion? To understand a fast-revolving machine it must be slowed down. If you stop it, it is a dead thing and a dead thing can never be understood. So, a mind that has killed thought by exclusion, by isolation, can have no understanding; but, a thought can be understood if its process is slowed down. If you have a slow-motion picture of a horse jumping a hurdle, you will see in detail the marvelous movement of the muscles. Similarly, when the mind is slowed down, it can understand each thought as it arises; then only there is freedom from thinking, not controlled or disciplined thought.

Only in meeting the new as the new, the fresh as the fresh, is there creative being. So long as the mind is a recorder, the gatherer of memories which are vivified by challenge, thought process must go on. To be aware of each thought is arduous. But, if you are interested in thinking out one thought fully, you might experiment in putting down on paper the thoughts as they arise; by observing them after they are written down, you will find that your mind has slowed down without discipline, without compulsion. Thus, the mind is free from the past and the mind becomes tranquil; for, it is no longer the creator of problems. Into this tranquillity reality comes into being.

March 7, 1948

Ninth Talk in Bombay

Existence is action—action at different levels of consciousness. Without action, life is not possible. Action is relationship. In isolation, action is not possible, and nothing can exist in isolation, so relationship is action at different levels of consciousness.

Consciousness, as I have been explaining, is experiencing, naming, and recording. Experiencing is the response to challenge. The challenge is met by conditioning responses. This conditioning is called experience. This experience is termed and thereby put into the frame of reference which is memory. This total process is action. Consciousness is action. Without experiencing, terming, recording, there is no action. This process is going on whether one is aware or unaware of it.

Action creates the actor. The actor comes into being when the action has a result and an end in view. If there is no result in action, the actor is not. So, the actor, the action, and the end are a unitary process, a single movement. Action towards a result is will. The desire to achieve an end brings about will, and so the actor comes into being. The actor with his will and the action towards a result are a single process. Though we can break it up and observe them separately, they are one. With these three states we are familiar—the actor, the action, and the result. This is our daily existence. These three make up action which is a process of becoming. Otherwise, there is no becoming. If there is no actor and no action towards an end, there is no becoming.

Our life is a process of becoming, to become at different levels of consciousness. This becoming is strife and pain. Is there an action without this becoming, with its conflict and misery? There is, if there is no actor and no result. Action with an end in view creates the actor. Can there be an action without an end, without a result and so not giving birth to an actor? For, where there is an action with a desire of a result, there the actor is. So, the actor is the source of strife and misery.

Can there be an action without the actor and without seeking a result? Then only, action is not a process of becoming, in which there is confusion, conflict, and antagonism. Action then is not a strife. This state of action is the state of experiencing without the experiencer and the experience. This is simple to understand. Our life is conflict and can one live without conflict? Conflict is disintegrating, bringing wave upon wave of confusion and destruction. Only in creative happiness can there be a revolutionary, regenerating state. Our problem is, can we live without strife? So, we must understand action. As long as action has an end in view, there must be the experiencer who gives continuity to becoming and so, to strife. This becoming creates contradiction. So, can there be action without contradiction? There can be freedom from contradiction only when there is no action with the desire for a result. Action then is a state of constant experiencing without the object of experience, and so without the experiencer. Can you live in a state of experiencing all the time without creating the actor?

Take any experience that you have had. In that moment of experiencing, there is no awareness of the experiencer and the experience; there is only a state of experiencing. As the state of experiencing fades away, the experiencer and the experience come into being—the actor and the action towards an end. We are living in a state of experiencing; only as the experiencing fades away do we give it a name, recording it, and thereby giving continuity to becoming. The very desire for the repetition of an experience gives birth to becoming, which prevents experiencing. Becoming prevents experiencing. This becoming is strife and pain.

So, our problem is how to be free from the conflict and misery of action. Without action there is no life. Action is relationship. Without action there is only isolation and

nothing can exist in isolation. There is freedom from contradiction in action when there is only a state of experiencing without the experiencer and the experience. This state of experiencing excludes the actor and his search for result. You can live completely, wholly, in action without conflict only when there is no terming or naming the experiencing, and thereby reviving it, which is to build up memory. Memory is a record of the result which is the outcome of action with an end in view. This experiencing is joy, is creation. To live in a state of constant experiencing, which is to live in constant regeneration or transformation, there must be awareness of the process of action with its search for result, which gives birth to the actor. We must be aware of that and nothing else. When we are aware of it and see the truth of it, being alert yet passively aware, then in that state there is experiencing without the experiencer and the experience.

Question: What is the relation between the thinker and his thought?

KRISHNAMURTI: Is there any relationship between the thinker and his thought, or is there only thought and not a thinker? If there are no thoughts there is no thinker. When you have thoughts, is there a thinker? Perceiving the impermanency of thoughts, thought itself creates the thinker who gives himself permanency; so, thought creates the thinker; then the thinker establishes himself as a permanent entity apart from thoughts which are always in a state of flux. So, thought creates the thinker and not the other way about. The thinker does not create thought, for if there are no thoughts, there is no thinker. The thinker separates himself from his parent and tries to establish a relationship—a relationship between the so-called permanent, which is the thinker created by thought, and the impermanent or transient, which is thought. So, both are really transient.

Pursue a thought completely to its very end. Think it out fully, feel it out and discover for yourself what happens. You will find that there is no thinker at all. For, when thought ceases, the thinker is not. We think there are two states, as the thinker and the thought. These two states are fictitious, unreal. There is only thought, and the bundle of thought creates the 'me', the thinker. The thinker, having himself permanency, tries to change thought, to modify thought, thereby to maintain himself. But, if every thought is thought out and felt out without resistance, without choice, without condemnation, then there is no entity as the thinker. When thought ceases to create the thinker, that state is experiencing. It is action in which there is neither the experiencer nor the experience.

Only when the thought process is completely understood, in that passive awareness where every thought is allowed to unroll itself deeply and widely, is there freedom from all thought. Only in that state is there experiencing.

Question: I would like to help you by doing propaganda for your teachings. Can you advise the best way?

KRISHNAMURTI: To be a propagandist is to be a liar. Propaganda is mere repetition and a repetition of a truth is a lie. When you repeat what you consider to be the truth of another, it ceases to be truth. Repetition has no value, it only dulls the mind and wearies the heart. You cannot repeat truth, for truth is never constant, is never fixed. Truth is the state of experiencing, and what you can repeat is a static state, and so it ceases to be the truth.

Propaganda, which is repetition, does infinite harm. A lecturer who goes out doing propaganda for an idea is really a destroyer of intelligence. He repeats an experience which he or another has had. Truth cannot be repeated. Truth must be experienced by each one.

Now, with this understanding, what can you do to help further my teaching? All that you can do is to live it, to live that which you understand completely and vitally, enthusiastically, with vigor. Then, like a flower in a garden, the perfume is spread abroad. So likewise, the perfume of your life will be carried by the winds. You do not need to do propaganda for the jasmine; its perfume, its loveliness bring life. Only when you have not the loveliness, the beauty, you talk about it and thereby cover your own emptiness and ugliness by words which have little meaning.

But, when you yourself have an understanding, then you inevitably talk about it and shout about it from housetops. A dead thought can never be systematized and spread abroad through propaganda. A living thought cannot be the instrument of exploitation; a living thought cannot be accepted from another, you must discover it. As the bees come to a flower, and as the flower does not do any propaganda for itself that it has honey, so a living thought creates the nectar. But without this nectar, to do propaganda is to deceive people, to exploit people, to create division among them, and to breed envy and antagonism. But, if there is that nectar of understanding, however little, then it will nourish people.

If there is understanding in your heart, that itself will bring about the miracle of regeneration, not tomorrow, but from moment to moment. There is understanding only in the now. Love is not in the net of time. You either love now or never.

Question: The fact of death stares everybody in the face. Yet, its mystery is never solved. Must it always be so?

KRISHNAMURTI: Why is there a fear of death? When we cling to continuity, there is the fear of death. Incomplete action brings the fear of death. There is fear of death as long as there is the desire for continuity in character, continuity in action, in capacity, in the name, and so on. As long as there is action seeking a result, there must be the thinker who is seeking continuity. Fear comes into being when this continuity is threatened through death. So, there is fear of death as long as there is the desire for continuity.

That which continues disintegrates. Any form of continuity, however noble, is a process of disintegration. In continuity there is never renewal, and in renewal only there is freedom from the fear of death. If we see the truth of this, then we will see truth in the false. Then there would be the liberation from the false. Then there would be no fear of death. Thus, living, experiencing, is in the present and not a means of continuity.

Is it possible to live from moment to moment with renewal? There is renewal only in ending and not in continuity. In the interval between the ending and the beginning of another problem, there is renewal.

Death, the state of noncontinuity, the state of rebirth, is the unknown. Death is the unknown. The mind which is the result of continuity cannot know the unknown. It can only know the known. It can only act and have its being in the known, which is continuous. So, the known is in fear of the unknown. The known can never know the unknown, and so death remains the mystery. If there is an ending from moment to moment, from day to day, in this ending the unknown comes into being.

Immortality is not the continuation of 'me'. The 'me' and the 'mine' is of time, the result of action towards an end. So, there is no relationship between the 'me' and the 'mine' and that which is immortal, timeless. We would like to think there is a relationship, but this is an illusion. That which is im-mortal cannot be encased in that which is mortal. That which is immeasurable cannot be caught in the net of time.

There is fear of death where there is search for fulfillment. Fulfillment has no ending. Desire is constantly seeking and changing the object of fulfillment, and so it is caught in the net of time. So, the search for self-fulfillment is another form of continuity, and frustration seeks truth as a means of continuity. Truth is not continuous. Truth is a state of being and being is action without time. This being can be experienced only when desire, which gives birth to continuity, is wholly and completely understood. Thought is founded on the past. So, thought cannot know the unknown, the immeasurable. Thought process must come to an end. Then, only, the unknowable comes into being.

Question: I have plenty of money. Can you tell me what would be the right use of money? Only do not make me squander it by distributing coppers to the poor. Money is a tool to work with and not just a nuisance to be got rid of.

KRISHNAMURTI: How do you acquire money, how do you accumulate it? Through acquisitiveness, through exploitation, through ruthlessness. To accumulate money one must be clever and cunning, dishonest and ruthless. After accumulating, you want to know how to use it. Either you become a philanthropist or you distribute it. Having accumulated wrongly, you want to use it rightly. Don't laugh at the rich. You, too, desire to be rich. Through wrong means you cannot come to a right end. Should one give away to the poor and become oneself poor? Your action will depend upon your heart and not upon your calculating mind. That which has accumulated cannot be generous. A hard mind, the calculating mind, can only act on its own level and therefore its problems will remain, though modified. Love alone can resolve this problem, not the mind and its inventions, which are systems and organized philanthropies.

If you have love, then you will know what to do with your money; and according to the dictates of your hearts you will act. To be in communion with the promptings of a loving heart is difficult, especially for those who are rich. So, what to do with the money which you have inherited or accumulated is not so important as the cultivation of the heart. When you have money and no love, then woe unto you. It is an empty heart that gathers money, and having gathered, the problem of what to do with the accumulation arises. But, the problem is not with the accumulation, but to awaken the beauty of the heart. When it is awakened, then it will know how to act.

Without love, trying to become a philanthropist is another form of exploitation. Love will show the way to the rich man and to the poor man. Love alone will solve the contradiction of existence. Love alone will show the way of true action when the mind is caught in the net of ugly actions.

Question: I am a writer and I am faced with periods of sterility when nothing seems to come. These periods begin and end without any apparent reason. What is their cause and cure?

KRISHNAMURTI: The problem is not how to be creative all the time. Why is there insensitivity? Why are there moments of dullness in which creativity ceases? Creativeness comes into being; it cannot be invited, it cannot be artificially sustained. Why do these moments of dullness come? Obviously, insensitivity must come into being through dull thoughts, dull feelings, and dull actions. How can there be sensitivity when there is greed, ruthlessness, and envy? Envy, though it gives

a certain activity to the mind as the search and the achievement of power, will inevitably make the mind and the heart dull. Without understanding the causes that bring about insensitivity, we cling to those states in which creativeness has been. We long for creativeness, which is another escape from *what is*. In the understanding of *what is* without creating an opposite, creativeness comes into being.

So, the problem is first to be aware of the causes of insensitivity, to be passively aware without choice and denial, without justification or identification of those periods that are dull. Then, in that alert, passive awareness, the cause of insensitivity is revealed. In just being aware of this cause without trying to overcome it, dullness begins to fade away. It is this period of silence in which there is no condemnation or justification—in this period of silent observation, the truth of that which is false is perceived. This perception of truth frees the mind from insensitivity.

But, the painter, the writer, the sculptor has to live. He is not merely content with the expression of his joy, he wants a result, he wants a recognition; and also he wants food, clothing, and shelter. If he is merely content with food, clothing, and shelter, then his life will be comparatively easy; but, like the rest of us, he uses these as a means of psychological expansion. So, his heart becomes a process of self-expansion and thereby brings about strife and misery and that insensitivity which prevents creative being.

There is constant renewal of creative being only when the 'me' and the 'mine' are absent. It is the 'me' that gives continuity, which brings about insensitivity. Only in the constant ending of the 'me', there is renewal. Then only is there that state in which no dullness, no insensitivity can exist.

Question: Is not the direct effect of your person helpful in understanding your teach-

ings? Do we not grasp better the teaching when we have the teacher?

KRISHNAMURTI: No, sir. When you love your neighbor, when you love your immediate relations, there is greater understanding. When you love your wife, your child, your neighbor—white or brown—when there is a song in your heart, then love brings understanding.

When you are listening to me, perhaps there is direct help, for you are giving your mind and heart to discover the truth of what is being said. If you do not want to discover it, you would not be here. In talking to a person who understands more clearly, your own mind and heart become clarified. But, if you make of that person your guru, your teacher, and only love him and respect him, then you have contempt for others. Have you not noticed, sirs, how very respectful you are to me and how very thoughtless and callous to your neighbors, to your wife, and to your servants, if you have any? This state of contradiction indicates your own disrespect to everyone concerned. It is of no great significance how you treat the teacher, but it matters enormously how you treat your neighbor, your wife, and your servant. Respect to me and denial of it to others is hypocrisy, which destroys love.

What brings understanding is love. When your heart is full, then you will listen to the teacher, to the beggar, to the laughter of children, to the rainbow, and to the sorrow of man. Under every stone and leaf, that which is eternal exists. But, we do not know how to look for it. Our minds and hearts are filled with other things than the understanding of *what is*. Love and mercy, kindliness and generosity do not cause enmity. When you love, you are very near truth. For, love makes for sensitivity, for vulnerability. That which is sensitive is capable of renewal. Then truth will come into being. It cannot

come if your mind and heart are burdened, heavy with ignorance and animosity.

These talks will have significance only as they affect directly the breaking down of thought process, the breaking down of the isolating process in relationship, and putting an end to greed and envy in your daily action. Intelligent and arduous inquiry is devotion. The very open receptivity for truth, the unknown, is devotion. Where there is love there is understanding.

March 14, 1948

Tenth Talk in Bombay

One is apt to put new wine in old bottles. Those of us who have studied and experienced sufficiently are likely to interpret what I have been saying according to their previous knowledge, or to put it in the framework of their prejudice. What brings about understanding is direct experience, and not putting it into the framework of their particular terminology and experience. Most of us have accumulated knowledge and according to it, we interpret and act.

Self-knowledge does not demand accumulated knowledge. Accumulated knowledge becomes a burden to self-knowledge. Self-knowledge, the understanding of the total process of oneself, does not demand any previous knowledge. Previous knowledge about oneself brings misinterpretation and misunderstanding. Self-knowledge is constant movement without accumulation. This knowledge is from moment to moment, for self-knowledge is a process of discovery of the activities of the self. Only when there is the process of accumulating knowledge, then it is in opposition to creative being.

Our existence can be likened to an iceberg. Only one-tenth of it shows on the surface and the rest of it is below the waters. We are so occupied with the superficial existence that we have not the time nor the inclination to inquire into the depths, where most of our existence is. But to inquire within so deeply, there must be a certain alert watchfulness for the intimations of these deeper levels of consciousness. It is these deeper layers that control and shape action. Merely to be occupied with the outward actions of these superficial layers brings about destructive contradiction. These contradictions between the different layers of consciousness make for frustration and despair. To escape from frustration, thought seeks other activities and so multiplies frustration. Frustration will come to an end only when all layers of consciousness are related without contradiction. So, self-knowledge is essential for the freedom from corroding frustration. Self-knowledge brings joy and freedom.

Question: What is it that comes when nationalism goes?

KRISHNAMURTI: Intelligence. The implication in this question is what can be substituted for nationalism. All substitution is an action which does not bring about intelligence. Substituting one political party for another, one religious belief for another, one guru for another, one leader for another, is an act of ignorance.

How does nationalism or patriotism cease? Only in understanding its full implication outwardly and inwardly. Outwardly, it creates division between people as class, as races, as economic frontiers, and so on, ultimately bringing about strife and war. Inwardly, psychologically, nationalism is the outcome of the craving to identify oneself with something greater, the greater being the family, the group, the race, the country, and the idea. This identification is a form of self-expansion. Living in narrow circumstances in a village or in a town, you are nobody. But,

if you identify yourself with the larger, with a class, with a group, with a country—call yourself a Hindu, a Christian, or a Muslim—then there is a sense of gratification whose prestige gives vanity. The psychological necessity for identification is the outcome of inward poverty. Self-expansion through identification breeds mischief and destruction. In understanding this process there comes freedom and intelligence, and not substitution.

When you substitute religion for nationalism or nationalism for religion, both become the means for self-expansion and so lead to contention and misery. Any form of substitution, however noble, leads to illusion. Substitution is bribery. Only in understanding the problem at its different levels, outward as well as inward, intelligence comes into being.

Question: What is the difference between awareness and introspection and who is aware in awareness?

KRISHNAMURTI: The examination of oneself in order to modify or change is generally called introspection. To look within with an intention to change the responses of the self is what most people indulge in. In this process, there is always the observer and the observed, the observer having an end in view. In this process is involved not the understanding of *what is,* but only the transformation of *what is.* When that end, that transformation, is not achieved, there is depression, there is frustration, that peculiar moodiness that goes with introspection. In this there is always the accumulating process of the 'me', the dualistic conflict from which there is no release. In this introspective action, there is a battle of the opposites in which there is always choice and the endless strife that it breeds.

Awareness is entirely different. Awareness is observation without choice, condemnation, or justification. Awareness is silent observation from which there arises understanding without the experiencer and the experienced. In this awareness, which is passive, the problem or the cause is given an opportunity to unfold itself and so give its full significance. In awareness there is no end in view to be gained, and there is no becoming, the 'me' and the 'mine' not being given the continuity.

In introspection there is self-improvement which causes self-centeredness. In the process of awareness there is no self-improvement; on the contrary, it is the ending of the self, the 'me' and the 'mine' with its idiosyncrasies, memories, demands, and pursuits. Self-introspection implies identification and condemnation, choice and justification. In awareness there are none of these things. Awareness is direct relationship without the intermediary of persuasion, like, or dislike. Awareness is being sensitive to nature, to things, to relationship of people and of ideas. It is an observation of every feeling, thought, and action as they arise from moment to moment. Awareness is not condemnatory; there is no accumulation of memory as the 'me'. Awareness is the understanding of the actions of the self, that of the 'me' and the 'mine' in its relationship to things, people, and ideas. This awareness is from moment to moment and so it cannot be practiced; so awareness is not the cultivation of habit. A mind that is caught in the net of habits is insensitive. A mind that is functioning within a pattern of action is not pliable. Awareness demands constant alertness and pliability.

Introspection leads to frustration, to conflict, and misery. Awareness is a process of release from the activities of the self. To be aware of your daily actions, your movements of thought and feeling, to be aware of another, there must be that sensitive pliability which can only come with inquiry and interest. To know oneself fully, not just one or two layers of oneself, there must be that alert, expansive awareness and freedom so that the hidden intentions and pursuits are revealed.

Who is aware in awareness? In the state of experiencing, there is neither the experiencer nor the experience. It is only when the state of experiencing has gone, there emerges the experiencer and the experience, which is the division in memory itself. Since most of us live in memory with its responses, we invariably ask who is the observer and who is it that is aware. Surely, this is a wrong question, is it not? At the moment of experiencing, there is neither the 'me' which is aware nor the object of which he is aware. Most of us find it extremely difficult to live in a state of experiencing as it demands easy pliability, swift movement of thought and feeling, a high degree of sensitivity. All this is denied when we are pursuing a result, when achievement becomes far more important than understanding. Only a man who is not seeking an end, who is free from that bargaining spirit, who is not becoming—such a man is in a state of constant experiencing. You can experiment with this yourself and observe that in experiencing the experiencer and the experience do not exist.

The improvement of the self-expansion process can never bring truth. This self-expansion is ever self-enclosing. Awareness is the understanding of *what is*—the *what is* of your daily existence. It is only when you understand the truth of your daily existence that you can go far. But, to go far, you must begin near. Without understanding the near, we look to the dim, distant future, which only brings confusion and misery.

Question: Is marriage a need or a luxury?

KRISHNAMURTI: The sexual urge is legalized by marriage. Society demands the protection of children. That is one of the reasons for the so-called marriages. Marriage also takes place because of psychological reasons. One needs a companion, a person to possess, to dominate, who will give one psychological as well as physical comfort. Thus, either the man or the woman dominates and makes the other a dependent. Sexual possession or economic possession gives gratification. So, possession becomes extraordinarily important in relationship, which leads to all kinds of agony, distrust, and suspicion. Where there is possessiveness and gratification, there can be no love. How can there be love when in your livelihood you are ruthless; when in your business you are cunning and competitive? You cannot exploit your neighbor, starve him out, go home and have affection in your heart for your wife and children. The exploitation of another destroys the love for your wife and children. When children become the means of self-perpetuation or are used as self-fulfillment or treated as mere toys, then there can be no love. Only love and intelligence can solve the complex problem of marriage.

To understand our human problems there must be love. Mere legislation cannot bring about the tender intelligence which brings understanding in relationship. You cannot be ambitious and yet tender. You cannot be a captain of industry, a politician, the head of an organization, and be merciful. Our human problems need to be understood and not condemned or justified. This understanding comes through being aware of *what is*.

Question: Who is he that feeds, if not the exploiter? How are you free from exploitation when you exploit the exploiter?

KRISHNAMURTI: When one uses another for psychological purposes, then exploitation begins. All exploitation is based on psychological poverty of being. There will be no exploitation of man by man when this poverty of being is understood. Exploitation will not cease through mere legislation. There will be exploitation in different forms—at home, in public—as long as this psychological emptiness exists. You will be content with little, with the necessities of life, when you are inwardly rich.

The questioner asks me if I am not exploiting the exploiter. I don't think I am. I am fed by him as I would feed myself if I went out and earned money. I am not using him as a psychological necessity, nor am I using you, the audience, as a means of self-gratification. Psychologically, I do not need you. As I go out and earn money for my needs, I am preaching; and for this I am clothed, fed, and sheltered.

Where there is no self-expansion, where there is no use of another psychologically, there is no exploitation. One is content with little not because of an ideal but because inwardly there are beauty, riches, and ecstasy. Without this inward simplicity, merely to put on a loin cloth means nothing. You seem to give too much importance to outward exploitation, and there is legislation to prevent this brutality. The psychological exploitation is far more subtle, more mischievous, and destructive; it cannot be done away with through legislation. This exploitation will cease only with the transformation of the individual. This transformation is not of time; it is ever in the present. In this inward revolution you bring about a transformation in the world in which you live, the world of your relationship.

Question: Is not stilling the mind a prerequisite for the solution of a problem, and is not the dissolution of the problem a conditioning of mental stillness?

KRISHNAMURTI: Is not the stilling of the mind a prerequisite for the solution of a problem? The mind is not a few layers of superficial consciousness. Consciousness is not just the dull actions of the mind. When a problem is created by the superficial mind, the superficial layers have to become quiet in order to understand it. When you have a business problem, what do you do? You switch the telephone off. You stop your secretary from interrupting you and you study the problem. This is what most of you do with regard to your various problems. In studying the problem, only the superficial layers have become comparatively quiet, temporarily at least. Only when every problem is completely understood, the problem leaves no residue, no memory. Consciousness is a process of experiencing, naming, and recording, which is memory. This process is going on continuously, consciously or unconsciously.

How can a mind be made still without understanding the whole content of consciousness? The mind cannot be made still by discipline, which only makes the mind dull and weary. Only by allowing every movement of thought and understanding its implications, stillness comes into being. As the pool becomes serene when the breezes stop, so the mind becomes extremely quiet, and the problems are dissolved. A stillness of mind comes only through self-knowledge, not through denial or acceptance, but through being aware of every thought and feeling. To cultivate stillness destroys creative understanding. When you pursue stillness, you are exercising will, which is the outcome of desire; and desire, in its very nature, is disturbing. It is only by inviting sorrow that you can understand reality, not by escaping tribulation.

Question: Since the motive power in the search for power is interest, what creates interest? What creates the interest is a relevant question. Is it suffering?

KRISHNAMURTI: When there is no interest, there is no search. This very search is devotion. There is no path of devotion to reality. Where there is search there is action and there is no separate path of action. Where there is deep inquiry into *what is*, there is the action of wisdom and there is no separate path as wisdom.

How does this interest come into being? Earnestness comes with the understanding of sorrow. Understanding ceases when we seek to run away from sorrow. This escape from sorrow through social activities, through gurus, through amusement and knowledge dissipates earnestness. The difficulty is not in understanding sorrow, but we dissipate our energies in trying to overcome it. What is overcome is to be conquered again and again, and so we suffer again and again. Suffering does not lead to intelligence. Only in understanding it is there intelligence. Only when all escapes from sorrow are put to an end— and in facing sorrow, you will find there is first a shock—and when the mind is no longer escaping from suffering, the causes of suffering are revealed, and you do not have to search for the cause. To search out the cause is another form of escape. If you are aware of suffering, then the content of suffering unfolds itself. The more you understand the book of suffering, the greater the wisdom. When you are escaping from the suffering, you are escaping from wisdom.

Only through passive yet alert awareness, truth comes into being, and it is truth that liberates man from sorrow. It is truth that gives bliss. All positive action towards sorrow is an action of escape. It is only through negative thinking—which is the highest form of thinking—is there the dissolution of sorrow.

March 21, 1948

Eleventh Talk in Bombay

Most of us have many problems and many anxieties, conflicts, and strife, for which we are not able to find a lasting solution. We do not see the problem clearly and precisely. We do not read the intricacies and the implications of the problem deeply and simply. The problem is blurred by the many screens that we have created within it and ourselves. Whatever the problem—economic or social, superficial or psychological—we have conclusions and ready-made answers for them. We approach them either with apprehension or with preconceived formulations. These prevent the deep and lasting understanding of the problem; for, the answer is not away from the problem but in the problem itself. Our whole difficulty, then, is to view the problem clearly and simply because the problem is never the same, it is never still, it is ever undergoing a change. To understand a problem we must understand the creator of the problem, which is the mind, the self, the 'me'.

We are sufficiently content with things either produced by the machine, by the hand, or by the mind, by thought, by belief. The things made by the hand or by the mind are both sensate. The things made by the hand soon wear out and so do things produced by the mind. The evaluations of the mind are soon established, fixed in a framework of references, but this standardization cannot be permanent. So, there is constant strife between the search for permanency and the things that soon wear out and pass away. The things produced by the hand are misused by the mind. Food, clothing, and shelter are given wrong values by the mind. It is the false psychological valuations of things made by the mind that breed conflict and misery. So, in the misuse lies our misery. So, the mind with its will and its capacity for valuation, which is the intellect, must be understood. As long as will, which is the

expression of desire, and the capacity for evaluation, which is the outcome of craving, are not clearly and wholly understood and their subtlety and significance are not perceived, there will be conflict and misery. This understanding of the ways of desire with its will and evaluation, with its choice and justification, with its identification and denial, is self-knowledge. Self-knowledge makes straight that which is crooked. Self-knowledge makes straight that which is corrupt. So long as there is no self-knowledge but the process of the mind, there must be the wrong valuation which inevitably breeds confusion and antagonism. Self-knowledge is the beginning of wisdom, and without understanding there is no happiness. Thus, the awareness of *what is*—however complex a problem may appear—without distorting it, is the dissolution of the problem. To see the problem deeply and swiftly is not possible without self-knowledge. Without meditation there can be no self-knowledge. Meditation is a process of perceiving the truth of every thought, feeling, and so, action. Meditation is not the exclusion of all thoughts and the fixation on a particular object, image, or idea. It is a constant awareness of every thought and feeling as it arises without choice, condemnation, or justification. It is the perception of truth in the problem that frees thought from the problem. With the unfolding of self-knowledge, the sorrow that comes with wrong valuations of things, of people, and of ideas, fades away. This knowledge is not of the higher or lower self, which is still within the field of the mind, which is a false and self-protected division without any reality. This knowledge is the total process of one's own being. So, as long as there is no self-knowledge, the multiplication and reformation of our problems will continue. For this reason only, the individual becomes greatly significant. He can alone transform himself. He alone can bring about revolution in his relationship, the necessary regeneration in the world of his relationship. This transformation can only come about through the knowledge of the self; it cannot come about through book knowledge, through inference, through another, however great. This knowledge is not in antagonism to the world about us. It is not a process of self-isolation. He cannot be without relationship. The understanding of this relationship to things, to people, and to ideas will alone bring happiness. Happiness comes not with the evaluation, not with the choice; it comes when the chooser, the actor, the mind, is not occupied with himself. When the mind is silent, truth and bliss come into being. Such a man is blessed.

Question: Why don't you do miracles? All teachers did.

KRISHNAMURTI: To be healed physically is not so important as to be healed psychologically. In the past, I have healed physically. Now I am concerned with the healing of the inner, which is far more important. Is it not? If the mind and the heart are diseased, they affect the body, which in turn affects the mind. If we give too much importance to the outer and neglect the inner, the inner will always overcome the outer.

This desire for the miracle, this transformation of the inner, is what you are looking for. You want a miracle to happen, which is really a sign of laziness, of irresponsibility. You want somebody else to do the job for you. The healing of the outer may make for popularity, but that will not lead man to happiness. So, we should understand the inward emptiness, the inward disease and corruption. None can heal you inwardly and that is the miracle of it. A doctor can heal you outwardly; a psychoanalyst may make you normal to fit into a decaying society; but to go beyond, to be inwardly true, clear, uncorrupted—that

you alone can do and none else. This is the greatest miracle, to heal yourself completely.

This is what we have been doing here during the last three months—to understand ourselves, the causes of our disease, conflict, and contradiction, to see things as they are, clearly and simply, without distortion. When a thing is seen clearly, then a miracle takes place; then, that which is, is perceived without distortion, and the truth that understanding brings, heals. The truth of that understanding can come only through your own awareness and not through a miracle performed by another. Miracles do happen, but only we are unaware of it. You are not the same as you were yesterday. If you can follow the inward nature of the mind easily and swiftly, then you will see that miracles will happen, the miracles of newness, of life, of beauty, and of happiness. But, you cannot follow the swift movement of life if you are tethered, bound to your own achievements and belief. A man who knows, who is caught in what he knows—there can be no miracle for him. But a man who is uncertain, who asks nothing—to him life is a miracle, for there is constant renewal, a renewal without an end.

Question: You have said that some transformation has taken place in all your listeners; presumably, they have to wait for its manifestation. How then can you call it immediate?

KRISHNAMURTI: As long as you are looking for transformation, a result to be gained, there will be no transformation. As long as you are thinking in terms of achievement, in terms of time, there can be no transformation. For then, the mind is caught in the net of time. When you say you are thinking in terms of immediate transformation, you are thinking of yesterday, today, and tomorrow. Such transformation within time is merely change, which is modified continuity. When thought is free of time, there will be a timeless transformation.

As long as a problem is thought about, the problem will continue. Thought creates the problem. That which is the result of the past, the mind, cannot solve the problem. The mind can analyze, can examine, but it cannot resolve the problem. The problem, however complex and however close, ceases only when the thought process comes to an end. When the mind, which is the result of many yesterdays, with its reasons and calculations, ceases, then only the problem comes to an end. That which is the result of time cannot bring about transformation; it can and will bring about a change, which is modified continuity or rearrangement of a pattern, but such action does not bring about freedom.

What do we mean by transformation? Surely, the cessation of all problems, cessation from conflict, confusion, and misery. If you observe, you will see that the mind is cultivating, sowing, and harvesting as a farmer cultivates, sows, and reaps. But, unlike the farmer who allows the field to lie fallow during winter, the mind never allows itself to lie fallow. As the rains, the storms, and the sunshine recreate the earth, so during that passive yet alert fallowness of the mind, there is rejuvenation, a renewal. So the mind renews itself and the problems are resolved. The problems are resolved only when they are seen clearly and swiftly.

The mind is constantly distracted, escaping, because to see a problem clearly might lead to action which might create further disturbance; and so the mind is constantly avoiding facing the problem, which only gives strength to the problem. But, when it is seen clearly without distortion, then it ceases to be. So long as you think in terms of transformation, there cannot be transformation, now or hereafter. Transformation can come only when every problem is immediately understood. You can understand it when there is no choice and the seeking of a result, when there is no condemnation or justification. Where there is love, there is neither choice nor search for an end, nor condemnation, nor justification. It is this love that brings about transformation.

Question: What are the foundations of right livelihood? How can I find out whether any livelihood is right? How can I find a right livelihood in a basically wrong society?

KRISHNAMURTI: In a basically wrong society, there cannot be a right means of livelihood. Such a livelihood will inevitably contribute to general misery and destruction. This society is founded upon envy, ill will, on acquisitiveness, and on the desire for power. Such a society will breed soldiers, police force, and lawyers. These products of such a disintegrating society inevitably bring further division, further strife, and further pain. These disintegrating factors also breed the big businessman and the politician with his party politics and ideologies. So, all this has to be transformed to form a right society in which there can be right livelihood. Such a revolution is not an impossible task. You and I have to do it. It can be brought about only when you and I are not envious and seeking power, are not antagonistic and acquisitive. Then, we will be able to create a new society; then, we will find a right livelihood even in a disintegrating society; then, we will be able to create a new society in which man is not held by its static demands, and in which there will be those who will not ask reward for their actions, those who have no authority or power over another. They are inwardly rich, for truth has come to them. It is only the man that seeks reality who can create a new social order.

Only love can bring about transformation in the world of corruption.

Question: How can a man who never left the limits of his mind go beyond his mind to experience direct communion with truth?

KRISHNAMURTI: When you know the limits of your mind, are you not already beyond it? To be aware of your limits—surely it is the first step, which in itself is difficult, for the limits of the mind are enormous. To be aware of a limitation without condemnation is to be free of that limitation. To be aware of a prejudice, a limitation, without choice, condemnation, or justification is to be free of that prejudice. There cannot be experience of direct communion with truth if the mind does not know its limitations. The awareness of limitation is the beginning of self-knowledge. Self-knowledge is not a goal. Self-knowledge is the experience and discovery of oneself from moment to moment, the discovery of truth from moment to moment. Truth is not continuous and is not bound from moment to moment. 'You', the limitation, can never be unified with truth. 'You' can never find truth. 'You' must cease for truth to be. 'You' are the limitation. So, you must understand the extent of your limitation and be passively aware of it. Then, into that passivity, truth comes into being.

Darkness cannot be unified with light; ignorance cannot become wisdom. Ignorance and darkness must cease for wisdom and light to come into being. Wisdom has no ultimate end. It comes into being when ignorance from moment to moment is experienced, discovered, and dissolved.

Question: Attachment is the stuff of which we are made. How can we be free from attachment?

KRISHNAMURTI: Surely, attachment is not a problem, is it? Why do you want to be detached and why are you attached? Why have you this constant strife of attachment and detachment? Why are you attached? What would happen if you were not attached?

Without attachment you would be lost, you would be empty. Without property, without name, you are as nothing. Without your bank account, if you have one, without your beliefs, what are you? You are an empty shell, are you not? So, afraid of being nothing, you are attached to something. Attachment brings with it many problems of fear, of frustrations, of cruelty. Being caught in the net of suffering that attachment brings, you try to become detached, then you try to renounce your property, your family, your ideas; but you have not really solved the problem, which is the fear of being nothing. Strip yourself of your titles, of your capacities, of your jewels, and all the rest of it, what are you? Knowing inwardly that there is a void, an emptiness, a nothingness, and being afraid of it, you depend, you are attached, and you possess. In possession, in attachment, there is cruelty. In the possession of another, you are not concerned with that other, but only with yourself; and this you call love. So, why do you not accept that which is? That which is, which is nothing—not that you should become nothing, but that you are actually nothing.

This recognition of *what is* frees the mind of all its renunciation, from attachment and from detachment. Then only is there beauty, a richness, and a blessing which cannot be understood by a man who is afraid of *what is*. But, to a man who is afraid of this emptiness, life is a struggle and a pain; then he is caught in the conflict of endless opposites. A man who is nothing knows love, for love is nothing.

Question: Is extensional awareness the same as creative emptiness? Is not awareness passive and therefore not creative? Is not the process of self-awareness tedious and painful?

KRISHNAMURTI: If awareness is practiced, made into a habit, then it becomes tedious and painful. Awareness cannot be disciplined. That which is practiced is no longer awareness, for in practice is implied the creation of habit, the exertion of effort and will. Effort is distortion. There is not only the awareness of the outer—of the flight of birds, of shadows, of the restless sea, the trees and the wind, the beggar and the luxurious cars that pass by—but also there is the awareness of the psychological process, the inward tension and conflict. You do not condemn a bird in flight; you observe it, you see the beauty of it. But, when you consider your own inward strife, you condemn it or justify it. You are incapable of observing this inward conflict without choice or justification.

To be aware of your thought and feeling without identification and denial is not tedious and painful, but in search of a result, an end to be gained, conflict is increased and the tedium of strife begins. In awareness there is no becoming, there is no end to be gained. There is silent observation without choice and condemnation, from which there comes understanding. In this process when thought and feeling unfold themselves, which is only possible when there is neither acquisition nor acceptance, then there comes an extensional awareness. In this extensional awareness, all the hidden layers and their significance are revealed. This awareness reveals that creative emptiness which cannot be imagined or formulated. This extensional awareness and the creative emptiness are a total process and are not different stages.

When you silently observe a problem without condemnation or justification, there comes passive awareness. In this passive awareness, the problem is understood and dissolved. In awareness there is heightened sensitivity, in which there is the highest form of negative thinking. When the mind is formulating, producing, there can be no creation. It is only when the mind is still and empty, when it is not creating a problem—in that alert passivity there is creation. Creation can only take place in negation, which is not the opposite of the positive. Being nothing is not the antithesis of being something. A problem comes into being only when there is a search for result. When the search for result ceases, then only is there no problem.

Question: What do you mean by love?

KRISHNAMURTI: Love is the unknowable. It can be realized only when the known is understood and transcended. Only when the mind is free of the known, then only there will be love. So, we must approach love negatively and not positively.

What is love to most of us? With us, when we love, in it there is possessiveness, dominance, or subservience. From this possession arises jealousy and fear of loss, and we legalize this possessive instinct. From possessiveness there arises jealousy and the innumerable conflicts with which each one is familiar. Possessiveness, then, is not love. Nor is it sentimental. To be sentimental, to be emotional, excludes love. Sensitivity and emotions are merely sensations. A so-called religious person, who weeps over the object of his adoration, is indulging in sensation. Sensation and emotion are the process of thought, and thought is not love. Sentimentality as emotion is a form of self-expansion. Emotions are cruel; in them are like and dislike. An emotional person can be stirred to hatred and to war.

Mercy and pity, forgiveness and respect are not emotions. There is love when sentimentality and emotion and devotion cease. Devotion is not love; devotion is a form of self-expansion. Respect is not for the few, but for man, whether he is low or high. Generosity and mercy have no reward.

Love alone can transform insanity, confusion, and strife. No system, no theory of the left or of the right can bring peace and happiness to man. Where there is love, there is no possessiveness, no envy; there is mercy and compassion, not in theory, but actually to your wife and to your children, to your neighbor and to your servant. When you are respectful to your servant as well as to your guru, then you will know love. Love alone can transform the world. Love alone can bring about mercy and beauty, order and peace. There is love with its blessing when 'you' cease to be.

Question: May we request you to state clearly whether there is God or not?

KRISHNAMURTI: Why do you seek my confirmation? Either I will strengthen you in your belief or shake you away from it. If I confirm, you will be pleased and you will go on with your rough and ugly ways. If I disturb you, you will soon cover up that disturbance and carry on with your daily routine. But, why do you want to know? This is far more important—to find out why you want to know—than if there is or if there is not God. To know reality, to know God, you must not seek Him. If you seek, you are escaping from *what is.* You want to escape from suffering to an illusion which you call God. Your books are full of God. The temples, with their images, do not hold God.

For reality to come into being, suffering must cease, and the mere search for truth, for God, for immortality, is an escape from suffering. It is more pleasant to discuss whether there is or there is not God than to dissolve the causes of suffering. He who discusses the nature of God can never know God. Reality cannot be caught in a garland of words. You cannot catch the wind in a fist. You cannot capture reality in a temple nor in ceremonies.

All escapes are on the same level, whether the escape is through the temple or through a drink. The search for God may not be so harmful to society as the escape through acquisitiveness. But, this search for God cannot bring about the realization of God. Until you understand and transcend suffering, reality cannot come into being. So, your inquiry whether there is or there is not God is vain; it has no meaning. Your inquiry can but lead to illusion. How can the mind that is caught in the turmoil of daily greed and suffering, in ignorance and envy, know that which is illimitable, unutterable? How can the mind which is the product of time know the timeless? It cannot. So, to think about truth, about God, is another form of escape. Thought is the result of time, the product of memory. So, how can thought find that which is timeless, eternal? It cannot.

When the thought process comes to an end, which is to understand suffering and not escape from it, suffering, which is not only on the superficial level, but at different levels of consciousness, is transcended. This means we must be open, vulnerable to suffering. You are suffering with an occasional ray of sunshine. Since you suffer, why not understand it thoroughly and resolve it finally? This cessation of sorrow is not so difficult. For a mind that is caught in the net of suffering, it is more difficult to search out God, for He is the unknown and you cannot search for the unknown. But, you can be aware of suffering, and in this awareness the cause of it is known. Since you run away from sorrow through many forms of escape, be aware of these escapes, and come directly, actually, face to face with suffering. Only then can sorrow come to an end. Then the mind is tranquil. This tranquillity is not a result; it is not the product of a disciplined, controlled mind. As the lake is still when the breezes stop, so the mind is still. Such a mind is a blessing, for it is then capable of receiving the highest. The experiencing of reality is not an illusion, but the experience which comes through an escape which you call God is an illusion.

So, to seek God is not to find Him. But to understand suffering and for the mind to free itself from its own self-created problems brings tranquillity. Then only, reality can come into being.

March 28, 1948

Questions

12. In truly great works of art, poetry, music there is expressed and conveyed something indescribable which seems to mirror reality or truth or God. Yet it is a fact that in their private lives most of those who created such works have never succeeded in extricating themselves from the vicious circle of conflict. How can it be explained that an individual who has not liberated himself is able to create something in which the conflict of the opposites is transcended? Or to put the question in reverse, don't you have to conclude that creativeness is born out of conflict?   18

13. The present is an unmitigated tragic horror. Why do you insist that in the present is the eternal?   19

14. You decry war and yet are you not supporting it?   20

15. You are very depressing. I seek inspiration to carry on. You do not cheer us with words of courage and hope. Is it wrong to seek inspiration?   21

16. You say that life and death are one and the same thing. Please elaborate this startling statement.   21

17. You said last Sunday that each one of us is responsible for these terrible wars. Are we also responsible for the abominable tortures in the concentration camps and for the deliberate extermination of a people in Central Europe?   23

18. I feel I cannot reach the other shore without help, without the grace of God. If I can say, "Thy will be done" and dissolve myself in it, do I not dissolve my limitations? If I can relinquish myself unconditionally is there not grace to help me bridge the gulf which separates God and me?   24

19. I an inventor and I happen to have invented several things which have been used in this war. I think I am opposed to killing but what am I to do with my capacity? I cannot suppress it as the power to invent drives me on.   25

20. Can I find God in a foxhole?   26

21. What is a lasting way to solve a psychological problem?   26

22. If we had not destroyed the evil that was in Central Europe, it would have conquered us. Do you mean to say that we should not have defended ourselves? Aggression must be met. How would you meet it?   27

23. In one's growth is there not a continuous and recurring process of the death of one's cherished hopes and desires; of cruel disillusionment in regard to the past; of transmutation of those negative phenomena into a more positive and vitalizing life—until the same stage is reached again on a higher spiral? Are not conflict and pain therefore indispensable to all growth and at all stages?   28

24. I have struggled for many, many years with a personal problem. I am still struggling. What am I to do?   29

25. I am intensely lonely. I seem to be in constant conflict in my relationships on account of this loneliness. It is a disease and must be healed. Can you help me, please, to heal it?   30

26. I have had what might be called a spiritual experience, a guidance, or a certain realization. How am I to deal with it?   31

Ojai, 1946

Madras, 1947

Bombay, 1948

Index

Acceptance: and desire to become, 134–35

Accumulation: and awareness, 81–81; as memory, 67; and the self, 75; and self-knowledge, 22; and the unknowable, 67. *See also* Environment; Heredity; Past

Acquisition: desire for, 95–96; and path to war, 23. *See also* Exploitation; Security

Acquisitiveness: and exploitation, 134; and inequality, 95–96, 198. *See also* Craving; Greed; Power

Action: and consciousness, 165; and existence, 195–96; and inward revolution, 102

Active stillness: and cessation of fear, 51; and well-being, 37. *See also* Silent Awareness; Still mind; Stillness; Tranquillity

Actor: and action, 195–96

Actual: understanding, 159. *See also* Real; Reality; Truth

Aggression: dealing with, 27. *See also* Violence; War

Aloneness, 75, 154. *See also* Emptiness; Isolation; Loneliness

Ambition, 39; and conflict, 11–12; and worldliness, 13–14. *See also* Acquisition; Becoming; Craving; Self-expansion

Anger: and choiceless awareness, 117–18. *See also* Emotion

Artist: versus creativeness, 14–15; and psychological expansion, 199; and the still mind-heart, 18

Assassination: causes of, 168

Attachment: and fear of emptiness, 208. *See also* Dependence; Detachment

Attack: and defense, 27–28

Authority: craving for, 44–45; as end to self-knowledge, 141; futility of, 33; as hindrance, 115; as hindrance to self-knowledge, 78; and relationship, 142; the search for, 46; without self-knowledge, 71; and tranquillity, 23; and understanding, 8. *See also* Gurus; Leaders; Masters; Society; State; Teachers

Awareness: and action, 196; without condemnation, 190–91; defining, 69–70, 112–13, 201–2; versus effort, 209; as end to conflict, 71; and escape, 166–67; of limitations, 64; necessity for, 142; the process of, 208–9; technique for, 73; three stages of, 26–27, 74; transcending thought through, 73; and transformation, 75; understanding, 143–44. *See also* Self-awareness; Self-knowledge

Becoming, 29; and authority, 163; and conflict, 56; as denial of *what is,* 135; and levels of consciousness, 195; and memory, 190; and process of understanding, 51–52; and will, 42. *See also* Ambition; Being

Becoming still: versus being still, 12, 26

Being, 191; versus becoming, 111; understanding, 51–52. *See also* Becoming; Truth

Belief: examining, 103–4; as hindrance, 120, 151, 157, 159; and need for security, 88; as search for security, 124–25. *See also* God; Religion

Believer: as prisoner, 113

Bondage: through belief and dogma, 63

Books, 106, 142–43

Brahmins: significance of contribution, 90–91. *See also* Past; Religion

Bureaucracy: *See* State

Catastrophe: cause of, 16

Cause and effect, 42–43; 50–51

Celibacy, 177. *See also* Chastity; Love; Sex

Change: inner and outer, 17; necessity for, 16. *See also* Reform; Revolution; Transformation

Chastity: and the intellect, 13–14. *See also* Celibacy; Love; Sex

Children: and education, 108. *See also* Love

Choice: and conditioned thinking, 44; and opposing desires, 11; and the self, 179–80

Choiceless awareness, 23–24, 66; and the real, 44

Choiceless passivity. *See* Silent awareness

Christian. *See* Religion

Clarity: and self-awareness, 1

Class and acquisitiveness: as the highest values, 98–99

Collective worship: and regimentation of thought, 75–76. *See also* Conformity

Communication: as mutual understanding, 104

Communion: *See* Communication; Relationship

Earnestness, 78–79; and effort, 64; and inquiring
awareness, 57; and interest, 167; understanding
sorrow, 204
Education, 106–8, 187; importance of, 107–8; as
producer of experts, 89
Effort: as activity of the will, 64; and becoming,
111–12; and happiness, 117; as hindrance, 70; and
intelligence, 66; and sorrow, 176; and the will of the
'I', 60
Ego: *See* 'I'
Emotion: and love, 209–10
Emptiness: and search for wisdom, 72; understanding,
86. *See also* Aloneness; God; Loneliness
Enlightenment: centers of, 85
Environment: and blunting of sensitivity, 4; and
heredity, 161; influence of, 139–40. *See also*
Conditioning
Escape: awareness of, 63; and concentration, 181;
methods of, 159–60; search for methods of, 30; types
of, 210–11; through war, 192. *See also* Conflict;
Suffering
Eternal: as the present, 12. *See also* God; Real; Reality;
Timeless; Truth
Evil: justification of, 168, 177–78; of killing, 3
Exclusiveness: as breeder of inequality, 49. *See also*
Superior
Existence: pain of, 32. *See also* Life
Experience: without authority, 23; and conditioning,
195; and consciousness, 186–87; defining, 1; of
momentary ecstasy, 31; and the real, 15–16; and
renewal, 36
Experience of being: and conflict of becoming, 28. *See
also* Truth
Experts, 88. *See also* Gurus; Leaders; Livelihood;
Masters; Occupation; Professions; Teachers
Exploitation: inward and outward, 133–34; levels of, 87;
process of, 95–96; and psychological emptiness, 203;
types of psychological, 134. *See also* God; Masters;
Religion
Exploiter: and exploitation, 94–96; as leader, 103

Faith: *See* Confidence
Family: and responsibility, 96
Fear: as hindrance to understanding, 57; of life and
death, 51; and search for security, 32; of the
unknown, 77. *See also* Conformity; Death;
Reincarnation
Feelings: and consciousness, 186–87; naming, 131–32.
See also Anger; Emotions
Followers: and creation of tyranny, 102–3; and leaders,
187–88. *See also* Authority; Conformity; Gurus;
Leaders; Masters
Food, clothing, shelter: availability of, 84–85. *See also*
Needs

Freedom, 49; from conditioning, 97–98; conditions for,
44; defining, 193; and education, 106; through
knowledge of hindrance, 59; of mind, 154; from
nationalities and sects, 91; from the old, 173; and
right meditation, 47; through truth, 71; and virtue,
79–80. *See also* Liberation
Frustration: understanding, 86
Fulfillment: for man and woman, 145–46; and
self-expansion, 59. *See also* Happiness; Reality; Truth

Gandhi, Mohandas K., 85, 90, 167; death of, and
identification with, 167–168; and desire for
continuity, 169. *See also* Leaders; Reincarnation
Generosity: and accumulation, 198–99
Goals: as hindrance, 79; understanding, 55
God: belief in, and hypocrisy, 16; false pursuit of,
174–75; futility of search for, 113–14, 184; and
illusion, 210–11; as an investment, 116; necessity for,
24; and prayer, 90; and right meditation, 75; search
for, 26, 210–11; as a word, 191. *See also* Authority;
Belief; Continuity; Real; Reality; Religion; Truth
Good men: defining, 115
Good will: versus the means, 85
Government: as the individual, 192; as instruments of
violence, 187. *See also* Bureaucracy; Exploitation;
Society; War
Gratification: and relationship, 50–53, 123–24; search
for, 179
Greed, 71–72; and awareness, 73; and desire for power,
95. *See also* Acquisitiveness; Craving; Power
Group: without authority, 40
Gurus: and disciples, 122; and search for God, 178–79;
and self-gratification, 129–30. *See also* Authority;
Leaders; Masters; Teachers

Habit: and awareness, 70; conquering, 10–11
Happiness, 175–76; and absence of conflict, 11;
achieving, 91, 104–5; as goal, 107; and renewal,
110–11; and sorrow, 61. *See also* Joy; Love; Real;
Reality; Self-knowledge
Happy man, 183; defining, 174
Healing: inward and outward, 206
Heredity: and environment, 161
Hindrances: of ideals, 185–86; to truth, 81, 169–70. *See
also* Conflict; Conflict of opposites; Escape
Hindu: *See* Religion
Human conflict: and need for change, 16
Human essentials: proper distribution of, 84–85
Humanity: loss of, 24
Human problems: and static approaches, 83
Humility: and conflict of opposites, 131
Hypocrisy: and war, 3

Self-consciousness: and conflict, 11
Self-discovery: and truth, 56
Self-expansion, 55, 56, 59, 60; and awareness, 78; and intelligence, 65; need to transcend, 62; as structure of thought, 62. *See also* Craving; 'I'
Self-fulfillment: and continuity, 198; of followers and leaders, 103
Self-hypnosis: and meditation, 100
Self-interest: and daily needs, 57
Self-knowledge, 66, 139, 160; without accumulated knowledge, 200; achieving, 68, 74; as choiceless awareness, 92–93; and consciousness, 166; and enlightenment, 16; and happiness, 105; without leaders, 188; and meditation, 34–35; and meditation without authority, 182; need for, 120; and right action, 141–42; and right thinking, 8; as solution, 182; and true meditation, 46–47; and truth of security, 99; and understanding of desire, 179–80. *See also* Happiness; Reality; Truth
Self-perpetuation, 67–68
Self-probing: for self-knowledge, 74
Self-responsibility: for life, 17
Self-transformation: for outer transformation, 188
Sensate values: and chaos, 97; and confusion, 160; and creativity, 177; as hindrance to happiness, 92; as individual enterprise and collective action, 92; and self-expansion, 164; and truth, 139–40. *See also* Craving; Love; Sex; Stimulation; Values
Sensitivity: achieving, 4
Sensory values. *See* Sensate values
Separation: as corrupter, 89. *See also* Divisions
Sex: reasons for problem of, 118–20; and social stimulation, 176–77. *See also* Celibacy; Chastity; Love; Sensate values; Sexual urge
Sexual urge: naming, 187. *See also* Sex
Silence: achieving, 41–42; and creativeness, 174; and perception of truth, 199. *See also* Active stillness; Silent awareness; Slowed down mind; Still mind; Stillness; Tranquillity; Wisdom
Silent awareness, 8, 14, 51; and thought-feeling, 25; and understanding, 23. *See also* Choiceless awareness; Silence
Silent moment: and joy, 166. *See also* Reality; Silence; Truth
Simple mind: and the real, 192
Simplicity: as approach to life, 88; and cessation of self, 75; and exploitation, 203. *See also* Complexity
Sinner: and the righteous man, 113. *See also* Evil
Sleep: and consciousness, 165–66. *See also* Dreams
Slowed down mind, 127. *See also* Diary; Silence; Thought
Social disintegration: and worship of authority, 163. *See also* Society; War
Social problems: and approaches to solutions, 138–39

Social reform: and outer change, 17. *See also* Transformation
Social reformation: through individual awareness, 92
Social structure: need for new, 162; and self-expansion, 56. *See also* Change; New; Revolution; Society
Society, 160; the acquisitive, 207; disintegration of, 162–63; and growing complexity, 41; as individual, 17; as war machine, 20. *See also* Authority; Inequality; Nationalism; Peace; War
Solitude: and psychological state of, 37. *See also* Aloneness; Emptiness; Loneliness
Sorrow, 104–5; and causes of, 61–62, 92, 160; desire to transcend, 61; escape from, 204; and search for purpose of life, 129–30. *See also* Conflict; Confusion; Escape; Happiness; Pain; Suffering
Soul. *See* Spiritual entity
Specialists. *See* Authority; Experts; Gurus; Leaders; Masters; Occupations; Professions; Teachers
Specialization, 66; as hindrance to understanding, 87–88
Spiritual entity, 170. *See also* Continuity; Reincarnation; Religion
Spirituality: versus spiritual leadership, 85. *See also* Authority; Gurus; Masters
Spontaneity: and the conditioned mind, 106
Starvation: and caring, 89. *See also* Needs; Philanthropy; Religion
State: as the individual, 92; and organized force, 16; and organized religion, 16; as power of the few, 164. *See also* Exploitation; Government; Society
State brutality: and sensate values, 23–24
State control: and education, 107–8
Still mind: and reality, 175, 210–11. *See also* Silence
Stillness, 143–44; achieving through craving or search, 125–26; and awareness, 74; experiencing, 125–26; and self-knowledge, 204; and timeless, 12–13; and truth, 172. *See also* Silence
Stimulation: and fear of dependence, 21. *See also* Inspiration; Sensate values
Success: and ambition, 14–15. *See also* Acquisitiveness; Becoming; Craving; Power
Suffering, 175–76; acceptance of, 130–31; and awareness, 134–35; and escape through God, 210–11; and invention of Gods, 175; as noble, 190; and relationship, 153; understanding, 130–31. *See also* Confusion; Escape; Pain; Sorrow
Superior: desire to be, 62–63
Superiority: and inward insufficiency, 63
Symbols: as distraction, 191. *See also* Nationalism; State
Systems, 178; and confusion, 140; and deprivation of physical necessities, 163–64; and education, 106–8; and futility of book knowledge, 94; and hindrance to world problems, 88; versus human needs, 84–85; and ideology, 154–55; and inequality, 128